Back Where You Came From

Harper's
MAGAZINE PRESS

Other Books by Bruce Franklin

THE WAKE OF THE GODS: MELVILLE'S MYTHOLOGY

FUTURE PERFECT: AMERICAN SCIENCE FICTION OF THE 19TH CENTURY

WHO SHOULD RUN THE UNIVERSITIES? (with John A. Howard)

FROM THE MOVEMENT: TOWARD REVOLUTION

THE ESSENTIAL STALIN

Back Where You Came From

A LIFE IN THE DEATH OF THE EMPIRE

H. Bruce Franklin

HARPER'S MAGAZINE PRESS
Published in Association with Harper & Row
New York

 For information address Harper & Row, Publishers, Inc., 10 East 53rd Street, New York, N.Y. 10022. Published simultaneously in Canada by Fitzhenry & Whiteside Limited, Toronto.

FIRST EDITION

Designed by Gloria Adelson

Library of Congress Cataloging in Publication Data

Franklin, Howard Bruce.
Back where you came from.
1. Franklin, Howard Bruce. 2. Radicalism—United States. I. Title.
HN90.R3F7 1975 322.4'4'0924 74-27301
ISBN 0-06-122525-8

75 76 77 78 79 10 9 8 7 6 5 4 3 2 1

To our children—Karen, Gretchen, Robert—and to all
the other young comrades of the world born in the
red dawn of freedom

Contents

Introduction

IT WAS JUST AFTER DAWN on December 19, 1972. Jane, my wife, was drinking coffee and reading the San Francisco *Chronicle* in our home in the suburban community of Menlo Park, California. The dog began to bark. Jane went to the front door and saw several short-haired men in suits and ties crouched on the porch. She rushed down the hall and called, "Bruce, wake up! I think the police are here." She got back to the front door just as it was being kicked open.

Twenty men poured through the door with leveled 12-gauge shotguns. "FBI! Don't make a move! Put your hands up!" they yelled. Jane took a step backward and one of them knocked her down onto the couch. Another pointed a shotgun at her chest and snarled, "Where's your father?" Jane was then, like me, thirty-eight years old. A second agent, standing behind the first, sharply whispered in his ear, "It's her *husband*, Jim."

Then a bunch of them charged down the hall to the bedrooms. Our nine-year-old son, Robert, was still asleep in the first room they came to. They threw open his door and ran in. One pointed a shotgun at his head and shouted, "Stay in bed! Go back to sleep!" Our fourteen-year-old daughter Gretchen was just getting up. She grabbed a pair of jeans and pulled them on, but was still bare from the waist up. When she picked up her shirt, one of them pointed a shotgun at her chest and shouted, "Put that down!"

While they were running down the hall, they were yelling, "Franklin, don't move! You're under arrest! Put your hands up! Come out of that room!" I had gotten out of bed and pulled on a pair of slacks. Through my mind flashed the images of Fred Hampton and Mark Clark, murdered in just such a raid in Chicago—Fred riddled with bullets and shotgun slugs while still in bed—and Bobby Hutton, who was gunned down in Oakland because according to some police he was "running away" while according to others he was "possibly going for a weapon," although he was standing still with his hands over his head. If I walked out of the room toward them, they could claim I was making an "aggressive" move. If I stepped away, they could say I was trying to escape through the window. So I raised my hands and stood still.

They rushed through the doorway, grabbed my arms, pulled me into the hall, shoved me face first up against the wall, handcuffed my arms behind my back, and searched me. I had been arrested a few times before and have been since. It is always frightening, and you must acknowledge your fear if you are to act with the necessary courage. Take the feeling you have when you see the red light of the highway patrol behind you and hear their siren. Add to that the knowledge that you are now in the hands of men who hate and fear you, men who have vowed they will kill you if they ever get the chance, men who have tortured some of your close friends and who have already killed a number of people they consider dangerous. Then there was something especially chilling about this one. For this was that nightmare world of the arbitrary secret police raid, or of Kafka's realistic fantasy of finding yourself a criminal without ever being aware of the crime. I had no idea what they were claiming I had done this time.

"What's the charge?" I asked, in as noncommittal a voice as I could manage.

"Harboring a federal fugitive," said a voice someplace behind my head.

I felt a mixture of relief and apprehension, because this didn't even sound like a plausible charge. I almost asked, "Who?" but checked myself, figuring that this might sound to them as if I had harbored so many federal fugitives that I didn't know which one they meant. I wondered whether I could be held without bail on this charge, how long it would be before I would see Jane again, whether they would torture me, and whether this might be just a pretext for them to kill me "trying to escape," like George Jackson, or whether, on the opposite extreme, it was just a little show of their power to try to put a scare in us.

Karen, our older daughter, was in the shower, getting ready to go to her own trial that day. Two days before we had celebrated her sixteenth birthday. It wasn't much of a celebration. We spent most of the day interviewing witnesses and listening to tapes of police radios. This was the seventh time she had been arrested since she was twelve. The local police, frustrated in their attempts to put Jane and me behind bars, seemed determined to take it out on Karen.

Her first arrest, at the age of twelve, came as she and another girl were walking home after working on a community newspaper. A man with a mod hairdo drove up in an old car and yelled, "Hi, girls." They kept walking. He then jumped out, identified himself as Palo Alto Police Officer Donald Criswell, and arrested them for "loitering." Later that night down at the police station she was released into Jane's custody. When the booking officer returned her personal belongings, Karen pointed out that her house key was missing. Officer Criswell reached into his pocket, took out the key, and handed it to her.

Donald Criswell was now chief investigator for the Palo Alto Police Department's "red squad." On Halloween, he had once again arrested Karen, this time charging her with "disturbing the peace" for allegedly swearing in the presence of his wife. The District Attorney demanded that Karen be taken away and made a ward of the court. She was eventually tried for this crime in Superior Court, Criminal Division, San Jose. The prosecution's witnesses were

Officer Criswell and his wife. Cross-examination, including replay of the police tapes, so clearly proved they were lying that the judge threw out the charge without hearing a defense.

But that lay in the future. At the moment, the FBI were dashing around with their guns in our home, and, in front of a house in Palo Alto, where the FBI were arresting two other political activists, Criswell was running up and down yelling, "The revolution is over! The revolution is over!"

With the shower running, Karen at first didn't hear the FBI agent banging on the bathroom door and bellowing, "FBI! FBI! Let me in!" When she heard, she stepped out, still wet, her shower cap on, wrapping a towel around herself.

"What are you doing?" she asked, staring into a leveled shotgun.

"Arresting your father," came the stern reply.

"What for?"

"Harboring a federal fugitive," he said grimly, clutching his shotgun.

"Who, me?" asked Karen, deadpan.

I was driven in handcuffs to San Francisco, booked, jailed, arraigned, and released on $10,000 bail. On January 5, 1973, the charges against me and the other three activists arrested that day for "harboring a federal fugitive" were dismissed for lack of evidence. But the U.S. attorney announced that he was asking a federal grand jury to bring in new indictments, either on this charge or others, a promise he has since kept for two of the other people.

A few days later, I called Larry Freundlich, editor of Harper's Magazine Press. Back in February, 1971, Larry had written to suggest I do a "political autobiography." I had then called him to ask, "How can someone who hasn't really done anything write a political autobiography?" Now I was calling to accept his old proposal. I guess what changed my mind was realizing that, whether I had "done anything" or not, the state considered me a dangerous enemy, and this fact itself is significant. What I have done is express some revolutionary ideas, and the state apparatus has responded as though its very existence had been physically attacked.

I was fired from my tenured associate professorship at Stanford University for giving analytical political speeches, on the grounds that these speeches "encouraged" or "urged and incited" unspecified violence. Senator James Eastland's Subcommittee to Investigate the Administration of the Internal Security Act and Other Internal Security Laws published in 1970 a report in which I am proclaimed to be a prime supplier of automatic weapons and explosives for the Black Panther Party and other groups. In 1972 the House Internal Security Committee, headed by Congressman Richard Ichord, published a volume which gave me credit for even more far-reaching activities, including masterminding a plan for guerrilla warfare featuring the "takeover" of the entire United States sometime between 1973 and 1975. And so on.

I have been beaten by police a number of times (the number depends on what you count as a beating). Although arrested five times, I have never been convicted. The one case that went as far as a jury decision taught me (and apparently the state) a useful lesson. Eight of us had been arrested for "failure to disperse" from a demonstration on election night, 1968. Our trial lasted five weeks. The jury not only acquitted us, but some of them became interested in revolutionary politics. The foreman of the jury, an engineer from Sunnyvale, has since then twice had me invited to speak on Marxism to the congregation of his church. One of the signs of our times is that my arrest record is quite modest for a political activist, and the failure of the government to win a conviction is typical in cases that are brought to public attention. The state has lost every big public political conspiracy case in the last six years—Benjamin Spock, the Berrigans, the New York Panther 21, Bobby Seale, Angela Davis, the Chicago 8, Vietnam Veterans against the War, Wounded Knee—although thousands of political activists whose trials did not get media coverage are still in prison today.

From all this I begin to understand the danger posed by people like me. The state is less afraid of what we may do than of what we are saying. But surely a torrent of words is not going to sweep away the government of the United States and all the powers behind it. Exactly. The government is not afraid of my words themselves any more than it is afraid of my physical body planting bombs or harboring fugitives. By fearing what we say, the government shows that it is mortally afraid of the people, the one historical force capable of implementing revolutionary ideas.

Furthermore, I am not some great genius with uniquely original ideas, but almost exactly the opposite. My ideas are commonplace, in every sense of that term. Although few American readers will believe this at the moment, the truth is that my thinking coincides with that of the vast majority of people on this planet, who daily see and feel the vital need to finish off the dinosaur system embodied in the United States. When average people in this country have an opportunity to hear these ideas, they seem to find them quite useful in understanding this system and what to do about it. The internal threat to the state is not me or any other single individual, but the millions and millions of people in the United States who, as our rulers fear, might agree with the simple, common ideas I express and attempt to act upon.

Political thought in the United States is so provincial, even though we live in the heartland of the world's greatest empire, that people whose thinking does conform to that of the majority in the world still seem to be a mere "dissident minority," "a lunatic left" that appears to have dropped in from the moon. Every reporter who has ever interviewed me has at some point asked this question: "How did you ever get to be a communist?" The tone of the question suggests that the transformation from an average American citizen to a communist revolutionary must be something like waking up one fine morning to find you have turned into a cockroach. But to people who have become communist revolutionaries the process is mostly just that—a process, a development, quite gradual up to a point, and in fact inevitable given the actual concrete conditions of this society. It is no surprise to me that my own political evolution closely resembles that of tens of thousands, possibly hundreds of thousands, of U.S. citizens within the last several years alone.

One of the guerrilla groups operating in Guatemala encountered a similar problem among the peasants and villagers, who were looking on the revolutionaries as if they were alien beings. So they switched methods. When they talked to the people of a village or a plantation, instead of giving political lectures on how the people are oppressed and why their only hope lies in the path of armed struggle toward a socialist society, they began by speaking of their own lives. They would tell of their own childhood, and trace the steps they had taken to become armed fighters ready to give their lives for the people. The peasants and villagers were then able to see the common experience in their own lives, and they understood there was actually a possibility they themselves might become revolutionaries.

Back Where You Came From

Perceptions of Stanford: Or "Can We Have Quiet, Please"

The overwhelming majority of professors at this university are actively engaged in the explanation and repudiation of Communism and Marxist ideologies.

Robert E. Miller, Jr., University Relations Officer, Stanford University, 1964 (Stanford *Daily*, December 2, 1971).

We are highly dubious whether *rehabilitation* is a useful concept in this case. Professor Franklin's announced convictions about the guilt of the university appear deeply-held, and his opposition to the institution in its present form seems implacable. We believe him when he expresses his regret that his role in converting the university to "serve the people" is restricted by practical reasons to advocacy rather than action. "Rehabilitation" might appear to Professor Franklin as a highly unfair mandate to change his convictions. Barring a dramatic change in perception he is unlikely to change his conduct; thus "rehabilitation" is likely to fail, whatever the sanction.

In the Matter of Professor H. Bruce Franklin, Decision, Advisory Board, Stanford University, January 5, 1972, p. 12.

WHEN THE PRESIDENT'S ADVISORY BOARD arrived at this decision to fire me from my tenured associate professorship at Stanford because I was not a suitable case for "*rehabilitation,*" they explained that the cause of my incurability lay in my "perception of reality." (It is worth noting that one of the five gentlemen who wrote this decision was then chairman of the Department of Psychiatry.) With sadness for me and concern for the security of Stanford, they pointed out that my "perception of reality . . . differs drastically from the consensus in the university." Then they went on to outline this "perception of reality," which they elsewhere characterized as "bizarre":

> In his opening argument Professor Franklin proclaimed deep convictions about the evils of American foreign and domestic policy and about the inevitable influences of our socio-economic system in shaping that policy. Essential to this perception is a mistrust of the allegedly intricate interrelationship between the economic power of America's "ruling class" and the maintenance of policies that are imperialistic abroad and oppressive at home. Of crucial importance in the present case is his expressed view that the university, run by and for this ruling class, possesses a substantial institutional guilt for the ongoing prosecution of those policies. (p. 12.)

Stanford University displayed its own institutional perception of reality in response to the suit brought by the American Civil Liberties Union to force my reinstatement. The university argued that the suit should be thrown out of court because the First Amendment to the Constitution of the United States does not apply to Stanford University, since Stanford is a "private" institution, an issue yet to be resolved.

My deviant perception sees the story of Stanford University beginning on a festive occasion on January 8, 1863. As the band plays merrily, construction begins on the Central Pacific Railroad. The first ceremonial shovelful of earth is thrown onto the embankment by Leland Stanford, Governor of the State of California, who happens, coincidentally, to be President of the Central Pacific Railroad.

The previous year, the U.S. Congress had passed the Railway Act of 1862, granting to the newly-incorporated Central Pacific vast lands and monies if it would do the country the kindness of building a railroad. The money alone amounted to $16,000 for each mile of track laid over plains and $48,000 per mile in the mountains. The Central Pacific immediately paid a team of geologists to define practically every proposed mile as in the mountains. In April, 1863, the California legislature, then entirely under the control of the Central Pacific, passed a bill giving the Central Pacific an additional $10,000 per mile in state funds, plus a state land grant to augment the federal one. Governor Stanford signed the bill, no doubt after careful consideration. But the western railroad lobby in Washington, made up chiefly of the Central Pacific and the soon-to-be-amalgamated Union Pacific, explained to a sympathetic Congress that more was needed. So Congress passed the Railway Act of 1864, doubling the land grant of 1862; the two railroads were granted ten tracts of land per mile within twenty miles of either side of the track, a total of 12,800 acres per mile of track. Not too many objections were heard, because after all most of the land belonged to Indians, who certainly were not going to use it to make profits and who even thought that people who believed they "owned" land were a little crazy.

Meanwhile, the Central Pacific had conducted an arduous search to find a construction contractor capable of this undertaking. They selected Crocker and Company, the tiny personal firm of Charles Crocker, one of Stanford's three co-partners in the Central Pacific, who had allowed the other three gentlemen to invest equally in his company. Stanford, Crocker, Huntington, and Colton then decided that "Contract and Finance Company" would be a more convenient name for the company that was receiving all the construction contracts.

The work conditions were so miserable, the pay so low, and the job so dangerous that the Contract and Finance Company had to go all the way to Canton, China, to find laborers. Ten thousand Chinese "coolies" and three thousand Irishmen built the railroad.

The Chinese worked for one dollar a day. Hundreds died on the job.

Meanwhile, Stanford and his associates sought additional public financing, this time from the towns through which the railroad might—or might not—pass. Henry George, the great nineteenth-century American sociologist, writing first in the San Francisco magazine *Overland Monthly* and later in *Progress and Poverty*, compared this operation of the Central Pacific to that of a gang of bandits: "A railroad company approaches a small town as a highwayman approaches his victim. . . . And just as robbers unite to plunder in concert and divide the spoils, so do the trunk lines of railroads unite to raise rates and pool their earnings, or the Pacific roads form a combination with the Pacific Mail Steamship Company by which toll gates are virtually established on land and ocean." (*Progress and Poverty*, 1879, pp. 192–93.) For example, Los Angeles County decided to give to the Central Pacific a total of 5 percent of the assessed valuation of the entire county, including a controlling interest in the existing railroad (the Los Angeles and San Pedro), $377,000 in cash, and sixty acres for a depot.

Neither Leland Stanford nor any of his three partners put up any of the money for the building of the railroad. It was financed by the United States, the state of California, and local communities, and it was built, by virtual slave labor, on land mostly stolen from the Indians. Yet the railroad, like its offspring, Stanford University, was "private" property. The four associates sucked vast private fortunes out of the railroad, and left it a shell, $57 million in debt, dangerously flimsy in construction, and reliable only in its continuing rapacity.

Leland Stanford used some of the millions he had "earned" to establish several imitations of feudal baronies, including a palatial structure on Nob Hill which seemed to many visitors and residents to reduce the rest of San Francisco to the image of the feudal township clinging to the heights of the lord's castle. But his favorite was "the farm" in Palo Alto, fourteen square miles of private estate. When Leland Stanford, Jr., died in 1884, his father, then U.S. Senator Stanford, and his mother, Jane Lathrop Stanford, looked for a suitable memorial. They decided to turn the Palo Alto "farm" into Leland Stanford Junior University, an act legally accomplished in November, 1885, when the Founding Grant of the University turned the property over to twenty-four white San Francisco men of business and "public affairs," the first Board of Trustees, representing primarily the western railroads and banks, and the Pacific shipping and mercantile trusts.

Instruction began at Stanford University on October 1, 1891. Two years later, Edward A. Ross, a young professor of economics, joined the Stanford faculty. Professor Ross was by no means a political revolutionary. But he had made a study of the Central Pacific and its subsidiary, which had since absorbed the parent, the Southern Pacific. It was suspected, though never proven, that Professor Ross believed that the railroad should be owned by the state or by the municipalities through which it passed. He began to give public speeches hinting of this view.

Mrs. Stanford, who had become a widow in 1893 and who now personally managed the Stanford financial empire, heard about these speeches and immediately wrote to the first president of the university, Dr. David Starr Jordan: "I must confess I am weary of Professor Ross and I think he ought not to be retained at Stanford University. . . . I think he should now be dismissed." Jordan remonstrated; but it was to no avail. On November 14, 1900, Ross was forced to resign. As he did so, he declared: "I have long been aware that my every appearance in public drew upon me the hostile attention of certain powerful persons in finance in San Francisco, and they redoubled their efforts to be rid of me. But I had no choice but to go straight ahead."

One student protested. He was called "a perpetual freshman" and thrown into Lake Lagunita, a lake on the campus, by his fellows. The student newspaper, the *Daily Palo Alto*, said this of the incident: "He spent most of the morning at the front entrance of the Quad talking disrespectfully of the men in charge of the university. Quite a number of juniors and seniors took exception and dealt him some punishment."

A sizable minority of the faculty, however, put up some fight. Professor George N. Howard of the History Department delivered a lecture to his class entitled "Commercial Absolutism and the Place of the Teacher in the Discussion of Social Questions," which vigorously supported Ross. Later the same day Professor Howard issued a public statement saying that Professor Ross's dismissal "is a blow aimed directly at academic freedom" and "a deep humiliation to Stanford University and to the cause of American education." This blow, he declared, "proceeds from the sinister spirit of social bigotry and commercial intolerance which is just now the deadliest foe of American democracy." Mrs. Stanford, then in Rome, got wind of this new incitement and swiftly wrote to President Jordan, now demanding that Professor Howard also be banished from the Stanford estate. Other professors now protested against Professor Howard's dismissal. By the time the confrontation was over, nine members of the faculty had been forced to leave.

In the heat of the struggle at the young university, the meaning of academic freedom at Stanford was accurately defined by Professor John Casper Branner, who was later to become president of the university. Professor Branner published his credo in the *Daily Palo Alto:*

> Are professors in this institution at liberty to attack the university management in the presence of classes?
>
> If such a liberty is looked upon as academic freedom, then I beg to say once for all that such freedom (if such is the word) is not and will not be tolerated in this institution so long as it is under its present management.

President Jordan had been forewarned by an administrator at another university that Ross might not have "tact enough to steer clear of possible difficulties," and that, in regard to his study of the Pacific railroad, "I have heard him say very strong language on that score that would not do to put into the mouth of a professor of your university." So the administration was more cautious in its subsequent hiring policy. Nevertheless, they soon discovered another thorny weed in their garden. But they had learned one lesson well from the Ross affair: when firing a politically controversial professor, it's best to find a nonpolitical pretext. So, when they dismissed Thorstein Veblen from his associate professorship in 1909, it was allegedly for "personal" indiscretions.

In 1916 Veblen published *The Higher Learning in America: A Memorandum on the Conduct of Universities by Business Men.* Here he analyzed the contradiction between the ideal of the university, dedicated to the pursuit of "the higher learning," and the actual institution, created by and for the small-minded men of business. In those primitive early days, Veblen could still assert that "work that has a commercial value does not belong in the university," but he predicted that the "unstable compromise between the requirements of scholarly fitness and those of competitive enterprise" would have "a doubtful and shifting issue." And he recognized that it was the ethic of the capitalist, not that of the scholar, which ran the university of his day, described with his characteristic subtle irony:

> Its only ostensible reason for being, and so for its being governed and managed, competitively or otherwise, is the advancement of learning. And this advancement of learning is in no degree a business proposition; and yet it must, for the present at least, remain the sole ostensible purpose of the businesslike university. In the main, therefore, all the competitive endeavours and manoeuvres of the captains of erudition in charge must be made under cover of an ostensible endeavour to further this non-competitive advancement of learning, at all costs.

Veblen published this analysis in the midst of World War I, a year before the Russian Revolution, more than a decade before the Great Depression. It was still the heyday of free-enterprise capitalism, and the United States, which was still annexing parts of the North American continent, was just beginning to perceive its manifest destiny in fully global terms. Let us pick up the story of

Stanford University again after World War II, the collapse of most of the great European world empires, and the global expansion of the U.S. empire under the cover of unwilling world policeman in the "Cold War."

By 1951, Stanford had become the matrix of two interlocked and interdependent complexes: the Pacific Basin (i.e., the lands washed by the Pacific Ocean) empire and a vast aerospace and electronics industry radiating from the San Francisco Bay area. The railroads and shipping companies had been dislodged from the Board of Trustees by the giant new industries created by the university itself, in partnership with the U.S. government. The master architect for the new design was Professor Frederick Terman of the vast Electrical Engineering Department, who taught William Hewlett and David Packard, became Dean of the Engineering School, and then Provost of Stanford University. Years later, Terman looked back and eloquently described the institution he had helped plan and create:

> We have been pioneers in creating a new type of community, one that I have called a "community of technical scholars." Such a community is composed of industries using highly sophisticated technologies, together with a strong university that is sensitive to the creative activities of the surrounding industry. This pattern appears to be the wave of the future.

This "community of technical scholars" did not emerge in an historical vacuum. Its overall purpose was described with great precision in a few well-chosen words by another key designer of the Stanford empire, Jesse Hobson, who spoke in 1951 as Director of Stanford Research Institute, then a wholly owned subsidiary corporation of Stanford University:

> This nation occupies six percent of the land area of the world, has seven percent of the world's population, but it now produces fifty percent of the world's goods and possesses sixty-seven percent of the world's wealth.
>
> Research must be the heart, the foundation, the life blood of our present defense economy if we are to maintain this position.

The "Pacific Basin" or, as it is also called, the "Pacific Rim" concept was developed by Stanford University theoreticians. The Board of Trustees of Stanford consists of representatives of the banks and corporations that interlock around the Pacific Basin, together with representatives of the giants of the war industry that safeguards the investments of these banks and corporations and rips open new areas for them.

The trustees are not just run-of-the-mill directors of these companies. At the time of my firing, they included the actual board chairmen of fifteen corporations, including Northrop, Wells Fargo Bank, American Express, Hewlett-Packard, and General Dynamics, the nation's largest war contractor. (The Chairman of the Board of Northrop, producer of the F-5, principal counterinsurgency fighter-bomber of the Free World, Mr. Thomas V. Jones, resigned from the Stanford Board of Trustees in 1974, shortly after pleading guilty to a felony. In the Nixon impeachment hearings, it turned out that Mr. Jones—about a year after voting to fire me—had taken $50,000 of Northrop's funds, which he later falsely alleged was personal money, to a clandestine meeting in San Diego, where he handed it to Herbert Kalmbach, to be used as a payoff for the silence of the Watergate conspirators.) The industrial corporations represented on the Board of Trustees together produce more quantities of advanced military equipment than is now possessed by any but three nations in the world. For instance, they turn out nuclear submarines, the Poseidon missiles fired by these submarines, and all the navigational and other equipment needed to run undersea combat missions. They manufacture advanced fighter-bombers, the F-111 as well as the F-5, together with all the radar, weapons systems, fuel, and ordnance needed to run strike missions in Indochina, even down to the "Beehive" and flechette projectiles in the latest antipersonnel bombs still being used in Vietnam and Cambodia. They constructed the B-52 bases in Thailand. They manufacture dozens of varieties of missiles, including the Minuteman and the Atlas ICBM. Nor do they disdain mundane ground warfare. They produce everything from the various tanks and personnel carriers specifically programmed on the Stanford computer for use in an air-sea invasion plan of North Vietnam down to the small arms, ammunition, and even body armor and the "people sniffers" designed for counterinsurgency in the caves and jungles of Vietnam, Laos, Cambodia, and the Philippines.

Together with the banks on the Board of Trustees—such as Wells Fargo, Chase Manhattan, and Bank of America—these corporations have vast investments around the world, particularly in South Africa and the Pacific Basin, including Thailand, Laos, Cambodia, Vietnam, Malaysia, Singapore, Indonesia, the Philippines, Australia, Hong Kong, Korea, Japan, and Taiwan. (In the last two, Stanford has graduate campuses.) Union Oil, Shell Oil, and U.S. Natural Resources, all heavily represented on the Board of Trustees, are busy working their offshore oil concessions throughout Southeast Asia. Meanwhile, in the cities of these Asian lands, production facilities are set up by some of the subsidiaries of the trustees' companies, such as FMC's branch "FMC Far East Ltd." and Castle and Cooke's operations known as the "Thai-American Steel Works Co." and "Castle and Cooke East Asia Ltd." Good old American Standard, whose president is a Stanford trustee, keeps diversifying until it becomes one of the largest military research and development contractors, but not at the expense of its traditional line, for it secures a monopoly on the manufacture of toilets in Thailand (as well as at Stanford University). Many of these noble enterprises fulfilling the white man's burden are financed by the friendly banks on the Board of Trustees, such as the Bank of America, which put up a $20 million bond to help Utah International (also on the Board) to build one of its B-52 bases, and which, through such disinterested public service, managed to increase its overseas investments from $7.2 billion in 1946 to $65 billion in 1968.

A large piece of Stanford University land has been converted into the Stanford Industrial Park, which forms a home for many corporations represented both on the Board of Trustees and in the administration of the Stanford School of Engineering, School of Business, and School of Earth Sciences. Together with Stanford Research Institute and Stanford itself, the Industrial Park forms the nerve center of the highly technical electronics "defense" industry of the United States. For instance, there is Applied Technology, set up by a Stanford group including Professor Oswald Villard, Director of the Stanford Radioscience Laboratories, and Professor William Rambo, Director of the Stanford Electronics Laboratories. Rambo was the first Stanford professor exposed as a CIA researcher and one of the founding members of the Association of Old Crows, the key military research organization dedicated "To foster and preserve the art of electronic warfare," whose motto is *Non Videbunt* (They Will Not See). Applied Tech was bought in 1967 by ITEK, which is now also set up in the Industrial Park. There are Granger Associates, whose directors include former Stanford Provost Frederick Terman and Electrical Engineering Professor Allan Peterson; Flour-Utah, which built those Thailand B-52 bases, whose directors include not only a trustee but also the Stanford University Vice-President for Business; Beckman Instruments; Optics-Technology, one of whose directors is chairman of the Stanford University Physics Department; Hewlett-Packard, whose directors include four Stanford trustees and whose chairman, David Packard, was Chairman of the Board of Trustees before becoming Assistant Secretary of Defense (a position he relinquished to become head of Nixon's 1972 campaign in California); Varian Associates, whose chairman is a former Stanford engineering professor; Wells Fargo, which not only has its chairman on the Stanford Board of Trustees but also has among its directors the present Dean of the Stanford University School of Business, the Stanford Vice-President for Business, and another Stanford trustee; Teledyne; Control Data; Kaiser Aerospace and Electronics, whose parent company is on the Board of Trustees; Precision Instruments; ITT Semiconductor Division; Watkins-Johnson, heavily represented on the Board of Trustees; Fairchild Semiconductors; Lockheed Missiles and Space, whose president was a Stanford trustee until his death in 1971; and so on. This list includes fewer than a third of the "defense"-related companies in the Industrial Park.

Stanford University has made some spectacular contributions to the research parts of the "defense" economy and strategy outlined by Jesse Hobson of SRI. The "Strategic Hamlet" plan for Vietnam, otherwise known as the Staley Plan, under which hundreds of thousands of Vietnamese peasants were rounded up and put in concentration camps, was designed at Stanford, principally by Professor Eugene Staley of the School of Education. The ill-fated McNamara Line, the "Electronic Battlefield," and the electronic air war in Indochina all were produced by Stanford research and utilized sophisticated electronics components manufactured by the companies represented on the Board of Trustees and housed in the Industrial Park. The Hoover Institution on War, Revolution and Peace, which has open connections with the FBI and CIA, is one of the world's main centers of anti-Communist propaganda. It was set up, in the words of its founder Herbert Hoover, "to demonstrate the evils of the doctrines of Karl Marx . . . thus to protect the American way of life"; and, according to the *Wall Street Journal* (June 2, 1967), it now has "a network of agents around the world" employed, among other things, to steal documents for the Hoover archives.

Veblen accurately analyzed how the university's financial dependence in the early twentieth century limited and defined the ideas acceptable within it. "What is especially to be conciliated," he wrote, is the current range of convictions "among those well-to-do classes from whom the institution hopes to draw contributions to its endowment. . . . Which comes, broadly, to saying that a jealous eye must be had to the views and prepossessions prevalent among the respectable, conservative middle class; with a particular regard to that more select body of substantial citizens who have the disposal of accumulated wealth." Veblen's analysis still partly holds. In 1971, Stanford University received gifts, from businesses and affluent individuals, and nongovernment grants, principally from corporations and private foundations, totaling $15,251,928. Tuition and student fees, mainly paid by families of the social classes described by Veblen, brought in another $27,926,775. By this point in history, Stanford University is an independent business as well, with 1971 investment income adding up to another $15,835,868. But one thing has qualitatively changed since Veblen's time, the heyday of free-enterprise capitalism. We are now in a period of rapidly consolidating state capitalism, reflected in Stanford's interconnections within the military-industrial-educational complex. The income so far mentioned, all at least ostensibly derived directly from "nongovernment" sources, adds up to $59,014,571. In that same year, 1971, Stanford received income from out-and-out government grants in the sum of $69,349,656, with an additional income from government contracts of $16,063,049, for a total income from the government of $85,412,705. When we consider that the income from tuition includes a substantial amount from government grants and loans, the balance shifts even more toward government financing. Furthermore, many of the sources listed as "nongovernment" receive much of their funds from government loans, grants, and contracts. And the companies Stanford itself invests in do much of their business with the government. Even the gifts of individuals can hardly be described as purely "private." David Packard, for instance, who gave $2.6 million to Stanford two days after I was fired, derived this from the $18 million he "earned" from his investments while serving as Assistant Secretary of Defense.

The mere existence of complex ties among Stanford, the "defense" industry, and the government does not of itself prove that war and empire constitute the main business of the university. In addition to its research, which we shall come back to, one of the main functions of the university is education; that is, it teaches the future managers, technocrats, businessmen, diplomats, researchers, propagandists, corporation lawyers, engineers, secret police, and politicians how to run, maintain, and defend the empire. Whenever there is the barest hint of a threat to this training process, the university shows by its response that this is its life blood.

Recruiters from the government, the military, and big business pour into Stanford searching for these highly trained university products. In 1972, a movement developed in protest against direct military and war recruiting at Stanford, which was held to be in open conflict with the avowed purposes of the university. The Committee on Services to Students, set up by the administration itself, recommended, by an 8–1 vote, that military recruiters not be allowed to use student services facilities and that there be a binding referendum on whether these facilities should be used by corporations doing over $100 million war production annually. They rejected a previous student referendum, which had overwhelmingly voted against all military and war recruiting, and they recommended that all recruiters be allowed private conferences in professors' offices or other campus locations. President Richard Lyman promptly issued a public statement calling any limitation whatsoever on military recruiters "utterly irresponsible." He stated that because of congressional riders on "defense" funds, such action "would mean the loss to Stanford of more than $16 million annual research support on which about 1,000 faculty, staff, and students depend." The Faculty Senate hastily concurred with the president, voting thirty-one to six not to allow any restriction whatsoever on military or war recruiting at Stanford. The president and the faculty thus showed in practice that though they might call my perception of the real Stanford University a "bizarre mischaracterization" and kick me out for expressing this view in public speeches, the perception of Stanford upon which they act is remarkably similar.

What views should the professors of a capitalist university be allowed to express? The university's philosophy and policy were described perfectly by an ardent defender of Stanford, the San Francisco newspaper *The Argonaut*, in support of the firing of Professor Ross:

Suppose you had twenty millions of dollars. Suppose you endowed a great university. Suppose that within its halls there arose the jangled voices of what you believed to be false teaching. . . . Would you continue to use your vast fortune in the inculcation of what you believed to be false?

After Veblen's firing in 1909, Stanford did a good job of keeping out teachers who might incur the displeasure of the capitalist class until 1948, when Paul Baran joined the economics department.

In 1954, after he had acquired tenure, Professor Baran signed a petition supporting a left-wing school being investigated by the government. Fred Glover, special assistant to the president, immediately sent a copy of the petition to President Wallace Sterling, warning "Wally," in words that sounded like those applied to Ross sixty years before, "Baran, being in the Econ Dept., may give us real trouble some day." (This and the following quotations are from correspondence published in the *Stanford Daily*, December 2, 1971.)

Real trouble came in 1960 when Baran visited Cuba and came back to praise the revolutionary government. From that point on the official correspondence about Baran defined Stanford's academic freedom with great precision. When a Texaco Oil executive wrote in, emphasizing Texaco's recent $10,000 gift to Stanford and indicating that it was inconsistent to retain on the faculty a person who seemed to approve of Cuba's seizure of Texaco refineries, University Relations official Donald Carson wrote back, stating Stanford's policy in no uncertain terms: "I know that we would agree that Communism is the very antithesis of freedom, academic or otherwise. This is why Communists are not permitted to hold positions on the Stanford faculty."

But Baran was a problem. Fred Glover, writing to an alumnus from southern California, put it like this: "Baran has tenure. To fire him, we would have to have a reason which would stand up in court." Morris M. Doyle, then Chairman of the Board of Trustees, and now senior partner of the law firm representing Stanford in its attempt to make my firing seem legal, wrote his own letter to alumni advising them that "we must suffer" Baran until he does a specific act "which would warrant termination." But he assured them that it was only the law that prevented the administration from getting rid of him: "Dr. Baran is a continuing embarrassment and source of irritation to the administration at Stanford and to the Board of Trustees."

David Packard, Chairman of the Board of Trustees at Stanford just prior to his appointment by Nixon as Assistant Secretary of Defense, wrote a letter declaring that Baran's being an avowed Marxist violated the principle that "a professor should be a teacher, not an advocate." Since Baran had tenure, Packard proposed a punishment fitting the crime of expressing the "wish to destroy" capitalism: his salary should be reduced "proportionate to the amount which can be clearly identified as having come from sources other than Capitalism."

Packard's revealing solution was essentially the one implemented. Baran's salary was frozen (as was mine for several years). He was also subjected to increasingly vicious attacks both from within and outside the university. The attacks began to have their effect. In a letter to Paul Sweezy he said, "The business of freezing my salary, far from being treated as a secret, is being widely advertised to show that nothing would be done to encourage me to stay here." He added that the pressure "burns me all up, plays havoc with the nervous system." Donald Carson was able to write gloatingly from the University Relations office, "I doubt if he's enjoyed the harassment he has received," because "shortly after" giving a speech praising Castro as one of the century's greatest men, Baran "had a serious heart attack." His second and final heart attack came in 1964. Paul Baran's death removed Stanford's acute problem, the man *Business Week* called "the only Marxist professor on the faculty of a major U.S. university."

According to the administration, the Board of Trustees, the Advisory Board, and their supporters in the Business School, the Law School, the School of Earth Sciences, the Engineering School, the Hoover Institution, the School of Aeronautics and Astronautics, and so on, the cases of Ross and Baran have no relevance whatsoever to my case. Ross and Baran, it is now tacitly conceded, may have gotten into difficulties because of their public speeches. But Franklin was fired for what he *did*, not what he *said*. But what I did was to say things, that is, I made public speeches, as Ross and Baran had. There had to be a way to transform my speeches into acts. Hence the charge of "urging and inciting disruption."

According to law and to the obvious meanings of the words, "urging and inciting" is something quite different from advocacy. It is the use of speech to impel people into an immediate action by overcoming their rationality. A district attorney *advocating* that a jury sentence a person to death is not (at least according to the law) *urging and inciting* them. If he started chanting and screaming, "Kill him! Kill him! Now!" in an effort to make them leap out of the jury box and do it right then and there, that would be *urging and inciting*. But all this is beside the point; after all, the Advisory Board admitted, in an unguarded sentence, that my role was restricted to "advocacy rather than action." And the specific "crime," the one that put me beyond the hope of "rehabilitation," was advocating that the university should "serve the people." It took me years to arrive at this revolutionary idea.

In January, 1959, I arrived at Stanford as a graduate student. After graduating from college in 1955, I had worked half a year on tugboats in New York Harbor and then spent three years flying in the United States Air Force. I was a political liberal, an intellectual elitist, and an idealist, in every sense of the term. I loved literature and believed that its general overall effect was to civilize people. I considered myself a seeker after truth, and I wanted to be a teacher in order to help society become more civilized.

My view of the Stanford English Department, and my expectations of what I would have to do to become a "Doctor of Philosophy," had me in awe—for about a week. Then I began to discover that the English Department consisted almost entirely of prosperous white gentlemen whose main interest was divided between writing books to be read by each other and indulging in a comfortable life, with the majority inclining rather heavily to the latter. They mostly did what was called "professional scholarship."

A few made some pretense of dabbling in ideas. Not one was concerned with the major ideological questions of our century, including questions about culture and literature. They were universally ignorant of Marxism, and of Marxist criticism, as was I.

The only active intelligence was that of Yvor Winters, who had been socially ostracized by most of the department. Winters wrote an essay in which he accurately characterized his archetypal colleague as "Professor X," who is above all "a gentleman and a scholar":

> He conforms to established usages because he finds life pleasanter and easier for those who do so; and he is able to approve of Emerson because he has never for a moment realized that literature could be more than a charming amenity. He believes that we should not be too critical of literature; that we should try to appreciate as much literature as possible; and that such appreciation will cultivate us. Professor X once reproved me for what he considered my contentiousness by telling me that he himself had yet to see the book that he would be willing to quarrel over. Professor X, in so far as he may be said to have moral motion, moves in that direction indicated by Emerson, but only to the extent of indulging a kind of genteel sentimentality; he is restrained from going the limit by considerations that he cannot or will not formulate philosophically but by which he is willing to profit. His position is that of the dilettante: the nearest thing he has to a positive philosophy is something to which he would never dare commit himself; that which keeps him in order is a set of social proprieties which he neither understands nor approves. In a world of atomic bombs, power politics, and experts in international knavery, he has little to guide him and he offers extremely precarious guidance to others; yet by profession he is a searcher for truth and a guide to the young.

Since the graduate program at Stanford was designed by Professor X and his colleagues, it was not necessary for a graduate student to know even one work by a Black or Chicano author, to read even one article by a Marxist critic, or to be aware of even one fact about the history and culture of proletarian revolution. My own total ignorance of the relations between literature and class struggle of course posed not the slightest obstacle to my graduate work.

I gravitated toward Winters, despite the fact that I disagreed with many of his ideas, because he took ideas—and literature—seriously. It was in one of several courses I took from him that I encountered Herman Melville. In 1960 and 1961 I read each of Melville's works at least three times, and was beginning to form some dim understanding of the source and significance of his influence on me. But it was to take almost another decade of history and personal experience to comprehend Melville's full relevance for us (see my article, "Herman Melville: Artist of the Worker's World," *History in Literature*, San Francisco: Ramparts Press, 1975).

Early in 1961, before I had finished my doctoral dissertation on Melville, the Stanford English Department offered me an assistant professorship, the first time in thirty-three years they had asked one of their own graduate students to stay on. At the time, I took this as a testimonial to the brilliance and originality of my work. Looking back, I see it as a recognition that this work was harmless, insignificant, and highly professional, that is, it projected the alleged ideals of the profession within a methodological form acceptable to those who controlled the profession.

As an Assistant Professor of English and American Literature, I found myself right away, in September, 1961, placed in an unexpected role, but one that I accepted with pleasure, seeing in it still another way to spread intellectual and cultural enlightenment. The administration appointed me to the University Committee on Public Exercises, which had jurisdiction over all public events and ceremonies. I served on that committee through the spring of 1964, just before the summer that marked a new stage of U.S. history. During that three-year period, two major issues of free speech arose. By looking back on these controversies, we can see how far we have come since just before Mississippi Freedom Summer, the open use of U.S. troops in Vietnam, and the Free Speech Movement at Berkeley in the fall of 1964.

The first issue was: Should Stanford students (that is, the most privileged and presumably least dangerous of students) be allowed to have political free speech and, if so, when and where? Month after month our Committee on Public Exercises wrestled mightily with this question, in various forms. The issue reached a crisis in January, 1963, when the student government took the wildly controversial, radical, inflammatory, and menacing action of expressing "grave concern" because the FCC was withholding the license renewal of KPFA, the listener-supported FM radio station in Berkeley, during an investigation by the Senate Internal Security Subcommittee, headed by Mississippi Senator James Eastland. (It would have been entirely beyond the boundaries of my comprehension to have learned then, in some message from the future, that eight years later this same committee would accuse me of being a dangerous revolutionary leader who "had supplied explosives and weapons" to a Black revolutionary organization known as the Black Panther Party, as well as assisting "wounded members of the Black Panther Party in obtaining surgery.") The administration, sensitive to dangerous political potential and implicit threats to its control, thundered, threatened the students with immediate discipline, and reminded them of the existing university policy, which they officially reiterated in these terms:

> The President and the Board of Trustees have begun a review of the University's policies relating to institutional participation in and identification with political and social action.
>
> At the request of the President of the University, I am writing to inform you that, pending the policy review and until further notice, Stanford student organizations may not take public stands on issues affecting affairs beyond the Stanford campus without prior University approval. This provision applies also to officers of Stanford student organizations in their official capacities, although it does not limit the right of any student as an individual to participate in undertakings which are not identified with the University.
>
> H. Donald Winbigler
> Dean of Students

The other burning question to come before our Committee on Public Exercises was: Should a Communist be allowed to appear on the campus of Stanford University in order to give a public speech? Archie Brown, an official of the Communist Party, had been invited to speak on campus. The administration was opposed, but would allow our committee, which consisted of administrators, faculty, and three nonvoting student members, to decide.

During the committee discussions, the liberal professors argued in favor of Brown's speaking, but fell all over each other in assuring the administrators that they would never, never dream of allowing a Communist to *teach* at Stanford. It was good, they argued, for the students occasionally—very occasionally—to be exposed to such ideas, to be, as it were, vaccinated against them. But they were most firm in their argument that Communists were unfit to be teachers, since they had to follow a party line, were never permitted to think for themselves, and therefore could not participate in academic freedom, which provided for an unfettered expression of one's own ideas.

The resolution was a compromise. A Communist could come to speak at Stanford if there were a "balanced program." So the committee invited Fred Schwartz of the Christian Anti-Communist Crusade to come to balance things out.

Out of these two struggles emerged the concept of a free speech area on campus, one place where students, and possibly others, could give political speeches without university approval. The administration reluctantly acquiesced to this audacious proposal. So came into being White Plaza, Stanford's showplace of token free speech, its miniature Hyde Park, where, on February 10, 1971, I gave the principal speech for which I was fired.

In the summer of 1964, I left Stanford to accept a teaching job at Johns Hopkins University in Baltimore. The events of the next twelve months transformed me, as they did the rest of U.S. society. Exactly how they did I shall explore in later chapters, because this transformation produced all of us as we are today. Here let us just recall the three main events. The Black rebellions broke out that summer, developed into the pattern of the "long hot summers" of 1965, 1966, and 1967, and culminated in April, 1968, when in one week Black people in 110 U.S. cities rose up in a simultaneous rebellion. This was also the year when most people began to get inklings of what was going on in Vietnam. The third event had its roots in the first two: the emergence of a white student movement, which seemed to begin as an isolated outburst at Berkeley that fall.

It is now October, 1965, over a year later. An evening meeting in an auditorium at Stanford. A panel of four white gentlemen, all neatly dressed in jackets, ties, and white shirts, make brief presentations about Vietnam. One of them is introduced as an associate professor of English, who has just returned after a year on the East Coast. Somewhat shorter and looking somewhat younger than the others, but attired in the same gentleman's uniform, he begins his talk with a quotation from Herman Melville's *The Confidence-Man: His Masquerade*, in which a gruff, rifle-toting, eccentric frontiersman from Missouri confronts the Confidence Man with the question, "You are an abolitionist, ain't you?" The Confidence Man responds:

> "As to that, I cannot so readily answer. If by abolitionist you mean a zealot, I am none; but if you mean a man, who, being a man, feels for all men, slaves included, and by any lawful act, opposed to nobody's interest, and therefore, rousing nobody's enmity, would willingly abolish suffering (supposing it, in its degree, to exist) from among mankind, irrespective of color, then am I what you say."

The professor then quotes the Missourian's reply:

> "Picked and prudent sentiments. You are the moderate man, the invaluable understrapper of the wicked man. You, the moderate man, may be used for wrong, but are useless for right."

The speaker then applies his text to the Vietnam War:

> Yes, this is the class position—and the role—of the moderate man, whether in Germany in the 1930's or in the United States of America in the 1850's or 1960's. The moderate man refuses to recognize evil, refuses to call it by its right name, and refuses to oppose it unless it is absolutely convenient and comfortable to do so. He is a fine upstanding, law-abiding citizen who will obey that law no matter what it tells him to do. I would like tonight to say a word or two for immoderation.

He goes on to explain the importance of being "immoderately for good," but strongly cautions that "immoderation for peace" must remain absolutely "nonviolent." He advises those who are not ready to be immoderate in their nonviolent protest to write letters to government officials and "get informed." He asks those who still support the administration's Vietnam policy to join in discussion during an all-night vigil that will begin at the end of the meeting. That literary professor, with his tie and jacket, his moral fervor and slightly archaic style, and his immoderate commitment to such immoderate nonviolent actions as an all-night vigil, was considered part of the extreme ultra-left of the antiwar movement at Stanford in the fall of 1965.

I myself had remembered that speech as a fire-breathing call to radical action. When recently I found the written text buried in a file, I read it in disbelief. The speech shows nothing particularly noteworthy about me, but it reveals with almost dazzling clarity how far we have come since then. In terms of its own theme of moderation, we would have to put it today among those who are trying to impede activism by issuing calls for vigils, letter writing, and "nonviolence." But more significant is the political naïveté of the speech, its substitution of moral exhortation for political analysis. The fact that this speech could in late 1965 be taken as a "left" statement shows that we had only begun to stir from the intense stupor of depoliticization into which we had been drugged in the late 1940s and 1950s. Of course there were some individuals in the United States who in 1965 did have a political consciousness and a political vocabulary. But here I was at Stanford, cast in the role of radical and political activist, when I did not even know the political categories, or even have available the very words that would have made a political analysis possible. And I still didn't understand Melville.

White Plaza, that free-speech zone, was becoming the focal point of the public antiwar movement. I spoke there first toward the end of 1965 in support of a blood drive for the Vietnamese victims of U.S. bombing. When I very naïvely—and mistakenly—declared that Ho Chi Minh was a nationalist above being a Communist and a human being above being a nationalist, I was pelted with trash and called a "dirty Jew bastard" by the ROTC students who had been assembled in the plaza by their instructors.

By this time, I was on another university committee, the Committee on General Studies, which decided what student activities were to receive academic credit. The ROTC students who had attacked me, together with coeds in an Air ROTC support group called Angel Flight, were awarded activity credit by the committee for organizing a rival blood drive in the plaza, this one for U.S. soldiers. I moved that the people who had organized the original blood drive should also get activity credit. The motion died for want of a second.

In 1966, I helped build a movement to stop the construction of a napalm plant in neighboring Redwood City. Meanwhile, the first sit-in took place at Stanford. It was a protest against the secret CIA research contracts just discovered in the Electrical Engineering Department and against the continuing practice of giving Selective Service tests for student deferments on the campus. In contrast to the view widely publicized these days that the student antiwar movement was motivated largely by a desire to avoid the draft, it should be noted that this protest, like many others, called for an end to deferments for college students, arguing that they were unfair to working-class young men. I did not participate in the sit-in, for several reasons. The anti-napalm campaign in Redwood City was taking all the time I felt I could spare. I thought of the sit-in as an action by students and had doubts about whether any faculty member should participate (none did). I even had lingering doubts about whether this were not too militant a tactic, one that would isolate the few dozen students participating in it. So, together with about a dozen other professors more or less in the same boat, I limited myself to sponsoring some resolutions to the Academic Council, the assembly of the full faculty. Up until that time, the Academic Council was a purely ceremonial body which listened to and applauded the president's reports, routinely voted by acclamation to award degrees to lists of students, and held moments of silence for recently deceased colleagues. Our little resolutions—

to prohibit secret research ("research which could not be shared with all members of the Stanford community") and to ask that the draft deferment tests be held off campus—produced waves of outrage. We were all branded "radicals," and I was dumfounded to hear our mild motions labeled "irresponsible attacks on academic freedom and the personal liberties of Stanford students."

So far, I had had no direct confrontation with the administration. My first one came a couple of months later, during the summer of 1966, over a most unlikely issue. The student government, whose president was then David Harris, was sponsoring a summer film festival. The films included *Never Give a Sucker an Even Break, Scorpio Rising, She Done Him Wrong, Gold Diggers of 1933* (the musical with Dick Powell and Ruby Keeler), *High Mass for the Dakota Sioux, Flaming Creatures, Le Coquille et le Clergyman,* and Jean Genet's *Un Chant d'Amour*. The administration, acting through the Committee on Public Exercises, ordered the entire festival banned from campus on the grounds that the films, particularly the one by Genet, were "obscene" and "salacious." I denounced the administration and the committee in public, and invited the student government to show the films in a seminar I would give, open to anyone. Eventually a compromise was reached: the films would be sponsored by the English and French departments, there would be no admission fee, attendance would be limited to "members of the Stanford community over the age of 18," and I.D. cards would be checked by the student police.

That September I left for a year in France. There I participated in the antiwar movement, began to study Marxist theory seriously, worked with the Vietnamese, and started thinking of myself as a communist. When I returned in the fall of 1967, I began teaching Marxist theory in my classes. Shortly after I got back, there was a noisy but nonviolent demonstration against CIA recruiters who had come to campus. My Melville class voted to meet on the lawn outside the building where the CIA was recruiting. I spent the period reading to them passages about imperialism and capitalism from the first edition of Melville's *Typee*, passages which Melville had been forced to delete from subsequent editions. In the spring of 1968, there was a very large sit-in protesting the suspension of many of the anti-CIA demonstrators. This sit-in was a turning point in student consciousness, well described by Irving Louis Horowitz and William H. Friedland in the chapter "Sit-in at Stanford" in *The Knowledge Factory* (Chicago: Aldine Publishing, 1970, pp. 281–335). They accurately describe my role:

> The final speaker, H. Bruce Franklin . . . sought to refocus the issue most directly: the struggle of the students was only a part of larger struggles in society; it was the job of the students to take up those larger issues and to come to grips with them.

In the spring of 1969, a very large student movement, eventually supported by the vote of the majority of students, arose to protest a vast complex of secret war research being conducted at Stanford. Police were called in for the first time to arrest students and others engaged in a nonviolent sit-in. Two days later, hundreds of demonstrators laid siege to the Stanford Research Institute Center for Counterinsurgency in Southeast Asia. For the first time, they fought back against a police charge, setting fire to barricades and hurling most of the burning tear-gas grenades used by the police into the SRI Center, which never reopened.

A few days later, the kind of motion which was to become a ritual was introduced into the Academic Council. It commended the president for calling the police, praised the police for their great restraint, vilified the handful of "troublemakers" who had brought all this senseless violence to a peaceful campus, and called for "rational discussion" to solve all our problems. Professor after professor rose to express warm and orotund support for the motion. Nobody opposed it. Finally, when mine was the only hand remaining in the air, the president called on me. I managed to get out half a sentence—to the effect that violence on campus was not caused by a handful of troublemakers. Suddenly the faces of the professors, usually so unruffled, venerable, gentlemanly, and either white or mildly tanned by the California sun, writhed with snarls and reddened as they booed, hooted, and rhythmically stamped their feet (it sounded like a combination of Ebbets Field in Brooklyn and the old burlesque theater in Union City, New Jersey). After a minute or so, the president raised his arms, asked them to be quiet, and announced that he would allow me exactly one minute to finish my remarks—the first, and perhaps only, instance when a faculty member had a time limit imposed on speech to the Academic Council. At the close of the meeting, about a dozen professors came up to shake my hand, apologize for the conduct of "our colleagues," and express amazement at what they had just seen revealed.

The following fall, the English Department unanimously voted (with one abstention) that I be promoted to full professor. In January, 1970, the administration vetoed this recommendation on grounds that it was "premature." At the same time, the president secretly submitted to the Advisory Board a request that they begin proceedings to have me dismissed. The Board responded that the administration would have to supply them some charges.

In the spring of 1970, the United States invaded Cambodia. Most Stanford students, many Stanford workers, and, after a good deal of pressure, the majority of the professors shut down the university as part of the nationwide campus protest strike. In the midst of the strike, firebombs exploded at the Center for Advanced Study in the Behavioral Sciences and did considerable damage. The administration issued public statements blaming the antiwar movement. Later it was discovered that the firebombs had been hurled by an agent-provocateur in the pay of the FBI, then working tightly with the Stanford administration. Still later, during the Nixon impeachment hearings, it was revealed that one part of Operation Gemstone was to be a firebombing of the Brookings Institute, also in the spring of 1970. Operation Gemstone was one phase of the Nixon administration's overall plan (code-name Operation Cointelpro) to destroy the movement.

In January, 1971, Henry Cabot Lodge came to speak at Stanford as part of a program set up by the Hoover Institution to redefine the usefulness of the United Nations in view of the impending admission of the People's Republic of China. Lodge was heckled by the audience, and retreated from the lectern in a pique of petulance. Glenn Campbell, Director of the Hoover Institution, then canceled the speech, or rather rescheduled it for a more select audience. Within hours, the Stanford administration had begun a carefully orchestrated media campaign about Lodge being shouted down by a "mob." At the proper moment, they released the news through the media and private channels that I was being officially charged with being a principal participant in the "disruption." Exactly one year later, I was unanimously acquitted of this charge by the Advisory Board. They most reluctantly had to admit that during Lodge's entire appearance I was not, as contended by the administration's main witness (a retired army colonel now part of the Stanford administration), jumping up and down yelling at Lodge, but rather was sitting, not saying a word, with my son Robert on my lap.

In early February, 1971, news leaked out that the United States was supporting a massive invasion of Laos by Vietnamese puppet troops. The same week, workers at the $5-million Stanford University computer discovered on it a secret program, a detailed plan for an air-sea invasion of North Vietnam. The plan, code-named Gamut-H, was being run through the computer by Stanford Research Institute. SRI had been a wholly-owned subsidiary of the university until that 1969 protest movement had discovered its research in biochemical warfare and counterinsurgency in Indochina, South Africa, and the Black ghettoes of the United States. Overwhelming votes of the Stanford community had demanded that the university halt this SRI research. The Board of Trustees had responded by "selling" SRI, which they held in trust—to themselves (the majority of the Board of Directors of SRI still consists of members of the Stanford University Board of Trustees, thus showing that not everything has changed since the days of Leland Stanford and his associates). The trustees, however, had allowed one concession to the movement—fairly strict rules against secret research and SRI war research on campus. But the enforcement of these rules was then placed in the hands of a faculty committee dominated by some of the very professors most involved in war research and most directly linked to SRI. This committee professed to know nothing about Gamut-H or the relevant Stanford rules. The administration saw no relation between the invasion of Laos and SRI's secret use of the Stanford computer to plan another Indochinese invasion.

For my role in the protest against the university's direct involvement in the Indochina War, I was suspended and banished by injunction from the campus for seven months prior to any hearing. The hearing itself lasted six weeks and generated five thousand pages of transcript. It was held before the Advisory Board, whose function was to "advise" the president, who had brought the charges.

I was unanimously convicted on only one charge—making a speech on February 10, 1971, advocating a "strike," or rather "a voluntary boycott," "to shut down the most obvious machinery of war" at Stanford, beginning with the computer. The speech was declared to have "urged and incited" people "towards disruption of University functions and shutdown of the Computation Center." It was ruled irrelevant whether these were legitimate functions of the university or whether, even according to Stanford's own rules, the Computation Center ought to be temporarily shut down.

No laws were broken by the demonstrators at the Computation Center. In fact, they did not even break any Stanford regulations. None of the demonstrators was ever prosecuted by Stanford or in court. But the administration called a hundred-man police riot unit to the campus to break up the peaceful, noncoercive, lawful demonstration that took place inside the Computation Center. The demonstrators left the building before the police entered, and then stood around talking to other people on the lawns outside. The police illegally declared all people in the two-block area of the computer to constitute an unlawful assembly, threatened everybody with immediate arrest, and poised to charge. My unsuccessful efforts to get two official faculty observers to stay on the scene and to convince the police not to attack were defined as urging and inciting people not to disperse, a charge upheld by a 5–2 vote, with even the chairman of the Advisory Board and one other member acknowledging that I was merely exerting legal rights and attempting to prevent violence by the police.

Finally, I was charged for making a speech at a rally that night which allegedly "urged and incited students and other persons present to engage in conduct calculated to disrupt activities of the University and of members of the University community and which threatened injury to individuals and property." It was never specified what "conduct" I "urged and incited," what "activities" this conduct was calculated to disrupt, or how that conduct threatened injury to anybody or anything. The faculty board found me guilty anyhow, again by a 5–2 vote, this time basing their decision primarily on an earlier speech that the administration had officially declared to be "not contended by the University to be inciteful at all." The majority of the faculty board admitted that this speech was an effort to persuade people new to the movement to vote for the demand "Free All Political Prisoners," but found it criminal anyhow because "his way of undertaking this persuasion was itself inflammatory": "He made assertions of such hostile content in such an angry manner regarding the University and the police that . . . they must surely have intensified the resentment of many persons favorable to the 'movement' and thereby raised the probability of violent actions later." Earlier that day Stanford University had brought in over a hundred riot police in order to protect its ability to plan an invasion of North Vietnam. These police, according to uncontested testimony at the hearing, had indiscriminately beaten students, professors, and workers. A professor who stated those facts that night in an "angry" or "hostile" manner must be thrown out of the university.

The five-man majority of the Advisory Board had summed up the case in these terms:

Professor Franklin asserts that the university's actual function is to serve as a training and research center for the maintenance of an imperialistic hegemony over the "Pacific Basin Empire"; yet to most of his colleagues, that is a bizarre mischaracterization. Thus the basis of a pattern of conduct is itself subject to conflicting interpretations, depending upon the perception of reality from which it is being described.

Agreed. And, as the science of Marxism demonstrates, perception of reality is determined primarily by class relations to the means of production. Two members of the seven-man board voted not to fire me. I do not think it a coincidence that these were the only two not primarily dependent on government and corporation financing of their work. The only humanist of the seven—and the most innocent—was Robert McAfee Brown, Professor of Religion, whose definition of the business of the university is a mere anachronism (as out of date as Cardinal Newman's 1852 "The Idea of the University"):

> I believe very strongly that, however much I and many of my colleagues may disagree with what Professor Franklin says or how he says it, Stanford University will be less a true university without him and more of a true university with him. I fear that we may do untold harm to ourselves and to the cause of higher education unless, by imposing a penalty short of dismissal, we seek to keep him as a very uncomfortable but very important part of what this University, or any university, is meant to be.

Much more revealing than this utopian ideal is the actual identity of the five professors who voted for dismissal.

First there is Wolfgang Panofsky, Director of the Stanford Linear Accelerator Center, a two-mile-long machine built on Stanford land by and for the U.S. government, which supplies its entire operating income (in 1971 a sum of $28,803,879). Then there is Professor of Business George Leland Bach, consultant to the Treasury Department, member of the board of governors of the Federal Reserve, and the only member of the faculty allowed to sit with the chairman of Wells Fargo Bank and eight other trustees on the Board of Trustees' permanent Committee on Investments. Next there is Professor David Mason, chairman of a department wholly dedicated to the disinterested pursuit of pure truth and entirely removed from the influence of large corporations—the Department of Chemical Engineering.

The last two have a special role in the preservation of the empire: they train its professionals and ideological apologists. First is Stanford Dornbusch, Professor of Sociology, who teaches the standard introductory sociology course, based on a stabilization model, and focusing from that perspective on such topics as "the relation of the individual to large scale organizations and institutions." One must admit Professor Dornbusch's special qualifications to get ahead in this area, since he sits on the Board of Trustees' permanent Commitee on Academic Affairs and served on the faculty committee that chose Richard Lyman as president. The rest of that committee consisted of three other members of this Advisory Board, together with Professor Rambo (the CIA and electronic-warfare researcher), Professor Friedenthal, who headed the university committee which succeeded in expelling all the leading student antiwar protesters, and another member of that same disciplinary committee. Finally, there is David Hamburg, chairman of the Department of Psychiatry. Professor Hamburg also served on that presidential selection committee, and he sits on the three-man Advisory Panel on the Hoover Institution. I am grateful that Professor Hamburg was unable to use the experimental methods being developed by his department in the School of Medicine and the Psychology Department in the School of Humanities and Science to bring about my "rehabilitation" through behavioral modification. As soon as the hearing concluded, Professor Hamburg rushed off on a U.S. government grant to study the "causes of violence." Where do you think he went? To Africa, of course.

Sociology and psychiatry in their present form at Stanford are typical of the pseudo-sciences that have developed from what Veblen described back in 1916 as the typical "academic social sciences":

> Such a quasi-science necessarily takes the current situation for granted as a permanent state of things; to be corrected and brought back into its normal routine in case of aberration, and to be safeguarded

with apologetic defence at points where it is not working to the satisfaction of all parties. It is a "science" of complaisant interpretations, apologies, and projected remedies.

These days at Stanford, however, "remedies" are not just projected by the social sciences, but also implemented. For example, behavioral-modification techniques developed at Stanford are used on prisoners in California.

In 1972, the basement of the School of Education building was turned into a simulated prison, with students playing the roles of guards and prisoners so realistically that a number of the "prisoners" began to develop psychological problems. The experiment turned out to be part of a half-million-dollar contract that Professor Zimbardo of the Department of Psychology has with the Office of Naval Research, whose own Advisory Board includes J. E. Wallace Sterling, former president of Stanford University, now a Stanford trustee and director of Shell Oil, SRI, and Kaiser Aluminum and Chemical Co. At Stanford, the contract bears the official title "Individual and Group Variables Influencing Emotional Arousal, Violence, and Behavior," vague and innocuous enough to sound academically scientific. But the official title at the Defense Documentation Center (DDC) is more revealing: "Personnel Technology Factors Influencing Disruptive Behavior Among Military Trainees." The DDC also has on file the statement of purpose of the contract:

> U.S. military forces have recently experienced an apparent upsurge of problems involving negative reactions to authority, insufficient loyalty to the organization, failure to maintain (and even sabotage of) valuable government property, and racial conflict. This research aims at the production of a set of behavioral principles which could reduce the incidence of such undesirable behavior in the Navy and Marine Corps.

I'm thankful that this research was not concluded in time to be applied to Stanford's own problems of such "undesirable behavior" as "negative reactions to authority" and "insufficient loyalty to the organization."

So we come back again to "differing perceptions of reality," the phrase used by the Advisory Board. To these Stanford researchers, like the men in government who award them their contracts, authority and organization represent an absence of violence. To them, protest against this law and order is "disruption," and anything beyond mere protest is "violence."

The most educational moment of the entire six-week hearing came during a routine cross-examination of a university photographer, Mr. Charles Painter, called as a witness by the administration. While he examined his eight-by-ten photographs, the board and the large audience could see each print projected on a screen. One of these pictures showed several casually dressed demonstrators taping a sign to the front door of the Computation Center and a television crew shooting this newsworthy scene. In the foreground stand two policemen. One of the police is turned so one hip is pointing directly toward Mr. Painter's camera. Strapped to this hip is a .357 magnum revolver. Being very close to the camera, the revolver appears larger than the head of any of the demonstrators. This is how the cross-examination went, according to the official transcript, with Mr. Painter slowly and carefully studying this picture before each of his first three responses:

MR. FRANKLIN: Do you see anybody with any weapons?

THE WITNESS: No.

MR. FRANKLIN: Could you take a closer look and make sure you don't see anybody with any weapons?

THE WITNESS: What is your definition of "a weapon"?

MR. FRANKLIN: Well, something like a gun, maybe.

THE WITNESS: Yes. There are policemen with their holstered guns in the scene, right.

MR. FRANKLIN: Did you just not see those at first?

THE WITNESS: I just didn't think of them as weapons.

CHAIRMAN KENNEDY: Can we have quiet, please.

Where I Came From

My father was born in Jersey City in 1903. When he was a few weeks old, his family moved to Brooklyn, where he spent the rest of his life. My mother was born in Brooklyn in 1905 and lived there until 1966, a few years after my father's death.

My father attended high school for about five months. He dropped out at the age of fifteen to support his mother. His first job was as a runner on Wall Street, where he worked in various white-collar jobs the remainder of his existence, except for a brief try at his own business, a couple of stints doing assembly work in a radio factory, one job as a clerk in a furniture store, and another sanding floors. He died of cancer in 1963 at the age of sixty. During that forty-five-year period he went to work every single day, no matter how sick, except when he was unemployed, when his mother died, and when he himself was dying.

My mother completed a commercial-art program at Cooper Union. At different times she worked as an advertising artist, a clerk in the art-supply department of Abraham & Straus department store, and a saleslady in a wallpaper store. Most of the time that I can remember we lived on what my father earned.

My parents met in the mid-1920s. They got married in 1928. I remember their favorite reminiscences were about speakeasies and the fun they had had in the roaring twenties. My mother's father owned a little shoestore in a working-class neighborhood in Brooklyn. He helped my father set up his own one-man trading operation on Wall Street. It lasted one year, until the crash of 1929. My parents lost their home and furniture, as well as the business, and were forced to move in with her parents, in what was then the up-and-coming middle-class neighborhood known as Bedford-Stuyvesant. In 1930, my grandfather was forced to sell his shoestore. He died in 1935, and my grandmother lost their home, which went to pay back taxes.

My parents felt they couldn't afford to support children in the first few years of the Depression. So I was their only child, born in 1934. In 1936, we rented the bottom floor of a two-family house in the Flatlands section, an Irish-Italian low-income working-class neighborhood. My mother's mother lived with us there.

We never did own a home or have any other tangible assets, but we never lived in any physical deprivation that I can remember. We had a 1936 Packard, bought, I guess, in the early 1940s, until 1952, when my mother's uncle let us have his 1951 Ford. When my father died in 1963, he had total net cash assets of fifty dollars, the 1951 Ford, his clothes, and some household furnishings. He had no insurance.

My father never complained about the fact that all those years of labor had never produced any wealth or even security for the family. But in the few conversations he and I ever had about how he felt about his work, he told me that all his labor was useless or worse, that he hated looking back on a lifetime of work that had no meaning, that had produced nothing of any use to anybody. Once he said, "If only I had worked with my hands, there might be something to have come out of it all, something that people could use."

It has taken me a long time to comprehend the significance of my father's work life. Some combination of my own experience, Marx's 1844 philosophical essays, and Herman Melville's story "Bartleby the Scrivener: A Story of Wall Street" made me finally understand that my father's labor sums up what is most grotesque and perverted about most people's lives in capitalist society. It is, after all, not the creation of physical deprivation and misery that distinguishes capitalism from all other forms of political economy. What is unique about capitalism is that it forces almost all people to alienate themselves from their own essence by selling themselves on the "free" labor market. People must sell their ability to create, their purposeful labor, that which is most human about them, their very human essence—in order to purchase the right to their animal existence. Thus all human relationships are reduced to money relationships. Nowhere is the irrationality of decaying capitalism lived out with more futility than in the life of the white-collar worker, trapped in a work world defined by the walls of an office and forced to expend all that is creative on alien, meaningless pieces of paper, often the very documents which give to a handful of rich parasites the right to own everything of material value.

We lived in the Depression years of 1936 through 1940 on that floor in Flatlands. My father became very active in the local Democratic club, which consisted of a group of men from the neighborhood meeting quite frequently in a bar a few blocks away. One day he suggested to his friends that he run for local office. They laughed and told him that as the only Jew in the neighborhood he couldn't get elected dogcatcher.

Shortly after that, in late 1940, we moved to Flatbush, into a neighborhood of middle-income workers, shopkeepers, and professionals living in apartments and small houses. It had previously been almost entirely gentile, but was now changing rapidly, as large waves of Jewish refugees retreating before the Nazi advances in Europe poured in.

I went to P.S. 99, a big old brick four-story building that looked like a prison and was run like one. The first time my mother was called to school, it was to be told that they had decided I was a "genius" because of my I.Q. test and that I was being skipped a grade along with several other "exceptional" children. I soon found myself, along with the other chosen ones, part of a designated elite, constantly prodded in various subtle and blatant ways to consider ourselves superior to the other children. This was highly effective, particularly since the other kids of course responded by ostracizing us and trying to knock in our exceptional heads. By the eighth grade, I was finding the pleasures of being "exceptional" not as great as the pains. I decided to go back to being like everybody else. I even got admitted into a street gang. The next time my mother was called to school, it was to be informed that I was suspended for being "incorrigible."

In vain my mother protested, pointing to my "genius I.Q." I kept piling up demerits at school, while sliding into other trouble in the streets. My parents found a way out. They got me admitted on a part scholarship to Brooklyn Friends School, a Quaker school in downtown Brooklyn. This was in 1947, during the postwar boom that let my father earn the most money I could remember his bringing in. I was now definitely upward bound.

Brooklyn Friends was a tiny school where teachers and students were friendly with each other. To me this was like heaven. Most of the students came from well-to-do families, but there were some on scholarships. The upper ten grades were all white, but integration was beginning, as two children of the janitor were admitted on scholarships into the first two grades. We were encouraged to lead an active intellectual life, something I had never experienced, even when I was "exceptional" in P.S. 99. Here I encountered the first progressive ideas I had ever heard systematically formulated: a mild pacifism, an idealistic internationalism, and an aggressive anti-racism based on the equality of all individuals. It was assumed that each and every one of us was going on to college, which generally turned out to be true.

Our education was liberal in content and democratic in form, within the closed world of the school. In relation to the society as a whole, we were a tiny elite band, intended to be carriers of goodness and civilization into the upper reaches of our society.

In 1947, during the summer before I started Friends School, Jackie Robinson became the first Black player in major-league baseball. I remember some of my father's friends down in the remaining local Irish bar carrying on about Robinson as an "uppity nigger." They talked about how "colored" people just don't have the same ambitions as white people, that they were contented with their lot, that they were in fact probably happier than most white folks because they weren't caught up in the same rat race, and that one college-educated smart aleck like Robinson (none of them had been to college) could create a lot of trouble for innocent people, particularly by stirring up a lot of racism. When I tried to raise a question, I was told that I was just a typical thirteen-year-old boy who didn't know what he was talking about, particularly since I obviously had never known any "colored" people.

This was certainly true. Although I had grown up in a city containing almost two million Black people, that city was so carefully segregated I had never personally known one Black individual. The closest I had come was one time when my father had hired a middle-aged Black man who owned a pickup to help us move. Then the three of us had sat around in the kitchen, the two men drinking beer, joking, and telling stories. My father used to tell people about this as an event, and as an example of Negro and white people treating each other as equals.

The subway I took home from Brooklyn Friends was the Brighton Line of the BMT. When I got on at Lawrence Street, near Borough Hall, about one-third of the passengers were Black. A few more would get on at DeKalb Avenue, Atlantic Avenue, and Seventh Avenue. Then the train, which had been underground all this time, would go through its final long tunnel and emerge into the open air at the Prospect Park station. Every Black person, with only a rare exception, would then leave. I knew they were transferring to the Franklin Avenue line, which would take them to Bedford-Stuyvesant. That up-and-coming white neighborhood of the late 1920s had become a sprawling Black ghetto during the Depression and World War II, as rural Black families were swept off the land in the South into the urban centers of the North. I didn't know anything about this history then. All I knew was a rather abstract idea of an ominous Black neighborhood and the very real daily phenomenon of the subway car. I sometimes imagined that all the Black people were being manipulated by a strange external force, maybe some invisible dictator who was ordering them out all at once. Here we would be, riding along, all mixed up, Black and white, standing and sitting, dozing and reading newspapers and ads. Then suddenly, as though responding to a command, every Black face would point toward the doors on the right side of the car, every Black body would begin to move in that direction, and the white bodies that had been standing would move back away from the doors, many of them heading for the warm, just-emptied seats. I still thought of "segregation" as something practiced in the South, because there Black people had to ride separately in the back of the bus.

When I was fifteen, I got my first full-time summer job. My high-school coach was director of Camp Pratt, a large YMCA camp on the south shore of Staten Island. The camp took some of the poorest boys from the slums of New York and gave them two weeks of all the joys of summer camp—dampened only by a rigid barracks discipline and the polluted waters of Prince's Bay. I was hired as a dishwasher and snack-bar counterman. I was also expected to work on getting my soccer and basketball skills in shape for the coming year.

About two-thirds of the boys attending the camp and about half the staff were Black. I found my world expanding as I related for the first time in my life to Black people. I was never the kind of racist who had any objections to washing the dirty tin silverware and plastic cups and trays used by Black people or to taking orders from my immediate boss, the Black chef who was as eccentric, tyrannical, and quick-tempered as most cooks in charge of large kitchens. He ran the kitchen with an iron hand, one that sometimes brandished a meat cleaver, and I did what I was told, including eating second and third and fourth helpings whenever he and his wife thought that we kitchen workers were not showing the proper appreciation of their cooking. My racism was of a distinctly liberal variety. I took it for granted that all Black people would appreciate the society of a friendly white person like myself. I had never heard of Black nationalism.

In between doing the thousands of lunch dishes and getting supper ready, my main job was working behind a counter in the late afternoon when all the boys who had any spare change could stand in line to buy hot dogs, ice cream, and soft drinks. The other person who usually worked behind the counter was June, a Black woman who spent most of the day typing and keeping books in the front office. She was nineteen, and was working her way through CCNY. She was the most sophisticated woman I had ever known. I soon fell madly in love with her.

I had had no previous sexual experience, except for a few clumsy childhood encounters. So I had no idea how to bridge the chasm between the passionate visions that kept me awake at night and the presence of the real June during the day. June and I slept in the same building, but at opposite ends of a cavernous gymnasium-theater, which had sleeping quarters for the men workers upstairs in the front and for the women workers upstairs in the back.

The main office was also in this building, and at night a bunch of us used to hang around drinking beer and socializing. One night every seat in the office was filled when June walked in, looked around, and, to my paralyzing astonishment, sat on my lap. As the evening went on, I hardly dared to move a muscle. People started drifting away and other chairs became vacant, but June, amazingly enough, stayed sitting on my lap, sharing cans of beer with me. Eventually everybody else left, and we were still sitting there. I had no idea what to do next, and was still worried that she might be offended by anything I might do. We must have sat there in silence for at least a quarter of an hour, while I agonized in timidity and dread that she would say goodnight and leave. Finally, I thought of what seemed to me a properly sophisticated thing to say.

"You know something, June," I whispered in her ear.

"What?" she asked softly.

"I've never kissed you," I replied cavalierly, omitting the fact that about the only people I *had* kissed were relatives, friends of my parents, and girls in spin-the-bottle games.

"That's true," she said patiently. We spent most of the rest of the night in the office.

After that, we used to go to our respective sleeping quarters, wait until everybody else seemed asleep, then tiptoe downstairs to meet in the big hall, and walk down to the beach, where we would stay until just before dawn. I still can't figure out when either of us got any sleep.

A deeper mystery about our affair is what part her being Black played in my love for her. It was not that she was some kind of exotic curiosity, because I did love her very deeply. But I think we both enjoyed defying the white world, particularly the glaring white racist world of Staten Island, by being with each other during the day. On our days off we would, along with some other Black and white workers from the camp, take a bus about seven miles to a miniature golf course at New Dorp. Once June and I went off by ourselves all the way to the main Staten Island town of St. George to see a movie she was particularly interested in. She was the only Black person in a huge old ornate movie theater that seemed to be bulging with a menacing white audience. I didn't remember what film we saw until years later. It was Ayn Rand's *Fountainhead.*

Sometimes it seemed to me that June was much more open about our relationship among white people—even when that meant potential physical danger—than she was among Black people. With my liberal racist view, this puzzled me. Wouldn't Black people be happy to see a white man who was not only going with a Black woman but was actually in love with her? One night June and I were out watching the moon at the end of a long wooden pier along with James, a Black fellow worker about two years older than me and two years younger than her, whom I considered a close friend. We were sitting there, our backs to a railing, smoking and drinking beer, with June in the middle. After a while I put my arm around June. She took it away quickly and tried to tell me something. James stood up angrily and strode off down the pier without looking back. I thought he was just jealous, but June tried patiently to explain to me that James disapproved of any Black woman relating to a white man. "How could that be?" I insisted. "He just wants you to relate to him." James never spoke to me again.

At the end of the summer, June and I were more in love than ever, or at least that's what I thought. We each went back home to Brooklyn, she to Bedford-Stuyvesant, and me to Flatbush. I told her that I'd call her and we'd go out the first weekend. When my parents learned that I had been going out with a "Negro girl," their agony knew no bounds. We had a fight. They forbade me to see her. I said I might marry her.

I called June and we arranged to meet at a movie theater near the Atlantic Avenue BMT stop. When I saw her on the street in front of the ticket booth, she looked nervous and uncomfortable. We held hands in the movie, but we both knew the summer was over and we were back in Brooklyn. I don't know what movie we saw that day. We never saw each other again.

A Reactionary Worker for Communist Bosses

WORLD WAR II left the old empires of Europe in ruins. The fascist upstarts that had tried to take their place were even worse off.

Throughout Europe itself the old order was in deep trouble. In Eastern Europe all the monarchies and fascist military dictatorships had been overthrown by a combination of partisan forces, led by local Communists, and the Soviet army. Except for Greece, all now had governments that relied on the workers and peasants and that gave at least verbal support to the deepening world revolution. In France and Italy the industrial proletariat was highly organized, and the largest political party in each country was the Communist Party, which still preserved the discipline and leadership developed in the underground resistance movement.

Before the war, most of the world's population and area had consisted of European colonies. Now these colonies were being swept by national liberation movements. Between 1946 and 1949 alone, national independence, at least on paper, was achieved by Burma, Indonesia, India, Pakistan, Laos, Libya, Ceylon, Jordan, and the Philippines, countries containing about one-third of the world's population. Anticolonial rebellions were brewing throughout the so-called "Dark Continent" of Africa (dark at least to most of us white Americans, whose ignorance about it was total).

The heaviest blow to the European and North American colonial powers came in 1949, when the Chinese peasants and workers, led by the Communist Party, drove Chiang Kai-shek, together with his U.S. advisers and equipment, off the mainland and set up their own profoundly anticapitalist and militantly independent government. The worst nightmare of the empires of finance capital had just come true: a national liberation movement had combined with a Communist revolution. And their horrified eyes saw the same kind of thing happening in Korea and Vietnam.

Having suffered minimal damage in World War II, the United States was, in the opinion of its leaders, in an ideal position to dominate the rest of the world and restore international law and order. Its global strategy was beginning to take shape in the last stages of the war itself. U.S. occupation forces were rushed in to establish permanent bases on all possible territory, whether it belonged to ally (Belgium, France, China), foe (Germany, Italy, Japan), the colony of a foe (Korea), or the colony of an ally (Greenland). The Japanese offers to surrender were rejected just long enough to allow the demonstration use of nuclear weapons, which were designed as the ultimate threat for the ensuing years. U.S. economic hegemony was to expand rapidly throughout Asia, Africa, Latin America, and the war-ravaged West European heartland, where the old fallen imperial powers were to be revived and allowed to become junior partners of U.S. imperialism and allies in the universal Pax Americana.

To achieve this goal, the United States had to meet the growing world revolution with a strategy of global counterrevolution. In 1947 this strategy, named the Truman Doctrine, was made the official foreign policy of the United States. From now on the country would be committed to the economic, political, and military support of the most reactionary governments and forces in the world. Every tottering monarchy from Greece to Iran, every colonial regime from the French rule in Indochina to the Portuguese "provinces" in Africa, every white supremacist dictatorship from South Africa to Guatemala had Washington behind it. And at Washington's disposal was its Strategic Air Command armada, carrying nuclear bombs from bases in every part of the planet. The Central Intelligence Agency was also established in 1947, and the Department of War was reorganized and renamed the Department of Defense.

Internationally the first blow of the Truman Doctrine fell on Greece. During World War II the partisan forces in Greece, led by the Communists, had first defeated the invasion of the Italian Fascists and then by mid-1944 had chopped up most of the occupation forces from Nazi Germany and its ally Bulgaria. The country was free of foreign invaders, but only temporarily. In late 1944 the British sent an expeditionary force commanded by General Scobie to land in Greece, ostensibly to aid in the disarming of the defeated Fascist and Nazi troops. As unsuspecting as their comrades in Vietnam and Korea, who were to be likewise "assisted" in 1945, the Greek partisans were massacred by their British "allies," who deployed tanks and planes in an all-out offensive against them. The British even rearmed and mobilized the defeated Nazi Security Battalions. On February 12, 1945, the Greeks surrendered to the British, who then spent a year "pacifying" the country under their own occupation troops and the police force that had been loyal to the Nazis. By March 31, 1946, they were ready for "free elections," which were boycotted by most parties and won by the monarchists. In September, 1946, the monarchy was restored as the legal head of the right-wing military dictatorship. In March, 1947, Truman began sending massive U.S. economic and military aid, including U.S. "advisers," to crush the stubborn Greek resistance that still held out. By 1949 the popular forces were defeated, at least for the time being.

On March 25, 1947, thirteen days after announcing his global anti-communist crusade, Harry Truman issued the first in a series of executive orders requiring "security" checks for 2.5 million government employees. These orders were soon extended to 3 million members of the armed forces and 3 million workers in war production, now renamed the "defense" industry. Within two years, 20 million U.S. citizens had secret dossiers in the files of the federal secret police.

In June, 1947, Congress enacted the Taft-Hartley Act, outlawing mass picketing, secondary boycotts, the political use of union funds, and the right of Communists to hold union office. The transformation of the principal labor unions into state-dominated labor bodies on the Mussolini-Hitler model then proceeded smoothly—and swiftly. By October, 1949, the CIO began the process of expelling all its most progressive unions. First to go was the 450,000-member United Electrical, Radio, and Machine Workers; its charter was turned over to CIO national secretary James B. Carey, who then boasted at a public meeting in the Hotel Astor: "In the last war, we joined with the Communists to fight the fascists. In another war, we will join with the fascists to defeat the Communists." Carey didn't point out that this was exactly what had just happened in Greece. In the next few months, ten more unions were expelled, including the International Longshoremen's and Warehousemen's Union (ILWU), the International Union of Mine, Mill and Smelter Workers, and the 100,000-member International Union of Fur and Leather Workers.

The mass criminal prosecution of Communist Party members and sympathizers began in the same month as the passage of the Taft-Hartley Act. The first large group, including the novelist Howard Fast, were arrested in June, 1947, charged with contempt of Congress, and convicted for refusing to turn over to the House Un-American Activities Committee the names of contributors to committees to aid Spanish Republican and other anti-fascist refugees. Ten of the most noted writers and directors in Hollywood were indicted in December, and later sentenced to jail, for refusing to discuss their political beliefs and affiliations before the House Un-American Activities Committee. The U.S. Attorney General began publishing a list of 160 "subversive" organizations, while HUAC issued its own list of 608 "un-American" organizations.

On June 20, 1948, twelve members of the National Board of the Communist Party were arrested and charged with "conspiring to teach and advocate" the violent overthrow of the government. In a criminal trial lasting from January 17 through October 14, 1949, the defendants were all convicted by a hand-picked "blue-ribbon" jury before Federal Judge Harold R. Medina (millionaire landlord, former corporation lawyer, rabid anti-Communist). For this crime, not of teaching or advocating but of conspiring to teach and advocate, each was sentenced to federal prison for terms of three or five years.

The following year, 1950, the bellicose expansion of the U.S. empire reached a new stage. As late as January of that year, the U.S. government was still officially stating that the southern half of Korea and the Chinese province of Taiwan ("Formosa") were internal matters of the sovereign nations of Korea and China respectively. In fact, the administration indicated that its solemn wartime pledge to return "Formosa" to China had not been altered by the revolutionary change that had just taken place in the government of China, and it stated unequivocally that U.S. military forces would not interfere with the reunification of either China or Korea. Six months later its policy was exactly the opposite.

The government of the so-called Republic of Korea, made in the U.S.A. and led by the U.S. puppet Syngman Rhee (who had recently arrived from the U.S., where he had lived thirty-seven years), desperately tried to make itself seem legitimate and to prevent reunification. Korea had been under the occupation of Japan before and during World War II. The anti-Japanese resistance movement had been led by Kim Il Sung, who had become the hero of the entire nation and who was now head of the Democratic People's Republic of Korea. Kim was also a major international Communist theoretician. So the United States now faced the prospect of a reunified, independently nationalist, and Communist Korea within months of the Communist victory in China.

Washington's only hope now lay in Syngman Rhee, a long shot to say the least. To show that his government enjoyed real popular support, Rhee called for parliamentary elections in May. During the campaign, his American-trained secret police rounded up many of the opposition candidates and their supporters. Nevertheless, when the election was held on May 30, Rhee's party was able to win only 12 seats out of a total of 210. Reunification of Korea under Communist leadership now seemed inevitable.

On June 25 fighting broke out along the demarcation line drawn by foreign governments across the middle of the Korean nation. Whether this was begun by Rhee in order to bring the United States in militarily, or whether it was a preplanned "invasion from the North," remains a matter of dispute among world historians, with the balance of evidence against Washington's version. But there is little argument about what happened next militarily. Syngman Rhee's army quickly disintegrated. Many units went over to the other side intact and with their weapons. Others threw their weapons and uniforms away and merged back into the civilian population. As the DPRK army swept forward, it was welcomed by large cheering crowds. Popular uprisings and guerrilla fighting broke out in many areas behind the retreating lines of Rhee's army. The only foreign troops then on Korean soil were U.S. Marines, mostly stationed near the demarcation line. They quickly withdrew to the south and regrouped.

On June 27, Truman ordered U.S. air and naval forces into action in Korea and directed the Seventh Fleet to station itself in the straits between the mainland of China and the Chinese province of Taiwan. The same day, the United States jammed an interventionist resolution through the Security Council of the United Nations. China, of course, was still represented on the Council by the overthrown Chiang Kai-shek government. The Soviet Union, taken completely by surprise by all these events (an indication that if there was a preplanned invasion from the North, the U.S.S.R. was not in on it), was boycotting the Security Council in protest against Chiang's representation there. Even so, the U.S. resolution passed without one vote to spare. Three days later, the U.S. Army and Marines landed in Korea under the flag of the United Nations and the command of General Douglas MacArthur.

In September, the United States launched a full-scale land and sea invasion of North Korea, seizing the capital city of Pyongyang October 20. By November 20, the U.S. 7th Division had reached the Chinese border. MacArthur openly announced his intention of pushing right on into China. On November 26, 1950, the Chinese moved across the border.

Like just about everybody I knew, I accepted the visions conjured up by the radio and newspapers. I saw tightly-packed hordes of screaming Chinamen hurtling wave on human wave against the staunch lines of U.S. Marines, each man a veritable John Wayne, fighting on until buried by these unfeeling fanatics, with their Oriental disregard for individual human life. The Chinese in my mind had pretty much the same faces, and showed the same Asian cruelty, as the Japanese in my comic books during World War II.

Six years later, I was a squadron intelligence officer in the Strategic Air Command. When I wasn't flying, I worked in a supposedly bomb-proof vault, filing, and guarding with my .45, all our classified documents. One day I came across a top-secret report on the combat effectiveness of our troops during this Chinese offensive. I discovered that the Chinese force had been one-third the size of the U.S. force, that even the most elite units of the U.S. Marines had thrown down their guns and run for their lives, and that 85 percent of our men, according to their own admission, had been too frightened to fire their weapons.

After routing the marines, the Chinese and "North" Koreans drove the U.S., European, and Australian invaders completely out of the area north of the thirty-eighth parallel and actually penetrated seventy miles south of that arbitrarily drawn demarcation line. The offensive was not halted until the end of March, 1951. The Chinese broadcast and published elaborate claims that what had halted them was the extensive U.S. use of bacteriological weapons dropped from planes. I can still remember the hilarious accounts of these claims in the U.S. press, which of course ridiculed these "germ warfare stories" as the ultimate in absurd Communist propaganda. I can also remember a night I spent on alert in SAC seven years later, when three pilots in my squadron began reminiscing and joking about the germ bombs they had dropped on Chinese troops, and also on "North" Korean villages.

On February 1, 1951, the General Assembly of the United Nations declared China the aggressor in Korea. On March 25, General MacArthur declared that his "UN" forces were going to use air and naval attacks on China itself. On April 11, Truman removed MacArthur from his command.

I was a tremendous admirer of MacArthur, as both a military and a political leader, and I thought his announced plan was what should have been done all along. I was furious at Truman, and deeply suspected him of being under the influence of the Communists who had burrowed into the State Department and no doubt many other areas of the government. Fortunately, I thought, these Communists were finally being exposed and rooted out. Senator Joseph McCarthy was doing a fearless job of showing that Truman and his cronies were only pretending to fight Communism, and that they were the ones who had given away China in the first place. On Friday, June 1, I graduated from high school.

On Monday morning, nervous but outwardly brash, I began my first day of work at Mayfair Photofinishing Company down at the Coney Island end of Coney Island Avenue in Brooklyn. The little plant was flooded with undeveloped snapshots taken that weekend, and I was too busy learning my miscellaneous duties as a "batchman" to think about much else. When I finally got home around ten that evening, I was happy to see in the afternoon's New York *Sun* that the U.S. Supreme Court, by a six to two vote, had upheld the conviction of those Communist Party leaders sentenced to prison by Judge Medina for "conspiring to teach and advocate the violent overthrow of the United States government."

Mayfair was owned and run by three brothers, Ben Weinstein, Murray Weinstein, and Joe Winston. By that Friday I had very strong suspicions that two of my bosses, Ben and Murray, were Communists. I had never before known anyone I was sure was a Communist, but these two matched all my expectations. They were always defending Russia and telling us workers how great life there was, and they were always knocking America, particularly harping on racism and the warlike nature of what they called the capitalist system.

At lunchtime I used to go to the little candy store and soda fountain on the corner (at Avenue Z) to get a malted milk. One day during my second week at Mayfair, Ben came in while I was sipping my malt at the counter, went to the opposite end, and motioned Mike the counterman over. Mike reached under the counter, pulled out a rolled-up newspaper, and quickly handed it to Ben, who then left. The next day I was there when Murray went through the same routine. After he left, I asked Mike what the newspaper was. "The *Daily Worker*," he said in a low voice. "They get me to order a daily copy for them. I'm not too crazy about doing it, frankly. But they're good customers, so I do it as a favor. Besides, it's just part of the business anyhow."

Eventually I learned that both Ben and Murray were active in the Communist Party, and that both were apparently officers on some level. Of course I thought of Communists as wily, furtive conspirators who acted under direct orders from Moscow. Their ultimate goal was to destroy our democratic society and turn it into a Communist dictatorship. But distrustful as I was of Ben and Murray, I think my curiosity was stronger. I was eager to find out firsthand how Communists talked and what they did.

Some of my worst suspicions were confirmed. It was a bit like *Animal Farm*. Our bosses verbally attacked the capitalist system, but the place they owned and ran was a sweat shop. Mayfair was at that time one of the largest photofinishing operations in New York. Yet the work was done by only about a dozen people, including the three owner-brothers and their aged father. Throughout Flatbush, Coney Island, and the Rockaways, people would choose different drugstores and small camera stores to develop and print their pictures. We picked up the work at all these stores and also processed a large mail-order business. The typical summer work week for each worker went something like this: Monday, 8 A.M. to midnight; Tuesday, 7 A.M. to 1 A.M.; Wednesday, 8 A.M. to midnight; Thursday, 8 A.M. to 7 P.M.; Friday, 9 A.M. to 5 P.M.; Saturday, 9 A.M. to 1 P.M. In the developing room the temperature never got below eighty-five degrees, and in the drying room, where we worked in twenty- to thirty-minute stretches, any exposed metal was too hot to touch. Four of us were paid seventy-five cents an hour, plus time and a half for all hours over the first forty in a week.

The main political education I got from these two members of the Communist Party came from their exploitation of me and the other workers, including the long, unhealthy hours, the poor working conditions, and the piddling pay. I learned that even a capitalist, at least a very small one, can call himself a "Communist." Most of this merely confirmed the prejudices and stereotypes that filled my head and seemed to me original and creative ideas. But the lesson did have some value in the long run. I think it made it easier for me to grasp one of the central historical facts of life of the third quarter of the twentieth century: that capitalism is being restored as fast as possible in the Soviet Union by none other than the leaders of the "Communist" Party.

On the other hand, Ben and Murray, though co-owners of a small capitalist enterprise, were no manicured bureaucratic parasites. Both were physically and mentally tough and extremely practical. They worked as long and hard as any of us. Unlike most of the employers I have had in my life, they took no special privileges at work and never acted as if they thought themselves to be our social superiors. Although deeply hostile to most of their politics and resentful of their gouging me as a worker, I liked them personally and even had a grudging respect for them. If we had all shared a common goal in the work of the shop, our basic relationship would probably have been one of comradeship. But that is just a utopian fantasy, since they owned the plant and were exploiting my labor.

Any very positive relationship was also undermined by their continual clumsy attempts to hide their relation with the Party. Although an open secret, the subject itself was taboo. They even made some faint pretense of not being affiliated. This merely made them seem furtive, reinforcing the stereotype, and placed people like me in the constant position of someone who strongly suspects what they are not supposed to know. Certainly they would have made more headway with me, and people like me, if they had been quite open about their membership. But, having had a taste of the police terror they were living under, I am no longer so cocksure about this opinion. I still think it is downright dangerous for a communist to be better known to the secret police than to the people, particularly the people they are working with. But it's quite possible that Ben and Murray were doing something more important than trying to convert some opinionated seventeen-year-old whose political heroes were Douglas MacArthur, Robert Taft, and Joe McCarthy. And one thing must be conceded: no one who belonged to the Communist Party during the Korean War and the witchhunts of the forties and fifties can be considered a complete coward.

Ben and Murray's methods of political work in the shop seemed to me crude and ineffective, particularly since they already had the big handicap of being the bosses of the workers they were trying to convert to Communism. Their efforts at political education consisted of discussion during slack hours, ranging from debates about current events, mostly with the most opinionated and reactionary worker in the shop (me), to long sympathetic explanations of the plight of the only Third World worker, Maria, an eighteen-year-old woman who had recently arrived from Puerto Rico.

I can't remember much of what we debated about, except that they spent a lot of time trying to explain to me and the other workers that all my facts and opinions came from newspapers, radio stations, and book publishers owned by the capitalists. The clearest example I can recall concerned a big war scare when the newspapers all headlined an attack by Soviet fighter planes on an "unarmed" U.S. reconnaissance plane that had "accidentally strayed off course." I knew that our free press would not invent such an incident, and that the Communists were masters of deceit. Ben then actually produced his copy of the *Daily Worker*, which stated in no uncertain terms that the U.S. plane was armed, for it had fired on the Soviet planes, and that it was on an espionage mission over the

Soviet Union. The paper even went so far as to allege that such missions were almost a daily occurrence. I don't know what effect this had on the other workers, but Ben, Murray, and their *Daily Worker* only succeeded in confirming all I had ever heard about outrageous Communist propaganda and their use of the Big Lie technique. The reason that this particular example stands out in my mind is that it was etched sharply in place while I was a navigator and intelligence officer in the Strategic Air Command. I belonged to an arctic squadron of KC-97s, refueling planes. One of our principal missions was midair refueling of armed B-47s and B-52s flying espionage—and sometimes provocation—missions over the Soviet Union.

On one occasion Ben and Murray did get me personally involved in a political activity. It was in August, 1952, during the second summer I worked at Mayfair, when Paul Robeson sang at a concert in New York. At that time, Robeson was widely known and admired as a great actor and a magnificent singer. Today few people under thirty even recognize Robeson's name. It has been consciously obliterated for his crime of trying, as a Black man, to speak out against injustice in America. Ben was in charge of Robeson's personal security during his stay in New York. For several days he bustled around, looking very busy and very worried. I took this to be mostly self-conscious drama. I didn't know that Robeson's big concert in Peekskill, New York, two years before had been attacked by large, well-organized gangs of white thugs.

Ben and Murray worked hard for a good turnout. All the workers at Mayfair were expected to attend. With our bosses arranging our transportation, we all made it. The concert took place at night on Randalls Island, in the East River under the Triborough Bridge. The 21,000-seat stadium was packed, and there was a large standing-room crowd. I had never heard Robeson sing in person before, and his deep, powerful voice was thrilling. When he sang "Ol' Man River" with the occasional whistle of a tugboat on the East River and Harlem River in the background, to me it sounded like the voice of an entire people.

Although I can still almost hear Paul Robeson, the rest of the evening was very confusing, and I always had trouble remembering what happened. Most of the speeches seemed, at least in my memory, to have been saying nothing at all controversial. In fact they seemed to have been saying nothing at all. The rest of the music was also not too memorable. But I do remember one part of one speech. The last speaker made, toward the end, a declaration something like this: "Vincent Hallinan is a wonderful man. I have the greatest personal respect for him. But he has no chance of winning this election. We have to stop Eisenhower, and the only one who can do that is Adlai Stevenson. So I must cast my vote and throw my support to Stevenson, not to Vincent Hallinan." I had never heard of Vincent Hallinan, and was certainly not prepared for what now happened. Thousands of people were suddenly on their feet booing and angrily yelling. Thousands of others were clapping and cheering. A fistfight broke out right behind us. Scattered fights erupted in other parts of the stadium.

I was very interested in politics, particularly electoral politics. But I had a feeling that whole evening of being in a foreign country, merely observing political passions irrelevant to my own experience and society. After all, I had just been bitterly disappointed by the Republican convention, where the big East Coast ultraliberal bosses like Nelson Rockefeller had maneuvered their empty-headed puppet General Eisenhower into stealing the nomination from the politician I most admired, the brilliant intellectual and man of principle, Robert Taft. On the way home I asked Murray who Vincent Hallinan was, and he told me Hallinan was a lawyer running as the Progressive Party candidate for President. He added, with an air of impatience hinting he didn't have much hope for my future political development, that Hallinan was now in jail in San Francisco "for political reasons." The most farfetched thing he could have said would have been, "If you don't watch out, the same thing might happen to you someday."

Such was my memory of the Randalls Island concert and rally. After getting these impressions on paper, I decided to do some research to find out what it was really all about. I went first to the *New York Times Index* for August, 1952. As far as the *New York Times* was concerned, no such rally had taken place. The fact that about 25,000 people had turned out to a rally organized at least in part by the Communist Party in New York City at the height of the anti-Communist hysteria of 1952 was not part of all the news that's fit to print. Proof, no doubt, of the theory that events not reported do not happen.

Where could I turn? I thought of the old New York *Daily Worker*. But where could I find a complete set of the *Worker*? The best one was in the Hoover Institution of Stanford University. But I had been banished by court injunction from Stanford for giving speeches protesting the university's participation in the Indochina War. Risking jail, I slipped onto campus, sneaked into the Hoover Institution, and then bluffed my way into their basement archives, where the *Daily Worker* is stored.

Sure enough, a rally had taken place on Randalls Island on the night of August 20, a standing-room-only crowd had jammed the stadium, Paul Robeson had sung "Ol' Man River," and the last speaker, Jerome Davis, executive director of Promoting Enduring Peace, Inc., had stirred up some controversy when he announced that "he expected to vote for Governor Stevenson." All this convinced me that this was the rally I had attended. But what dumfounded me was the discovery that the entire rally had been a peace rally aimed at stopping the Korean War.

All during the years of the movement against the Indochina War, I had been telling younger people that there had been no organized movement against the Korean War, that I had never even heard of an antiwar rally while that war was going on. How could I now account for the fact that I had actually attended a very large antiwar rally without realizing what it was? Was I an idiot, or did I have a case of selective amnesia? Why couldn't I remember the political content of any of the speeches?

The account of the rally in the *Daily Worker* of August 22, 1952, cleared up the mystery. This account contained hardly any more politics than my memory of the rally. I could not remember the political content of the speeches because there hadn't been any. It was not that I was stupid, but that the speeches themselves were based on the assumption that the people were either too stupid or too reactionary to accept—or even to hear—an anti-imperialist analysis of the Korean War.

The rally was billed by the slogan "Peace Under the Stars." The *Daily Worker* called it "New York's biggest-ever outdoor rally for peace." But everybody is for peace, including peace in Korea. Even Dwight Eisenhower ran his campaign that year on the promise of bringing peace in Korea. If the rally were to have had any overt politics, it would have had to give an analysis of the causes of the Korean War, the forces represented by the two sides, and what people could do to stop it.

In addition to Robeson, the rally featured Mary Lou Williams ("noted pianist and her trio"), actors Morris Carnovsky, Howard Da Silva, and Karen Morley, Pearl Primus and her dance group, ministers, rabbis, union officials, and even some officials of the American Legion and the Veterans of Foreign Wars. The account in the *Worker* described the opening "prayers for peace": Reverend Edward McGowan, chairman of the New York Peace Institute, greeted the crowd, and "the audience broke into applause at his first mention of 'peace,' and the applause got louder as he urged an end to the fighting in Korea." Then followed various skits showing "the fight for liberty, democracy, and peace in America throughout the generations," punctuated by quotations from Thomas Jefferson, Abraham Lincoln, and Franklin Delano Roosevelt.

According to the *Worker*, apparently no speech analyzed the Korean conflict as part of the world strategy of the U.S. empire. The closest was a claim that "Wall Street" was making a profit out of the war. If this contains any anti-capitalist content, I suppose it is a suggestion that the capitalists wanted to have a war, which is nonsense. They always prefer to reach their imperialist goals peacefully, and they fight only as a last resort, though admittedly they don't like to avoid war quite as much as the people who have to do their fighting. After all, hadn't they tried to hold Korea by sending Syngman Rhee over there? There was not a word about the capitalist system itself, and the economic needs of this system to invest surplus capital in overseas neo-colonies. There was not a hint that U.S. corporations and banks intended to turn South Korea into a neo-colony where they could invest some of this capital, hire cheap labor, and establish military bases for further expansion in Asia. There was one vague mention of U.S. overseas bases, but not a hint of the reason for them. There was no word at all about the liberation struggles of the Korean and Chinese people, Syngman Rhee's fascist dictatorship, or the history of Korea under Japanese and U.S. occupation. Perhaps the most dangerous omission, considering what was happening to the Communist Party and many progressive people at this time, was the failure to make any connection between the world-wide expansion of the U.S. empire, particularly manifest in Korea, and the vicious escalation of political repression at home. Apparently this repression was accomplishing one of its main purposes, silencing the left to the point where there was nobody to speak the truth about the Korean War. Or perhaps the Communist Party was now so politically degenerate that its own leadership neither understood the Korean War nor saw any connection with their own fate. The image of Ben and Murray furtively receiving the same newspaper I was now reading back in that candy store on Coney Island Avenue slipped into my mind. Why did they take those risks to read a paper that issued bland calls for peace Eisenhower could have used in a campaign speech? And why in the world did people have fistfights over that last speaker's announcement that "he expected to vote for Governor Stevenson"?

Before leaving the *Daily Worker* collection and slipping out of the Hoover Institution, I decided to see if I could find out why Vincent Hallinan had been in prison. The August 10, 1952, *Worker* had the answer: "Hallinan has been serving a six-month 'contempt' sentence imposed on him during his defense of Harry Bridges in the famous 'perjury' trial two years ago." If Murray had at least told me about that, I might not have left Mayfair as reactionary as when I started. I left Stanford without being noticed by the FBI "researchers" at the Hoover Institution, the campus police, and the administration, so I was not arrested for contempt of court.

Amherst and Empire

GOING TO COLLEGE in the early 1950s wasn't a very educational experience. Very few of us who went through the academies in those days could possibly comprehend what was being done to us, much less understand why it was being done. The main thing we didn't learn was how these institutions fitted into the designs of the expanding U.S. empire and its so-called Cold War against Communism.

In September, 1951, I entered Amherst College. I had just worked the first of two summers at Mayfair Photofinishing. At Amherst, the world of work, the anti-Communist repression, and the Korean War were all irrelevant to the academic program. Or so it seemed.

The Korean War seemed to penetrate Amherst only in the form of ROTC. I enrolled in Air Force ROTC because it guaranteed that I could finish college rather than getting drafted as a foot soldier in Korea, and because I had a romantic image of myself as a future combat pilot. Except for ROTC, which taught obvious lies about what was going on in the world, most of the courses at Amherst seemed to have nothing whatever to do with a planet on which the U.S. empire was trying to expand in the face of national liberation movements and communist insurgencies, with a domestic society in the grips of a vast political repression aimed at crushing the labor movement and wiping progressive ideas from the media and education.

I did not understand at the time why this society had put me in college or what was supposed to happen to me there. I did not know that the empire needed millions and millions of engineers, bureaucrats, administrators, lawyers, linguists, experts in finance and banking, social scientists, advertising and publicity technicians and executives, military officers, and other propagators of "Western" (i.e., European and North American bourgeois) culture; and that to fill this need it would have to channel into its institutions of higher learning, even to some extent into its elite New England colleges, a large section of working-class youth. U.S. society had no need to educate my parents. But it had potential uses for me that demanded that I be both trained and acculturated. When I went to college I was undecided whether I wanted to be an engineer or do something with literature, teach it or write it or both. The idea of being a lawyer also crossed my mind. When people back home asked me, "What are you going to do after college?" or, better yet, "What are you going to *be*?" I certainly would not have replied, "I am going to become a loyal member of the class of professionals and intellectuals." But that is exactly where I was aiming, and being aimed.

I could not help but feel out of place socially at Amherst, and I was conscious of enormous pressures to change my manner, dress, style of speech, and outlook. At most of the New England elite colleges at that time, coats and ties were standard dress for men. Amherst had a tradition of scorning such formality, with a studied air of casual dress and manner, indicating that Amherst men were so sure of their position that they had no need to rely on a formal display of it. The white buck shoes had to be very dirty, the Harris tweed jackets should have leather patches or even threadbare spots on the elbows, and open necks were the rule. As on every campus, crew cuts were the norm, but any fairly short, neat haircut was acceptable. Amherst men were expected to say "Hi" as they passed each other on campus. I speedily abandoned my old dressy clothes that I wore in high school: a dark blue double-breasted suit with wide padded shoulders and slightly pegged pants, set off with wide flashy ties done with a broad V knot. After being accepted for admission to Amherst, I had followed the advice of the mailing sent by the college and purchased dark gray flannel slacks, a tweed jacket and a corduroy jacket with natural shoulders, and some narrow, striped ties. But, after conforming for a while at Amherst, I began to rebel in a private and no doubt laughable way by not shaving and slouching around in a dirty, torn-up old brown leather jacket.

Amherst had supposedly achieved all the advantages of the fraternity system without its vicious exclusiveness through a policy of "100 percent rushing." This meant that there was eventually a place in a fraternity for every man who wanted to be in one. The Amherst system was a far more powerful engine of social conformity than existed on most campuses, where only a minority were admitted to fraternities. Each and every freshman felt the full weight of the fraternities' social judgment. Over most of freshman year hung the dread of being doomed to "over-the-quota rush," when, after spring vacation, each fraternity absorbed one or two of the social undesirables left over from the regular season.

I guess the first "radical" action I ever engaged in was a campaign some of us mounted senior year to do away with fraternities. In my sophomore and junior years I had participated with some enthusiasm in a fraternity that had been kicked out of its national for recruiting two Black members. By senior year I had begun to realize that allowing a couple of token Blacks the dubious privilege of conforming to the social criteria of the fraternities did not balance the general social damage perpetrated by the fraternity system. I had also become deeply ashamed of my own loyal support of the fraternity, a feeling I have still not gotten rid of. Our antifraternity campaign did not use any militant tactics. We tried to persuade enough freshmen not to join fraternities so that the whole system would collapse financially. Our literature argued that fraternities are "anti-democratic and anti-intellectual." At one point a majority of the freshman class actually supported this campaign.

The most effective antifraternity organizers in the freshman class were a couple of vets of the Korean War. Both were several years older, more experienced, and more self-reliant than the other freshmen. When the fraternities all banded together to smash this threat to their existence, they very quickly singled out these two vets as their first targets. Each was taken out for an evening by a group of members of several fraternities. When they returned after midnight, both had become converts to the fraternity system, and they soon became leaders of the drive to make sure that each and every member of that freshman class join a fraternity, a goal that was entirely achieved. I never did find out how these two guys, whom I had deeply admired, had been transformed in a few hours, though each told me privately that at one point during the "conversation" they had been reduced to tears. But even the most sophisticated pressures toward social conformity were more obvious and less insidious than what was going on in the classroom.

Amherst had just developed a freshman English course that was becoming widely known as a model of sophistication and ingenuity. English 1 was designed to indoctrinate us into a set of beliefs based on the premise that only a highly select and rigorously trained intellectual elite could glimpse the essence of "reality," which lay in the total dependence of the objective world on the subjective. Form and content, we had to understand, were one and the same, and therefore the style of English 1 was the very heart of its lesson. Since the "real" world was merely perceptual, since being was mere consciousness of consciousness, since symbols were on a higher level of existence than objects, and since all these beliefs were far beyond the ken of ordinary people, our instructors' relationship to us was of priests to initiates. We soon learned our first lessons, that our teachers were brilliant, that they were in possession of some great mystery, and that they were to lure us into this inner sanctum with sly looks, bizarre questions, a thousand little suggestive ironies, cryptic comments on our papers, and, very occasionally, a dramatic physical act in the classroom.

One professor, one of the principal designers of the labyrinth, usually began his first class by stepping through the window and then sitting on the table. He would then silently stare at the class for several minutes, finally demanding, "What did I just do?" The bravest would pipe up, "You stepped through the window, and then sat on the table." "Nonsense!" he would bellow, pretending to be enraged by this crass, vulgar stupidity, "I entered through a door and am now sitting on a chair. Doors are things you walk in and out through, and chairs are things you sit on."

The textbook for the first few weeks was a map of the local area. We were to "define" such terms as "symbol," "map," and "here." Then one big assignment was to define "reality" in exactly half a page. When you received your written assignment back, it would contain between one and three obscure and puzzling comments. One that I can remember, next to a sentence I had just thrown in for a fill, was "Keep it up. You're on the right track!"

We could never figure out exactly what was going on, or what it was we were supposed to be learning. The closest we got was when someone discovered through an overheard conversation that some of the theory of the course, and all the map assignments, came from a book called *Language in Thought and Action* by some weirdo named S. I. Hayakawa.

English 1 was both fascinating and infuriating. It usually made me mad. Sometimes after class I would go back to my room and throw things against the wall or kick the wastepaper basket across the room, just to reassure myself about the physical world. For this I became a noted "character" in the dorm. But the game was intriguing, and at the end of the school year when I went back to Brooklyn I had great fun confounding my friends by showing them that only thoughts and words were real, though I didn't dare try that on Ben and Murray when I went back to work at Mayfair Photofinishing.

I have to admit that English 1 did me some good, mainly by

letting me in on the ways the cynical ideologues of the empire could manipulate language. During the height of the white student anti-Vietnam war movement, when window breaking at ROTC buildings and war-research centers was widespread, the professors, administrators, and media created a wild image of frenzied barbarians threatening the very foundations of civilized society. Key to this image was the word "violence." Many of the demonstrators tried to argue that throwing a rock through the window of a war-research center was not nearly so violent as the activities going on inside, where new invasions, chemical and biological weapons, and systematic torture were being planned. I used to go further in my speeches, arguing that throwing a rock through a pane of glass is not in itself a "violent" act in the language of the apologists for the status quo. I said that what makes it "violent" is the fact that it is an attack on private property, that it wouldn't be "violent" if the window were the property of the people throwing the rocks. "Suppose," I said, "the administration of a university decided to demolish an entire building, not just the windows, to make way for something else. Who would call that 'violence'?" Then in December, 1972, S. I. Hayakawa, no longer the obscure semanticist merely writing treatises on how to manipulate language, put my conjecture into action. In the words of the San Francisco's *Chronicle* of December 22:

> S. I. Hayakawa, the no-nonsense president of San Francisco State University, threw rocks at windows on his own campus yesterday. And was on target, too. Hayakawa, his famous tam o'shanter replaced momentarily by a hard hat, was publicizing the demolition of the campus' 20-year-old food service facility known as the Commons.

By the close of my sophomore year I had become so caught up in the elitist world of the Amherst English Department that I applied for admission into English honors, considered to be the most intellectual program. For the junior year the honors course consisted of a series of intimate seminars on select literary subjects. My responses still vacillated. My notes for one two-hour seminar consisted of a full page with "BULLSHIT" written in different styles and sizes. But it sure was a pleasant feeling to know that you were special, and that you could say and write marvelously obscure things about literary works only a handful of people could really enjoy and comprehend—the metaphysical poets, Alexander Pope, Matthew Arnold, T. S. Eliot, and James Joyce. Despite this, my underlying attitude toward Amherst was still alienation.

Senior year was different. I actually began to like the place, particularly after quitting my fraternity and spending most of my time with the other misfits who belonged to the Jeff Club, the alternative to fraternities. I still wore my old leather jacket, even to those thrilling but puzzling private conferences with the adviser of my senior honors thesis, Benjamin DeMott, who now seemed to accept it as just a little sign of eccentricity (though he never seemed quite at his usual ease). I didn't know what to write about, so DeMott guided me into an attempt to develop evaluative criteria for distinguishing between "great" and "inferior" plays on the basis of the "refinement" and "sensibilities" of the audiences for whom they were intended.

This outlandish project had the preposterous title "An Examination and Evaluation of Changing Moral and Social Perspectives in English Dramatic Literature." Its basic argument was that in each historical period "great" plays present "complex" views of human experience and avoid the "easy answers" of "inferior" plays. It begins with a comparison of two Jacobean tragedies, showing that the better play is the more intellectually sophisticated and emotionally complex. The next section proves that the greatness of Restoration comedy lies in its "sophisticated complexity of attitude," whereas the drama that followed, written for the rising middle classes, was silly and sentimental. Then came the payoff, the final section, which proved that the proletarian drama of the 1930s was just crude garbage, a point we could appreciate by comparing it with Shaw's *Pygmalion*. What was especially wonderful about Shaw was his understanding that "class terms are not the most important." I not only failed to see Shaw's own class outlook, but even accepted his view of Liza's rise from the subhuman working class to real womanhood, i.e., becoming a cultured, civilized, refined bourgeois lady:

> The final significance of Liza's transformation is not merely that she has moved from one class to another, but that she has become someone who can no longer be referred to as either inanimate or nonhuman. No longer can terms such as "squashed cabbage leaf," "this baggage," "that thing," "this unfortunate animal," or "a lost umbrella" be used to describe Liza. Galatea, much to the surprise of Pygmalion, has come to life.

Shaw's greatness, according to my argument, lies precisely in his refusal to indulge in either "sentimental love talk" or "sentimental class talk."

Shaw saw Liza's transformation, though comical, as a matter of life and death. It was for me, too. At the moment I became persuaded that Galatea had come to life by leaving the working class and entering the parlors of the bourgeoisie, a vital part of me ceased functioning and I was well on my way to becoming an instrument of the dying world of that deadly class. No doubt my transformation was also comical.

The final step in the honors program was to defend your thesis before all the professors and instructors of the English Department. I was scared stiff beforehand, but when I was finally confronted with this intimidating array I discovered that they had equipped me well, and I used all the weapons of irony and superstyle against those who chose to cross swords. When I finished, the great Professor Baird stood up, walked over, patted me on the back, shook my hand, and said, "Good job." Professor DeMott then ushered me out into the hall. When the door had closed behind us, he said, very quietly and with unaccustomed intensity, "I hope you realize what that praise from Professor Baird means." I was really in. I understood what DeMott meant, but I didn't discover the real meaning of that praise for years.

Twelve years later, in 1967, I met Tom Wilcox, a professor of English at the University of Connecticut. It was about eight months after I had begun to call myself a Marxist-Leninist. It turned out that he had graduated from Amherst in 1940. Each of us tended to think of his own experience, both at Amherst and afterward in the profession, as individual and disconnected. But as we talked until the early morning hours, we both began to understand that we were part of a common historical process.

Tom had gone to Amherst in the 1930s. Like many at the time he was greatly attracted to proletarian literature. His senior honors thesis was an attempt to arrive at some kind of literary evaluation of some proletarian works. He described his profound disappointment when he "discovered," with the help of his faculty adviser and much against his own desire, that the formal imperfection of this literature made it "inferior," not for merely aesthetic reasons but because it displayed inadequate moral perception. I then saw the direct development from the ideology of his Amherst thesis in the late 1930s to mine in the mid-1950s. Here was the rise and triumph of formalism. First, form is raised above content by proving that form is the essence of content. Once this is accomplished, bourgeois culture is proved superior to proletarian culture. Why? Because it has a more elaborate and self-conscious set of formal criteria, and its artists and critics have an extremely high level of formal training, due in large part to their monopoly on education. Once these bourgeois criteria are completely internalized, it becomes "obvious" or even "intuitive" that a bourgeois work, with its high degree of formal excellence and elegant complexity, is superior to a proletarian work, which seems simple and crude by comparison (particularly when its own formal traditions are ignored, as with Afro-American poetry). Thus the worst weaknesses of *decadent* bourgeois ideology, its irresolvable contradictions and irrationalities, are magically turned into their opposite. The hallmarks of literary greatness become complexity, irony, ambiguity. In the present era, formalism is the use of aesthetics to blind us to social and moral reality. It is the expression of the mentality of Mussolini's son, who was thrilled by the beauty of the bursting bombs he dropped on the Ethiopian villages.

New Criticism began as a conscious counterattack on rising

proletarian culture. It was crude and frankly reactionary formalism. We must remind ourselves of where and when the most influential new critics arose. Cleanth Brooks, Robert Penn Warren, John Crowe Ransom, and Allen Tate all developed within that citadel of reaction, Vanderbilt University, and then received further training in elitism at Oxford. Their first influential works appeared at the height of the Depression. Allen Tate's frankly titled *Reactionary Essays* came out in 1936, the same year as the first edition of Brooks and Warren's *An Approach to Literature*. In 1938 came John Crowe Ransom's *The World's Body* and the first edition of Brooks and Warren's *Understanding Poetry*. New Criticism, which emerged in the 1930s to halt the advance of proletarian culture, gained complete ascendancy in the early 1950s, radiating out and "down" from Amherst and Harvard. It became the main form of anti-Communist ideology in literary criticism. Tom Wilcox's 1940 thesis represented a form for that ideology at an early stage. My 1955 thesis, written just after McCarthyism had swept the campuses, expressed that ideology in the period of triumphant reaction.

CARB MFG CO

In the summers of 1953 and 1954 I worked at Carb Manufacturing Company, on the last block of Carroll Street down on the Brooklyn waterfront in Red Hook. Mr. Nathan Carb was the sole owner of the company and of about three-fourths of the city block, including the main factory, which was housed in an ancient dingy brick four-story building. From the outside, there was no way to tell where the factory ended and Mr. Carb's adjoining tenement houses began. As I soon discovered, there was no way to tell from inside either.

Carb Manufacturing did almost exclusively government contracts. Every now and then Mr. Carb would withdraw a large amount of cash and bustle off to Washington to get a new contract or to have the heat taken off for failing to fulfill the terms of an old one. While I worked there, we were making mostly furniture for the Navy and Air Force, principally couches and chairs made of aluminum, leatherette, and foam. Production seemed in no way to be affected by the end of the Korean War in midsummer, 1953, possibly because of something I knew nothing about, the increasing U.S. involvement in Indochina. I learned that the plant previously had been making parachutes, a thought that later haunted me throughout my flying career in the Air Force. Whenever I checked out a chute, I always made sure it wasn't marked "CARB MFG CO."

My first job was webbing springs and stuffing cushions in the upholstery department up on the fourth floor. This was the only floor in the plant where any English was spoken (except of course in the front office). On every other floor all the workers were Puerto Rican, except for a few Cubans. Up here, the main production was done by two lines of women, about half Puerto Rican and half Black. They sewed cushion covers together on sewing machines that looked as if they had been hijacked from the Smithsonian Institution. The only two men besides me were Black. One was my twenty-three-year-old foreman Sylvester, who had grown up in the Bedford-Stuyvesant section of Brooklyn. The other was Jasper, who had just arrived in New York from Georgia, where he had been working in the cotton fields for five years. He was my age, nineteen. Sylvester, Jasper, and I spent about half our time boxing, arm wrestling, weight lifting with rolls of leatherette, talking loudly about our sexual prowess, and doing anything else we could think of to impress the women, who were working too hard to pay much attention to us. Sylvester's younger sister got hired shortly after I did, and he and his wife and she and I used to go out together on Saturday nights, usually starting at the clubs in Harlem and ending up at Nathan's in Coney Island.

After I had been there a few weeks, Mr. Carb called me into his office one day. He told me that production was being held up by a bottleneck in the sewing lines, and that as a result we were falling way behind on an important contract. What he was going to do, he told me, was to put all the "girls" up there on piecework until we got caught up. "You're a bright young fellow, and about the only person around here I can trust," he said in a low voice. "So what I want you to do is keep track of each girl's production."

So I did. The rate of production more than tripled. The women on the lines now had a chance to make close to half a living wage. All small talk and horseplay disappeared. Each woman worked at top speed, and the cushion covers were liberally sprinkled with sweat. The ancient machines started breaking down. Mr. Carb refused to replace any of them or even pay to have them serviced. So I had to repair them, always with an operator anxiously watching, begging me to hurry. The small piles of finished cushion covers grew into towering stacks completely cutting off the sewing lines from the area where I used to cavort with Jasper and Sylvester.

Mr. Carb had given me our production targets. When we reached this goal, I dutifully reported that to him. "Well, let's just keep going and get ourselves a margin of safety," he replied, with a smile and a pat on the back. So the frenetic pace continued, until we had run out of storage room and were weeks ahead of the rest of the production process. Then Mr. Carb fired three-fourths of the women in the sewing department. He informed those who were left that he was now taking them off piecework, but that he had the production record for each one of them and he expected them to maintain that pace. Of course I understood how I had been used against the women, and how the women's own labor had been used to destroy their livelihood. But it was many years before I learned, through Marx's categories of alienated labor, that what I had seen in microcosm was the very essence of capitalist socioeconomic relations. For most of these years, I just thought of Mr. Carb as an especially vicious breed of boss.

Whenever I think of Carb Manufacturing, I think of rats. Since the plant was located only about a block and a half from the waterfront, hordes of huge wharf rats made their homes in the walls and debris of the building. To us they seemed the real owners, and none of us would have trespassed into their domain after nightfall. When we reported for work each morning, we first threw bolts and yelled into each room, then waited until we could no longer hear any scurrying, before entering. From time to time rats would come out onto the middle of the floor, even right next to us while we operated noisy machines. Sometimes one would sit up on its haunches staring at us until we actually hit it with a bolt.

On the ground floor there was a large warehouse area whose floor was covered with piles of materials from past contracts and for current production, all scattered about helter-skelter. When we ventured into this area, we walked on bridges we built of wooden planks, hoping that our work shoes would protect our ankles from the rats which infested that morass. One day I went to Mr. Carb's office and proposed to him that we collect all the old materials lying around the warehouse, inventory them, figure out what could be used, sell the rest, and then utilize the cleared space for production. Mr. Carb became livid with rage. "All those materials are mine, do you understand that? They are mine! I am the only one who can decide what is to be done with them. Do you understand that?"

When I first arrived at Carb, there was one other "white" worker (a more accurate term would be non-Third-World worker, for a few of the Puerto Ricans were blond and had blue eyes). This was Angelo, a barrel-chested tough old Sicilian who was foreman of the shipping department. He ran that department by thundering curses in a kind of pidgin Spanish, shoving anybody he suspected of "loafing" up against the wall, and severely beating any worker who "didn't know his place." One day, three of his workers stopped the rattletrap old freight elevator between floors and beat Angelo into a three-day coma. He was shipped to the hospital and I was recruited to take his place as foreman of the shipping department.

Here is where I first discovered the real operating procedures of Carb Manufacturing. Only about half the production went on in the main factory. The rest took place in small shops secretly scattered throughout the adjoining tenement houses. There, large families lived in squalid two-room apartments, taking shifts at night to keep the rats at bay. The rooms in which we worked were permeated by a heavy smell of garlic, used by all the tenants to overpower the stench of stale urine in the halls. Safely tucked away from the government inspectors who periodically visited the main plant, we assembled frames made of aluminum two or three grades below government specifications, added foam remnants, and covered the final product with paper-thin leatherette. We carried the finished products on our heads through subterranean tunnels into a secret passageway opening into the shipping department of the main factory. There we crated them up and shipped them out.

When crated, the couches weighed 275 pounds each. The workers were so poorly nourished that it would take six to carry one crate. Whenever we had to load onto trucks lacking hydraulic tailgates, the only people strong enough to handle the two-man job of lifting them to the inside of the truck were myself and a man nicknamed "El Grande" because of his great size, which was about the same as mine—five feet seven, 150 pounds.

In the main shipping room, where we crated the junk assembled in the tenement houses, we kept a fair supply of good furniture on hand, one or two of them partially crated, all covered by tarpaulins. When the Navy or Air Force inspector arrived at the front of the plant, someone was dispatched to come running back yelling, "El inspector! El inspector!" We quickly pulled the tarps off the good stuff and threw them over the junk. By the time the inspector got back there, we were busily crating a fine specimen. One day the head Navy inspector approached me.

"Hey, Bruce, you know old man Carb takes care of me, but I still got to be sure the stuff he's sending out of here isn't too crappy. Hope you're keeping an eye on it."

"You know me, Mel. It just wouldn't pay for us to lose this contract. Look right here, for instance. I'm sending this one right back up to have those scratches on the legs ground off."

I showed him a perfectly good couch, pointing out a couple of minor scratches on the back legs. He half smiled at what he took for my overzealousness.

"Oh, that's O.K., Bruce. You don't have to worry about minor stuff like that. I just want to make sure that no real crappy stuff is going out. I'll tell you what I'm going to do, because I trust you and I know you'll be careful. I'll let you have the stamp so you can stamp the crates yourself. That way you guys won't get jammed up down here, and I won't have to make so many trips over. You scratch my back, Bruce, and I'll scratch yours. But you got to promise to keep being careful."

So Mel gave me the official U.S. Navy stamp of inspection and approval, which I cheerfully smacked onto every crateful of junk we put together, sometimes even before we stenciled CARB MFG CO and the destination on the crate.

The Puerto Rican people who worked at Carb were mostly from the island nation itself. In 1952, as part of the U.S. global plan, Puerto Rico was officially turned into a "commonwealth" of the United States, thus magically transforming it from being a colony. The relationship was basically that of Algeria to France, with Puerto Ricans automatically becoming U.S. citizens. Like the Algerians, who were used as French shock troops in Indochina, Puerto Ricans would henceforth be drafted to serve on the front lines of "anti-Communist" struggle, including Indochina. What I was witnessing was the first great influx of cheap labor from the island, brought into New York to serve as part of the reserve army of the unemployed, a lever to be used against the better-established workers in the city.

My own attitude toward Puerto Ricans had been blatantly racist. I considered them lazy, dishonest, sneaky, treacherous, stupid, and primitive. The only Puerto Rican I had ever known personally—Maria, who worked at Mayfair Photofinishing—I was forced to consider an exception, since she was hard-working, honest, straightforward, kind, intelligent, and more sophisticated than I was. My only other direct contact with Puerto Rican people had been back in 1949, when two friends and I had gotten into a fight with a Puerto Rican gang in a Puerto Rican neighborhood a couple of blocks from the Brooklyn Navy Yard. We got pretty thoroughly worked over, and although we had known better than to intrude on someone else's turf, we nurtured our resentment. After I was all stitched back together, my father called over to our home a friend of his who was a police sergeant in that precinct. He and my father mulled over various schemes for revenge, which soon dissolved in their beer. At one point this brawny cop held up both his hands, knuckles out, to show me that almost every finger had been broken "beating the shit out of these little punks, for all the good that it does."

The people who had come from the island preserved many of the traditions of the countryside, including strong family ties. Their tremendous honesty I found hard to believe. Practically all of them were making seventy-five cents an hour and trying to support families whose average size must have been at least ten or twelve. The most skilled production workers at Carb were welders, and they made only eighty-five cents an hour. Once someone found a five-dollar bill on the floor behind a machine. This equaled almost a full day's take-home pay. Instead of putting it in his pocket, he went to each person working on that floor, to see who had lost it. It was claimed by about the twentieth person he asked. There has never been a doubt in my mind that this was the rightful owner.

But one could also see the traditional ethics breaking down in New York City, where, in that filthy, foreign, treeless jungle, Puerto Rican people were daily hunted down by rats, cops, unemployment, hunger, dope pushers, the draft, and disease, and where the best opportunity in life lay in working for the Mr. Carbs. The younger people raised in New York had a very different outlook from the older people who had come from the island. For them the only unit of security could be the street gang, which was beginning to take the place of the family as the center of loyalty.

Everybody's day dream was hitting a number and hitting it big. Some people actually dreamed numbers at night. Each day's number at that time was the last three digits of a parimutuel figure in the *Daily News*. When you picked a number, the odds were therefore 999 to 1 against your winning. If your number hit, the Syndicate paid you 500 to 1. This meant that they kept half of each day's money bet in the entire city. Every floor of our factory had a numbers runner, who was just one of the workers. Each floor runner gave his money to the head runner in our immediate area, and so on up the line. The Syndicate was absolutely reliable in its payments. The most exciting topic of conversation each morning was numbers—who had won, which of us had missed by only one digit, what numbers people had dreamed, what to bet, tales of famous hits. Numbers was the only chance most Carb workers had to ever find a way out of there. A dollar hit equaled a third of a year's pay, more money than most people there had ever had at one time. If you worked at Carb for a year and a half and never spent a dime you earned, you would not have as much as a five-dollar hit.

The plant was located in Red Hook, which was probably the toughest section of Brooklyn. While I was working at Carb, the Syndicate controlled the entire area. A lot of the young Italian guys who lived there had graduated from the teen-age street gangs into a fairly systematic livelihood based on car theft, mugging, and numbers running. Directly across the street from the front steps of the plant was a pool hall and beer parlor where some of these gangs hung out during the day. Being the only white worker in the plant, I was elected to go over there whenever we wanted some bottles of beer to wash down our lunch. As I approached the front door, I could always hear lots of conversation and the clicking of pool balls inside. As soon as I opened the door and stepped inside, there would be total silence. It was like everybody was a player in that game where you yell "Freeze!"—except that everyone would turn and stare at me. I knew that all I had to do to get myself in deep trouble was to return any of these stares. So I would keep looking at my shoes and occasionally glance up at the ceiling while I jingled some coins waiting for the guy from the bar to take and fill my order.

Mr. Carb was probably the cheapest scrooge I ever met. He would hire new workers to work four ten-hour days at seventy-five cents an hour (grand total, thirty dollars for forty hours) and then fire them so he wouldn't have to pay them overtime. When he had overseas shipments to make from piers fairly nearby in Brooklyn, instead of having the loading done by longshoremen, he would send me down with two truckloads of workers from the plant (all of course paid seventy-five cents an hour) and a pocketful of five-dollar bills to pay off the loading boss of the pier. We would do the loading under the belligerent stares of the longshoremen.

Because the plant was in Red Hook, Mr. Carb had a special economy plan for bringing in the weekly payroll, which had to be in cash because many of the workers had no way to cash checks. Rather than hiring an armored security service, which might have been jacked up anyhow, he would send me, dressed in my regular work clothes, to pick up the entire payroll. I would walk the long block to the corner, take a bus, transfer to another bus, walk two short blocks, go into the bank, hand a certain teller a sealed envelope, and be given the payroll in small bills. The way back to the plant scared the hell out of me. The last block that I had to walk always seemed about three miles long. I was prepared to surrender the payroll as quickly and cooperatively as possible.

Needless to say there was no union at Carb. One morning, four men and women greeted us at the door to the factory and handed us leaflets headlined on one side, "ONLY ONE WAY! JOIN THE UNION TODAY!" and on the other, "¡SOLAMENTE UN MEDIO! ¡INGRESAR EN LA UNION HOY!" A copy I still have explains in Spanish and English:

> Remember the laws of this Country protect you. Should your department head or any other supervisor discuss the Union with you or should they antagonize you in any way—report this to one of the organizers immediately—steps will be taken before the National Labor Relations Board to put a stop to this. The laws of this Country give you the right to join a Union without discrimination for doing so by your Employer.
>
> The Miscellaneous Industrial Employees Union, Local 138, D.R. & W.W.I.U. of A.—A.F.L. consists of intelligent members and responsible leadership. The policy of this union is to exercise utmost responsibility toward strife and quarrels.

Mr. Carb's office looked out over this area. Only three people stopped to talk with the leafleters. At noon, Mr. Carb called these three in, informed them they were fired for inefficiency, and gave them their paychecks. The next day, two of the workers in the plant tried to encourage people to send in applications to join the union.

Both were jumped and badly beaten on the way home by a gang of thugs that evening. Mr. Carb fired them for not reporting to work the following day. Other workers called the telephone number at the bottom of the union leaflet to report the situation. They were told that the union had decided that "the workers in Carb were not ready for a union," and they could therefore do nothing further to help.

The last month I worked there in 1954, Mr. Carb gave me the grand title of Supervisor of Production for the whole plant and raised my hourly wage to eighty-five cents. Then in my final week he proposed that I quit college and stay there, promising me that I would eventually have a really fine future working for him. Maybe that's why senior year at Amherst didn't seem so bad.

New York Harbor: 1955

It must have been near 7:30 p.m. toward the end of July, 1955, a couple of months after I graduated from Amherst College. The sun was close to setting behind us over Jersey City. Ahead of us and to the right, the skyscrapers of Wall Street were orange, with windows of burnished gold. New York, the Empire City, looked like a magical metropolis of gold and stone—pure, brilliant, soaring above the harbor. The water of the river, wrinkled by a light breeze, was dark blue flecked with more gold, mingled with rainbows created by floating oil.

I was the mate on a Pennsylvania Railroad tugboat heading for a pier just north of the financial district. As we approached the three barges we were supposed to tow, I climbed out over the bow and stood on the tug's bumper, a mass of old knotted-up towing lines fastened to the front of the bow. I was holding a heavy towing line, with a two-foot "eye" or loop spliced in at the throwing end. We slowly narrowed the distance between us and the closest barge. I began to calculate my heave. As I glanced down at the water, all now in shadow and covered with the usual patches of condoms and other New York City garbage, I noticed a dark blue patch of cloth billowing up above the surface as though it were attached to a large object underneath. Looking closer, I saw it was the back of a man's shirt on a body, floating, head down, under the water.

The stern-line man and the deckhand, who were both also ready to cast their lines, as well as the captain up in the pilot house, were all watching me for signals. We were about to drift over the body. I motioned to reverse immediately. The swirls from our propellers washed over the body and spun it slowly around.

Old Joe Barnes, considered the best railroad tugboat captain in the harbor, maneuvered us to within a couple of yards of the body and held even with it, while keeping the stern pointed out toward open water. I conferred with Sonny, the strapping, blond Irish deckhand, who had now lost his usual jovial and boisterous manner. We decided to drop a towing line under the body and try to hook one of its legs in the eye of the line. Each leg was swollen to double its normal size and was pushing through the rotting blue work pants. I dropped the line and swung it out, caught a leg on the third try, and Sonny began pulling in. Pieces of the pants and of the flesh on the leg stripped off in jellyish clumps. Those of us on the deck came close to being sick as a heavy, sweet, putrid smell wafted over the tug. As the line tore loose, the legs came up, then dropped down, rocking the head into view for the first time. Through the back of the neck was stuck a bag hook, the standard hand tool of the longshoremen. Tony, our wiry, dark, grizzled old Italian stern-line man, muttered, "It's another ILA execution."

In two months our fleet of thirty Pennsylvania Railroad tugs working out of Pier H, Jersey City, had picked up five bodies of longshoremen floating in the harbor, all executed in the same manner. The docks and the dockers were up for grabs that year, and control over them was being fought out by the International Longshoremen's Association, the American Federation of Labor, the stevedore and ship companies, and the governments of New York, New Jersey, and the United States.

We felt sorry for "those poor guys" working on the docks and were glad we had our own superior position. Our attitude toward the struggle raging around us was formed by the various aspects of our job. Years later, I found in Marx, Engels, and Lenin the term "aristocracy of labor" used to describe that section of the working class in a capitalist empire who are bought off with some of the superprofits of imperialism. If someone had dropped in on us while we were having one of our pleasant, relaxed, philosophical discussions on deck and said, "You men are a real aristocracy of labor," we would have enthusiastically agreed. We were all white, male, skilled, athletic, highly paid, and we had a union that represented us exactly as we wished to be represented. We didn't know that our fate was tied to that of the longshoremen and of people even more oppressed. But our work did lead us to comprehend much about the society we lived in.

Each tug had a captain, a deck crew, made up of the mate, the stern-line man, and the deckhand, and an engine crew, consisting of an engineer plus either two stokers on a steam tug or one oiler on a diesel tug. Most crews were assigned to one particular tugboat. After my apprenticeship, somewhat shortened because I had had some previous experience working on a fishing boat, I was assigned to one of the six "roustabout" crews, which rotated through all the tugs on the Pennsy fleet, taking each tug for two-day stints while its regular crew was off. We were supposed to be the most highly skilled crews, because we had to be able to handle both steam and diesel tugs as well as cope with the idiosyncrasies of each different vessel.

About half our fleet were steam tugs. Working on them gave a sense of the impending end of an era. They had all been built in the early years of the century, and were the last steam tugs working in the harbor, probably the last steam craft of any kind. We preferred them to the diesels for several reasons. They were considerably heavier than the newer diesel tugs, and were therefore a more solid platform to work barges around. Although the diesels could get up to top speed faster, this was no great advantage in our kind of work. When we got up a full head of steam, we easily outran the latest diesel tugs, and this kind of speed was useful for long hauls. The piercing steam whistle, which could be heard for miles, was a marvelous power to have for clearing a path in the harbor, which in those days was crowded day and night with liners, freighters, tankers, ferries, self-propelled barges, cruise boats, patrol boats, and hundreds of tugs shuttling back and forth with barges, lighters, and floats holding twenty railroad cars apiece. The steam tugs also shortened our work day, for we were allowed an hour and a half to pull the ashes out of the hold with a pulley and bucket and dispose of them. This time allowance provided for our sailing to one of the approved disposal areas and returning. We just posted a lookout for the harbor patrol and then dumped the ashes in any convenient hiding place, or, at night, even out in the middle of the river. But our pleasure with the steam tugs was dampened by the sure knowledge that their days were numbered.

Our tasks fell into two basic categories—float work and barge work. The simplest, but busiest, was ferrying railroad-car floats back and forth between railroad yards along the New Jersey shore and the fruit and vegetable markets in lower Manhattan. Each float had a track switch and rail sidings. The larger floats held twenty railroad cars, the smaller ten. Switchyard locomotives would shunt the cars on board the floats via an adjustable platform known as a bridge, which had tracks matching up to those on the float. We would slip between two loaded floats, and tow them one on either side. During the peak hours—between 5 P.M. and 1 A.M.—dozens of railroad tugs scurried back and forth across what we called the North River (the lower Hudson), towing forty railroad cars laden with fruits and vegetables on each trip.

As soon as the front of the floats touched the dock in New York, even while we were still securing them, dockside crews would trot on board stringing lights and opening up the cars. Inside the market, a series of vast warehouses between the river and the truck-jammed streets, fruits and vegetables were being bought, loaded, and trucked away as fast as we brought them over, with wholesalers, merchants, warehousemen, forklifts, and truckdrivers buzzing around like bees inside a hive. The appetite of the giant city seemed insatiable, consuming freight-car loads of perishables by the dozens and hundreds an hour. Faced with this awesome dependency of the city on the countryside, I often wondered what the city did that was worth it. After all, its main products did not come from the light industry like Carb Manufacturing or Mayfair Photofinishing or even the garment center, but from the labyrinth of Wall Street, where people like my father expended their lives pushing pieces of paper representing the basic property relations of the world's commerce: stocks, bonds, title deeds, promissory notes, insurance policies, contracts, mortgages. What, I wondered, did New York produce for the migrant workers who picked the cantaloupes that came in two-hundred-car-long trains on the Atlantic Coast Line?

Sometimes we towed cattle floats to the slaughterhouses on the west side of Manhattan. These floats were tall double-decked stockyards, several times the size of a tug. We did our work on the narrow catwalks on the outside of the lower deck. Slippery manure accumulated on these catwalks, often to a depth of two feet. (Securing a cattle float during a hurricane, I came close to an untimely and unpoetic end.) My father, whose brother had been a butcher in one of these slaughterhouses, used to tell me about an animal known as a Judas goat, but before I worked on the tugs I had always assumed it was a mythical beast, one of the creations of my father's fantasy. We secured the cattle floats to special docks in Manhattan fenced with a labyrinth of passageways. If the floats contained sheep, a goat would walk up to the exit of the float. When the gate was opened, all the sheep followed this goat up through the passageways to the top of a ramp. At the last moment, the goat stepped through a little swinging door to one side. The sheep kept right on walking over a ledge, where their hind legs were automatically roped together and jerked straight up. A butcher then slit their throats, kosher style, under the supervision of a rabbi. Even at that primitive stage of my political thinking, this seemed a perfect image of the relationship between workers and bosses, who always pretend to be the same kind of creature we are, all living happily in a classless society, while they live off our life blood.

The other category of work, towing barges and lighters, was even more educational, for it took us throughout the entire waterway system of New York Harbor, with its seven hundred miles of shoreline. We worked up and down the North River between Jersey and Manhattan, down past the Statue of Liberty into the Upper Bay, through Kill Van Kull into Newark Bay, into Arthur Kill west of Staten Island, across the Upper Bay to "Tough Tony" Anastasia's piers in the Bay Ridge, Red Hook, and China Basin sections of Brooklyn, on both sides of the East River, which is really a saltwater sluiceway between Long Island Sound and New York Bay, to the deadliest spot on this sluiceway, the aptly named Hell Gate, where the tidal rip is so fierce that all mooring lines have to be replaced every twenty-four hours, and up into the Harlem River, which makes Manhattan an island.

A typical barge and lighter assignment could last for almost an entire work day, take us from one end of the harbor to the other, and involve the towing of several dozen barges. We received a list of barges to be picked up from widely scattered piers, docks, and ship sides along with the various destinations to which we were to deliver them. We had to know the type of load carried by each barge and then solve a complicated set of problems involving tide, wind, current, weight, point of origin, destination, and relation to the other barges. The intellectual activity required exceeds by far, I am now quite convinced, that employed by most university professors of literature. We might have to tow at one time fourteen barges, with cargoes whose weight varied as much as cotton and steel. Barges were often moored four or more abreast along the length of a pier, forming five or six rows end to end. The particular barge we were after could be the third in a row of four that had four other rows between it and the open end of the pier. We might already have eight or ten barges secured along our bows and sides. This particular barge could be loaded with steel, so it would have to go right alongside the tug, balanced against another heavy barge on the other side. In this case we would have to let the barges already in tow go partly free, swinging in the tide, wind, and current, while at the same time also letting several groups of barges alongside the pier swing partly free. Then we would have to maneuver the barge into its proper towing position, while at the same time maneuvering all the loose barges and resecuring them. To accomplish this kind of job, the three men on the deck had to work in clockwork precision with each other and with the captain, who had to be just as precise in his relations with the engine room. Our operation had to be closely planned and timed to take into account the various natural and mechanical forces in a fluid environment.

Towing lines are thicker than a man's wrist. They are made of three equal strands. The first thing an apprentice deckhand learns is how to splice, particularly how to splice the eye into the throwing end of the line. The eye is made by unraveling the end of the line, and weaving it back into the main body so as to form a flat loop about two feet long. This eye is the main tool of the trade. Being double, it is twice as heavy as any other equal length of line, and it is this extra weight that makes it possible to throw the line some distance and then manipulate it. Throwing this kind of line is based on a different principle from that used with a lasso. Even with a dry line, it takes some strength just to lift the eye and the length to be thrown with it. When the lines get wet, a dreaded event, the weight to be thrown is heavier than the man throwing it. Instead of spinning it high in the air like a lasso, you lift the loop barely enough to clear the surface you are standing on, open it by folding it back against the line, and then begin to build momentum by giving it a pendulum motion. When you actually throw, you use your entire body in a smooth motion timed to coincide with the swing of the loop, thus giving it the necessary extra acceleration.

The target is either a bitt or a cleat on a barge, float, or dock, or on the tug itself if you are working from another point. A bitt is a round metal post tapering somewhat from the top down and thick enough to hold an ocean liner or a fleet of barges. A cleat is a thick iron bar, with a horn at each end, parallel to the surface it is attached to. When aiming at a bitt, the object is for the eye to reach its fully open position just as it's landing on top, with as little sideways motion as possible. With a cleat, you aim at one horn, so the line is going sideways toward the center of the cleat. When the line lands on one horn, you then use a special trick, impossible to duplicate until you learn the secret. This trick makes it possible to manipulate the far end of these extremely heavy lines at considerable distances. You hold your end of the line with both hands, then very smoothly, almost gently, flick your wrist and move your arm as though throwing something through the center of the line. What you "throw" is the desired twist, curve, lateral, vertical, or backward motion in the form of a wave that travels evenly down the length of the line. With one end of the eye hanging on a horn, with a line weighing several times your own weight stretched between and with vessels shifting in a fluid medium, you watch your wave undulate along the line until it reaches the loop. The loop opens, flops over the opposite horn, and encloses the entire cleat.

At some point you usually have to reverse the process and retrieve the other end of the line. With dozens of feet of churning, filthy New York Harbor water in between, and with heavy vessels moving around you, you can't just step out and go fetch it. So you throw a different wave, the line snakes, the eye opens and pops straight up into the air. If you don't react now at precisely the correct instant, the line will fall into the water, making it extremely heavy and difficult to work with, besides filling it with salt water, which will rot it until it becomes a potential death trap. Just as the eye rises off the cleat or bitt, you snap your wrist and arm quickly in the direction you want the eye to travel. Most of us could drop the eye back at our own feet as if we had magic power over it.

In order for a line to be thrown and secured, the two vessels (or the vessel and pier) have to be either stationary in relation to each other or slowly closing. If the space between the two is widening as the line is thrown and secured, the line is almost certain to snap, whipping back with enough force and speed to kill. If the space is rapidly closing, the line cannot be secured and the possible heavy impact can hurl you overboard to be crushed.

Danger lurked in the lines themselves, especially those kept on the barges, whose "captains" were mostly former tugboat men who had been crippled on the job and were now old and alcoholic. We didn't have the time and manpower to inspect these barge lines. On top, where the sun kept them dry, they would appear sound. But underneath, where salt water accumulated, they were often partly rotted, particularly at the core. In the midst of the trickiest barge operations, our key lines would often have to be these barge lines. Under the tremendous weights and forces in motion, even sound lines could snap. So we all had close calls.

After throwing a line, you belay or make fast your end, usually by throwing figure-eight knots or some other quick-release knot as fast as you can onto the bitt or cleat from which you are working. Your head is about a foot from the line and your hands are rapidly working close to the metal. The most common accident—and it happens just as often to the most experienced men as to greenhorns—is to have several fingers crushed or even sliced off by a sudden tightening of the line, which is why tugboat deck workers all wear oversized, loose-fitting work gloves. But if you concentrate too much on this danger, you can miss the only warning you will get of a line about to snap, the unraveling of a tiny strand a split second before the explosion.

Our work made us independent, self-confident, linked in a tight solidarity among ourselves. No employer could push us too far. But our jobs also made us feel superior to most other workers. We never thought of taking action together with the longshoremen, not to mention the Puerto Rican women working on rickety sewing machines in Carb Manufacturing Company and in the sweatshops of the garment district, or the Black workers who felt fortunate when they could get a service job at seventy-five cents an hour. Thus we left the way open for our own elimination and for the disintegration of the commercial life and physical usefulness of the harbor and the city.

There were no Blacks on any of the crews in our fleet. When the giant black iron bitts on piers were referred to as "niggerheads," it was just their traditional name, and nobody "meant any harm" by it. I would wince, but never admonish anybody. Ours was a white world, and a tight one. Even Jews were a rarity. Once Tony was sick, and the scowling, beer-bellied stern-line man who took his place made some reference to "dirty Jews" while eating lunch. I jumped up all excited and asked if he wanted his teeth for dessert or some such smart remark. Sonny tried to smooth things over by saying that the stern-line man hadn't meant any harm, and wouldn't even have said it if he had known I was Jewish. The stern-line man said, "That's right," and sullenly "took it back."

It was also a male world. During a day's work, we didn't even see many women. They existed for us mostly as the fantasy objects of our boasting and jokes. We would steer out of our way to run alongside any harbor cruise craft so we could ogle the women on board, show off for them, and call out hopeless invitations to get together. Sometimes we would get ahead of our schedule, hide the tug behind a ship at Hoboken, and go to one of the 240 bars in the square-mile downtown area of that small waterfront city. But we never had any luck there. The actual details of our personal lives we pretty much kept to ourselves. When we were working middle trick, about the same hours as swing shift in a plant, most of us went out after work, but we only went together if we didn't have dates. At the end of that trick, we would rush to finish early. After our last tow, we washed up and changed into our fancy stepping-out clothes. When we got back to Pier H and were securing the final lines, we had to prance around daintily in our bright blue or tan suits, white shirts, and broadly-knotted silk ties.

In September, I started going out with Jane Morgan, who had grown up on a farm in North Carolina, majored in English at Duke, and was then working in the United Nations. As work was ending, I would put on my blue suit and fix my Wildroot Cream–trained pompadour. Then I would rush off to pick up Jane at her Manhattan apartment close to midnight. In November, we decided we were going to get married. I never mentioned her to the crew, even when we sailed past the UN building where she worked on the East River.

Those of us who worked on the deck considered ourselves the social superiors not only of the men in the engine room, particularly the stokers and oilers, but also the engineer, who was every bit as skilled as we were and whose pay was about the same. We viewed the deck as a superior environment. In nice weather, we enjoyed getting a deep tan during the day and breathing in the fresh air at night. Even in stormy and freezing weather, while the engine-room crew stayed dry and warm, we reveled in our freedom and manly fortitude. Years later, Melville's *White-Jacket* and *Israel Potter* taught me that the same hierarchy prevailed on sailing ships, with the highest status accorded to the highest altitude. In both eras, it seems, this social rank derived from the particular kind of athletic activity, combining skills, coordination, quick thinking, and daring. We viewed with disdain the hardest physical activity in the engine room, stoking coal, which requires strength and endurance we might not have had, as well as the most intellectual activity, maintaining the engine, which required technical skills certainly none of us had. To us the proof of our superiority came at the semiannual picnics, where the men from the decks engaged in line-handling contests displaying our daily activities. There were no coal-stoking or engine-maintenance contests. We never mentioned the fact that the engine room was strictly taboo to us (most of us had never been inside one), while the engine-room crew were free to roam the deck.

We had our own union, the Associated Maritime Workers, International Organization of Masters, Mates, and Pilots (AFL). Internally, it was a fully democratic union. In fact, it still stands in my mind as a model of how to eliminate the ruling elite and achieve workers' power, though admittedly it was on a small scale and was itself a somewhat elite organization. The secret was that we had no union bureaucrats sitting someplace in an office building ruling over us. All the union officers worked on the tugs. These union officers, out there with the rest of us amidst the dangers of the harbor, were totally responsive to our wishes. They were honestly concerned about working conditions, particularly safety conditions. It was the only union I have ever known of where the younger members were represented as well as the older ones, no doubt because we were in just as good a physical position to make sure we were. Even the greenest spare deckhands, called in to stand by on Pier H in case any men were missing, were paid full hourly wages from the time they reported, whether or not they were assigned to a crew. If they were given crew assignments after waiting a couple of hours, these hours were added at time and a half to the hours actually worked. The egalitarian pay structure went so far that the wage differential between the lowest rank on the deck, the deckhand, and the highest, the mate, was merely seventy-three cents a day. Therefore, as soon as a young deckhand learned the ropes, if he was any good at all the crew usually chose him to be mate, because nobody else wanted the responsibility of making the decisions. That was how I got to be mate just a few weeks after getting on a regular crew. Of course the office was mostly a formality: when in any doubt, I asked Tony and Sonny what "orders" I should give them.

We did have a vague sense of class solidarity extending to all railroad workers. But, isolated in our utopian little union, we did not even contemplate collective action to preserve other railroad workers' jobs, much less to preserve the railroads themselves. The major railroads were all rapidly moving toward bankruptcy. No workers I knew, including myself—and apparently no management either—understood the reason: capitalism was beginning to enter its final stages of collapse. We thought it was just greedy and stupid management that was ruining the railroads. Of course there was some truth to this. The boards of directors were all following the well-established criminal ways of the railroad robber barons of the West (like Leland Stanford) and of the East (like Jay Gould, who had once boasted, "I can always hire one half the working class to kill the other"). The railroad managements were siphoning off huge personal fortunes even as the roads were going bankrupt. The largest recurring expenses went to pay off the interest on gigantic loans made to the railroads by banks owned and run by the railroads' own officers. Meanwhile, the management started a big advertising campaign blaming the problem on us lazy workers, who were just "featherbedding" (as contrasted, we imagined, to their hard lives).

In April, 1954, the New York, New Haven, and Hartford Railroad was taken over by new management, which announced a "vigorous" policy to save that major eastern line from bankruptcy. One of the first steps was to eliminate the jobs of many workers. Together with the managers of the other big railroads and their public-relations men on Madison Avenue, trained well at Amherst and Harvard to manipulate language, they made the term "featherbedding" a household word. People started picturing us railroad workers lounging around most of the time, protected by cynical unions, demagogic politicians, and archaic work rules. One of the first batch of jobs to go on the New York, New Haven, and Hartford was that of half the track-inspection crews. Minor derailings started occurring. Then on July 14, 1955, the Washington-Boston Federal Express jumped the rails at Bridgeport. The cause was officially blamed on the engineer, who could hardly argue the point, since he was killed in the wreck.

Their next target was the deck crews of the New York, New Haven, and Hartford tugboats, which they cut from three men to two. We read the ads about the lazy workers on the deck, three men who just threw a few lines about from time to time. Tony, who wasn't usually this talkative, suggested that we ask the management of the New York, New Haven, and Hartford and the smart boys who had written their ads to come down here and show us how two men could do barge work. But when these first cuts on the tugs were made, and the New York, New Haven, and Hartford tugs had a brief strike, all we did about it was sympathize. By 1970, the consolidated tugboat fleet of the Pennsylvania and New York, New Haven, and Hartford railroads consisted of only twelve tugs towing merely 150 railroad cars a day (see "Port Operations Leave Pennsy Head Gloomy," *New York Times*, October 2, 1970, pp. 49, 53).

Throughout the harbor we watched the accumulation of another gigantic fortune, this one siphoned directly off the commerce of the port. Part of every cargo loaded or unloaded any place in the port went directly to the Syndicate. The same cranes divided each cargo between two different enterprises. The only difference I could see between how "legitimate business" and "organized crime" received their respective shares was that most, though not all, of the trucks of "legitimate business" bore a company's name, while many, though by no means all, of the trucks of "organized crime" were unmarked. All kinds of commodities went to the Syndicate—radio sets, cotton, structural steel, aspirin, .45 automatics, fertilizer, canned goods, clothing, jeeps. The collusion was on such a vast scale, and the goods and materials were so varied, that it was obvious to everybody working down there that "organized crime" and "legitimate business" were partners as close as Siamese twins.

Ever since, I have been unable to grasp any distinction between "organized crime" and "legitimate business." What I have learned since I left the tugs is that business, particularly big business, is just *organized* crime, as compared with the casual anarchy of petty crime. The railroads, the cattle empires, the oil cartels, and the other giant amalgams of U.S. industry were all put together as conspiracies run by swindlers and cheats employing armies of hired gunslingers, some in uniform, and gangs of thugs and goons, some acting in the name of law and order. The most recent industries, aerospace and electronics, have emerged through illegal wars and illegal interpenetration with the government. U.S. industry as a whole rests on a capital base derived from the export of cotton produced by slaves who were kidnaped by the millions from Africa, and it is built entirely on land gained by swindles and massacres.

We ourselves indulged in the anarchy of petty crime. Unlike our bosses, who were stealing hundreds of millions, we knew we would be jailed if we got caught. While we were tying up floats at the fruit and vegetable markets, one or two men from the engine room would sometimes secure some special delicacies, such as grapes and melons, for us to eat. Another crew once found a barge loaded with ladies' fancy silk pajamas. They took a bunch for their wives and girl friends, and put them on under their work clothes to slip past the company detectives back at Pier H. One time, late at night, we were ordered to tow a single barge from upper Manhattan all the way to the army terminal across the bay in Brooklyn. We weren't told the cargo, which was very heavy, and it was most unusual to tow a lone barge such a long haul. We figured it must be something like hand grenades or .45 automatics. We waited until we were all alone in the middle of the bay. Then Tony and I climbed over onto the barge, and, without any lights to give us away, we broke in. Sure enough, the barge was filled with heavy cartons. We took about two dozen and passed them back to the tug, where the engine-room crew stashed them in the hold. After tying up the barge, we waited until we were back out in the middle of the bay before inspecting our loot. All twenty-four cartons were filled with cans of Campbell's bean-and-bacon soup. Unwilling to admit defeat, we ate the bean-and-bacon soup for three nights. On the third night, we capitulated and threw the rest overboard. I have never again eaten bean-and-bacon soup.

We would not have thought of stealing from each other or from any other working people. Our personal property was always safe. The worst crime we witnessed was the extortion of the labor and lives of the longshoremen. They were exploited by the stevedore companies and shipping lines, ripped off and terrorized by the ILA leadership, sold out by the AFL leadership, and subjected to what we called fascism by the governments of two states and the nation.

At the time, I knew almost nothing about labor history, except for stories told by the other workers, and so I could not comprehend the historical significance of what was going on. But now, using the direct experience of being part of the aristocracy of labor in this critical period, some study of the organized labor movement, and a Marxist analysis, I believe I understand.

Most of the early unions in the United States were organizations of the labor aristocracy. They had almost more in common with medieval guilds than with unions of the industrial proletariat. Actually, most of the unions that came together in the American Federation of Labor were explicitly organized *against* three groups: Blacks, women, and the industrial proletariat in general. These unions had overt clauses in their founding constitutions denying membership to Blacks and women, and the basic condition of membership was active work in a skilled trade or craft. Many of these unions were also highly nationalistic, and served as bulwarks against the waves of immigrants entering the labor market. The AFL has consistently preserved much of its original racist, sexist, antiproletarian, and nationalistic character to the present day. George Meany is just as fit an archetype and representative of the most reactionary aspects of the labor aristocracy as was Samuel Gompers, the first president of the AFL.

The CIO (Congress of Industrial Organizations), on the other hand, was based directly on the industrial proletariat, organized largely by Communists, and often spearheaded by Black workers. Its traditions were militant, internationalist, and opposed to the narrow divisions along trade and craft lines. But the anti-Communist onslaught against the CIO in 1948 and 1953 gutted the organization of its most progressive leadership. In December of 1955, the AFL gobbled up the CIO in what was euphemistically called a "merger." The battle on the New York waterfront in the summer and fall of 1955 was part of this larger struggle.

The operations of any large port are irregular. There must be a labor force available to load and unload the peak number of ships. Since this peak number is rarely in port, large numbers of workers are almost always without work. This built-in unemployed reserve allows for brutal exploitation by employers and other kinds of criminals and parasites.

When longshoremen in New York Harbor began to organize, the stevedoring companies brought in machine-gun mobs from Chicago to break up the union. In response, the union brought in its own gang, the Hudson Dusters, whose leaders soon gained power within the union structure. By the late 1930s, a close working relationship had developed between the employers and the leaders of the union, by then known as the International Longshoremen's Association. Work was assigned at "shape-ups" where the workers paid off their union bosses. The only strikes in the history of the union were wildcats, and these were quickly smashed by the union's goon squads.

After World War II, the port was booming with the expansion of the U.S. global empire. Raw materials were pouring in from the former colonies of Europe, and manufactured goods, including military hardware, flowed out to Europe, South America, Africa, the Mideast, and Asia. At the same time, unemployment had moved up sharply (the 1949 rate, 5.9 percent, was almost five times that for 1944, 1.2 percent), and thousands came to the waterfront looking for jobs. There were three possible ways the situation could develop. The ILA could go along as before under gangster rule, with shape-ups, kickbacks, and organized plunder. Or it could begin to follow the example of the ILWU, the West Coast longshoremen's union, which, under Communist leadership, had become a democratic union and had replaced the shape-up with a rotating employment system run through the union hiring hall. Finally, the longshoremen could be brought under conventional control within the monolithic structure of the trade unions working in close cooperation with the government.

As soon as the main purge of communists and other progressives in the labor movement was completed, the government and the AFL turned their attention to the ILA. In 1953, the New York State Crime Commission held hearings on waterfront crime, disclosing kickbacks, extortion, gang wars, and organized looting, adding up to $5 million per year. The AFL promptly kicked out the ILA and set up a rival union to win control of the waterfront.

In 1954, an official election was held between the ILA and its AFL rival. Every newspaper in New York except one supported the AFL. The exception, the Communist *Daily Worker*, pointed out that the ILA, with all its problems, could still be turned into an instrument of the dockers, while the AFL would simply subjugate the workers to the bosses and the state. The ILA won the election, which the National Labor Relations Board promptly declared invalid. A second election was held, and the ILA won more decisively. This was also declared invalid, but in the third election the ILA victory was overwhelming.

Meanwhile the state apparatus, in the form of a body created by the states of New York and New Jersey, the New York Port Authority Commission, was moving in on the dock workers. All longshoremen were required to have extensive dossiers and submit to fingerprinting. The ACLU futilely protested this "blatant statism." The Port Authority Commission technically took over all hiring, but in reality merely subjected the workers to more harassment. On the subway going to work one day, I read a newspaper account of how the shape-up had been eliminated and the workers were now much happier. Then I walked past the big shape-up on Pier F, owned by United Fruit (whose ex-president, Allen Dulles, Director of the CIA, and his brother John Foster Dulles, Secretary of State, had just overthrown the duly elected government of Guatemala). A glum gang of longshoremen were grudgingly dropping five-dollar bills into a can destined, they were being told, "to buy flowers for Johnnie Jones' widow Annie Jones."

By July, 1955, the Port Authority Commission had revoked the work permits of over six hundred working longshoremen with criminal records, as if these men could get any other jobs. Then, on August 22, the Commission lifted the work permit of Mickey McLoughlin, loading boss on Pier 57, the luxury-liner pier at West Seventeenth Street. McLoughlin was one of the original Hudson Dusters. The union bosses for once had something in common with the rank-and-file, and they quickly moved to exploit the widespread resentment against the Port Authority Commission. By nightfall, a third of the thirteen thousand working longshoremen were wildcatting against the Port Authority.

We began securing barges and floats during the next few days, as the strike developed unevenly, with the goon squads of the North River ILA leadership ranging all over the harbor. By the first week in September, most of the port was shut down.

On the morning of September 13, "Tough Tony" Anastasia, union leader of almost all the Brooklyn docks, announced that his men were going back to work. Anastasia, unlike most of the ILA bosses, had staunch loyalty from the rank and file. Although vilified continually by the *New York Times* and New York *Daily News*, which mingled his image with that of his brother Albert of "Murder Incorporated," Tough Tony was considered by the men on the Brooklyn docks to be a real fighter for their interests. During the attack on the ILA by the AFL and the government, Anastasia had actually sent representatives to get support from the Communist-led ILWU on the West Coast. When the ILWU membership had voted generous financial support, the New York press had warned of a red menace in Brooklyn. In June of 1955, Anastasia had begun to speak in favor of the ILWU system of rotational hiring. In July, the United States government had begun its fifth attempt to deport Harry Bridges, head of the ILWU. Now Anastasia, apparently trying to break the rule of the old Hudson Dusters, was openly challenging their power. By noon, he was asking for police protection, and the North River goon squads were visiting Brooklyn, closing the docks down one by one.

The strike faded out with no serious challenge to the power of the Port Authority. Gangster leadership was still firmly in charge of the ILA, and there was no hope in sight for the longshoremen. By early November, the ILA leadership was attacking the Port Authority on new grounds, accusing it of being lax in dealing with alleged Communists. At the end of December, the month the CIO was taken over by the AFL, I went off to the United States Air Force to help defend American democracy against the international Communist menace.

"Peace Is Our Profession": Flying with SAC

THOUSANDS AND THOUSANDS of us ROTC second lieutenants, the future flyboys manning the front line of America's global strategy, poured through Lackland Air Force Base, Texas, in the mid and late 1950s. Lackland was the main Air Force processing center. We all knew before we got there what our job was: building up a nuclear strike force awesome enough to be the world's only effective deterrent to Communist aggression.

The first day was just like summer camp. The second day we got our first "indoctrination" lectures. The best show was put on by a big, beefy lieutenant colonel, who chewed his cigar just like the commander of the Strategic Air Command, General Curtis LeMay. The colonel was the flight surgeon of the base.

"You men," he roared into the microphone, "are now nothing but a bunch of professional hired killers."

Our hearts warmed with pride. This was what most of us had always wanted to be when we grew up, swaggering out of the Saturday afternoon movies and shooting it out in the back alleys on the way home from school.

"So don't think," he went on, "that you're going to walk into my base hospital and get your skinny ass grounded just because your li'l ol' nosey caught de sniffles. Uncle pays you top dollar to do your job, and he's going to spend one quarter of a million little green ones to train each motherlovin' son here how to do it right.

Anybody here now who thinks he can't hack it in this man's world?"

"Don't be bashful," he thundered at the five hundred of us sitting in the auditorium. "Just raise your hand."

They did spend a quarter of a million dollars training me at Ellington Air Force Base, outside of Houston, Texas. It was on leave between Lackland and Ellington that Jane and I got married in the little Methodist church she had belonged to in Mount Pleasant, North Carolina. The pants on my only suit had a shiny seat which would show in front of the church, so instead I proudly wore my second lieutenant's uniform. It was a fit symbol, as Jane's function in life shifted to become for three years an Air Force officer's wife.

I worked hard at Ellington, partly because choice of assignment went according to class rank. We got our navigators' wings in December, 1956, and were shocked when we looked at the assignments. A few of us got to pick the handful of choice slots: MATS (Military Air Transport Service) and air refueling in SAC. But most of the list were for bomber crews, so the entire bottom three-fourths of the class went into B-47 and B-52 training. When we thought about it, we weren't too surprised that this was the big priority at the end of 1956, for now was the hour when we needed those bombers to stop the Russians. And when I started flying in an air refueling squadron, I wasn't too surprised that the bomber crews were often hopelessly lost; I remembered some of my classmates who had ended up doing their navigating.

I picked an assignment at Dow AFB, Bangor, Maine. Jane and I, with Karen, less than two months old, arrived there in February, 1957, and rented a house in the snow out in the country. Then I drove to the base. The sign at the gate said:

STRATEGIC AIR COMMAND
"PEACE IS OUR PROFESSION"
HOME OF THE 4060TH AIR REFUELING WING

I found the 341st Air Refueling Squadron and reported for duty.

"You're just in time," said the grizzled master sergeant who issued my equipment.

"For what?" I asked.

"To go with the rest of the squadron to Newfoundland."

For three months we flew out of Harmon AFB, Newfoundland, refueling B-47s and B-52s flying over the North Atlantic—and points north. How far north I was soon to discover.

Our squadron was about two-thirds KC-97Gs and one-third the older-model KC-97Fs. The G model had later equipment, and according to technical specifications could climb and fly faster than the F, despite the addition of seven-hundred-gallon fuel tanks under the tips of the wings of the G. So in mixed flights (called "cells") the G models always took off first, supposedly because it would be dangerous to have the slower planes up front.

My first refueling mission was on the lead ship of a four-plane cell. Our plane and number two were Gs; the other two planes were Fs. As we taxied out, the instructor navigator told me, "These G models are all heavier and slower than the Fs. Boeing just keeps selling the Air Force more shit to put on these planes to make money. So I want you to watch out for numbers 3 and 4 after takeoff."

As we made our turn into takeoff position, I noticed that the ice fog was so thick you couldn't see more than halfway down the runway. As we lifted off, it became so thick we couldn't see our own wing tips. Five minutes after takeoff, I noticed two blips on radar, each less than one hundred yards off either wing.

"What are these, Dave?" I asked the instructor navigator.

"Jesus Christ! That's numbers 3 and 4 climbing right through us. They don't even know we're here. Jesus Christ!"

We called the other planes and spent the next ten minutes vainly trying to re-establish our formation. Finally, we gave that up and decided that all four would meet at the orbit area, where we were supposed to await four B-47s. The center of the orbit was a set of coordinates in the North Atlantic three hundred miles northeast of the island of Newfoundland. All four planes arrived in the area and began orbiting. But, because the orbit pattern was an oval and we had long since lost track of who was where, we had no idea what order we were in. We decided to fire colored flares so we could find out who was who. Dave showed me how to do it. It was great fun, shooting off green double stars and red-green double stars. Though it did begin to strike me that this was not exactly how I had imagined a Strategic Air Command mission.

We finally did straighten ourselves out. The B-47s still hadn't shown up. Then, thirty minutes after the time scheduled for rendezvous, I picked up a squiggly green line on the scope of my transponder. This meant that my transponder unit had triggered the unit on the lead B-47. I established radio communications with its aircraft commander, and began to give him corrections to steer into the rendezvous. He informed me that they had gotten lost en route, were low on fuel, and would need all we could give them.

The B-47s were still at 39,000 feet, while we were circling at 15,000. This was normal procedure. At the proper range, I told the B-47 lead plane to begin the descent of their four-plane flight. Simultaneously, I gave the signal to our A/C (aircraft commander) to break out of our orbit and proceed down the refueling track, which was preplanned to coincide with the bombers' course. The other three ships in our cell followed us out on a diagonal line to our right at quarter-mile spacing. If everything went as planned, the four B-47s would hit this diagonal line at the same spacing, and we would refuel them in formation.

I watched with satisfaction as the green squiggles on my transponder scope followed my instructions perfectly and lined up directly behind us. I was a bit disturbed, though when the B-47 pilots could not see us as they crossed the half-mile range indictor. According to our written regulations, refueling was to be completed only if the bomber could see the tanker at one-half mile. I watched the signal approach, and radioed, "You are now at one-quarter-mile range. Do you have visual contact?" "Negative," came the reply. At this point, Dave, quite unperturbed, said, "Hey, Bruce, you may never get to see a refueling when you're on your own. So let me take over now, and you go on back and take a look."

I grabbed my chute and raced back past the double rows of fuel tanks that lined both sides of the body of the KC-97. I stopped just short of the pod in the tail, and squatted down so I could look out through the pod window. The boom operator lay on his stomach inside the pod, peering out back. He grasped the stick that controlled the rigid refueling boom that he actually flew, like a big model plane, behind the tail. When the bomber was in position, the boom operator would fly the boom toward the refueling receptacle and then extend its tip until a hookup was completed.

It seemed strange to me that the B-47 still wasn't in sight. After all, he had been only a quarter mile back when I left the control cabin. The boom operator kept peering through the soup. Suddenly, a vertical line appeared about three feet behind the pod window. What could that be? I wondered. Then I recognized it: it was the vertical stabilizer (the top part of the tail) of the B-47. This struck me as a strange procedure and a little different from that described in the books.

"Oh my God! Oh my God! Oh my God!" the boom operator yelled, partly into the intercom and mostly into the air. "He's right underneath us and he hasn't seen us! Oh my God! Please save us!"

It slowly dawned on me that the big jet was directly under us, and had to be so close that we were almost touching. And its crew hadn't the faintest idea that we were there.

Our A/C informed the B-47 about the situation, in the same tone you would use to someone standing about half an inch from a rattlesnake. The vertical stabilizer moved back from the pod window, and I could see the whole bomber slowly coming into view behind us.

Meanwhile we got a message over the radio. The other three B-47s had all homed in on our number two KC-97.

After twenty minutes, everybody got straightened out and we refueled all four bombers. After giving a bomber all the JP-4 jet fuel we had on board, we were supposed to let it have all the aviation gas we could spare. The B-47 (and the B-52) could burn our aviation gas, but one pint of their JP-4 back-flowing through our valves would cause fuel contamination and engine failure for us. I made my calculation of time en route back to Harmon, but Dave stopped me before I gave the figures to the flight engineer for his computations of fuel needed for an adequate reserve.

"You've computed a thirty-knot headwind component," Dave said. "It should be ninety knots."

"You can check my figures. I'm sure it's thirty knots at the outside," I replied.

"Oh, nobody told you about the navigator's life-insurance policy. Add ten knots headwind for each man aboard. If you'd rather, add ten knots for each child of a man on board. Then the engineer will add the engineer's life-insurance policy to that."

After we finally completed the refueling and headed for home, I asked Dave about some things I found puzzling.

"How come we completed this mission despite the fact that we were way below minimums for takeoff and refueling?" I asked, trying not to sound too chicken. "After all, wasn't it just a routine practice mission that could have been rescheduled?"

"Didn't you realize that these babies are going all the way?" he responded.

"All the way?"

"Sure, they are going to get another refueling and then go in over Russia."

I had heard through scuttlebutt in the squadron that many of our missions were refueling spy ships penetrating Soviet airspace for electronic surveillance. But I had understood that these were all radio-silence missions, conducted with great care so that the bombers wouldn't be detected and shot down. I asked Dave about this, but since very few readers would believe my report of what he said, let me give you a source you can check, one written by somebody totally sympathetic with the goals and methods of our missions:

> Electromagnetic reconnaissance carried out by ferrets furnishes Intelligence information essential to our national security, but ferreting is a highly dangerous activity. Between January, 1950, and May, 1964, there were 108 U.S. airmen killed or taken prisoner while ferreting. In most cases, their planes were flying near or across the borders of unfriendly countries. In all, there were thirty-eight reported incidents in which U.S. aircraft were fired upon by Red aircraft, antiaircraft guns, or missile batteries. Twenty-six aircraft were shot down or forced to land in or near Communist territory. . . .
>
> Although the Communists also carried out ferreting operations, no Red planes were shot down . . . the Soviet ferrets seldom crossed the borders of continental United States, while U.S. planes often intruded on Soviet airspace.
>
> The Soviet planes were able to gather much information about our electronic weapons by cruising one hundred miles or so from our borders because U.S. radar and radio men unfortunately kept their equipment operating all the time. But Soviet radar and radio men realized that when they kept their equipment turned on, U.S. ferrets could plot the locations of the stations and deduce their capabilities. Accordingly, the Soviets did not turn on their equipment unless they thought the U.S. plane was actually going to attack them.
>
> And so the restraint exercised by Soviet radar men forced U.S. ferrets to intrude on Soviet airspace and simulate an actual attack to get the Russians to turn on their radar. Once the Russians turned on their radar, they started shooting. (John M. Carroll, *Secrets of Electronic Espionage*. New York: E. P. Dutton, 1966, pp. 134–35.)

This last paragraph sounds fantastic, and in fact it is not true.

I saw only one of the B-47s on this mission, but that one was not a reconnaissance plane. The B-47 fitted out for reconnaissance, designated the RB-47, had one distinctive feature familiar to all air refueling crews: the refueling receptacle was not in the center of the nose but had been offset to the right side to make room for the extra electronic equipment. I flew on many subsequent missions on which B-47s and B-52s were heading for the Soviet Union. Some of these were reconnaissance planes, and in each case we refueled them on a radio-silence mission. Furthermore, our briefing, takeoff, and flight plans for these missions all carried a high security classification. But I also participated in many missions on which we were refueling B-47s and B-52s not fitted up for reconnaissance, and heading for the Soviet Union. Most of these were like the one I just described, filled with radio chatter, and often well within range of Soviet radio receivers. These missions could have only one purpose, the same one as Gary Powers' 1960 flight right across the heartland of the Soviet Union. That purpose: provocation.

These were the waning days of the U.S. nuclear monopoly and its ability to hold the socialist countries and the national liberation movements of the world under nuclear blackmail. In 1953, the Soviet Union detonated its first hydrogen bomb. At an air show in 1955, it displayed a jet, designated by NATO the Bison, comparable to the B-52. In August, 1957, the Soviet government announced that it had just tested an intercontinental ballistic missile. Many doubted this claim, but in October the Soviet Union launched Sputnik I, the first man-made satellite. Despite the opinion of most scientists and military experts that it would take several years for the Soviet Union to have an operational ICBM equipped with a nuclear weapon, panic swept many quarters.

Like almost everybody else in the United States, I believed that the Soviet Union had a fleet of long-range bombers, equipped with nuclear weapons, and well capable of devastating most cities in the United States. I had some doubts that they actually had more and better jet bombers (as General LeMay was trying to convince us), but that didn't make a fundamental difference anyhow. My assessment was pretty much the same as that of Henry Kissinger's book, *Nuclear Weapons and Foreign Policy*, published in 1957 for the Council on Foreign Relations by Harper & Brothers: "From the Chukchi peninsula the 'Bison' can cover seven-eighths of the United States with one aerial refueling and all of the United States with two refuelings." Kissinger raised some doubt as to whether the Soviet Air Force was capable of midair refueling, but the general line put out by SAC was that they were quite well equipped for it.

My secondary assignment, during most periods when I was not flying, was in Squadron Intelligence, and I eventually became the Squadron Intelligence Officer. I worked in a big vault, where we stored all our confidential, secret, and top-secret documents. The vault had explosive hinges. In the event of an enemy attack, one that didn't seem to me too likely in Bangor, Maine, I was to push a button setting off the charges and sealing myself in the vault, which I was then to defend with my .45. The documents were kept under combination locks in fireproof files, where there were also stored incendiary devices to burn the papers if necessary. If those documents had gotten out they certainly could have burned SAC.

One of our main jobs in SAC intelligence was to prevent anybody in the United States, and particularly our own flight crews, from knowing that the Soviet Union had no ability whatsoever to deliver a nuclear attack. Their main bomber fleet consisted of a few hundred TU-4s, copied from the B-29, with a maximum range of 2,200 miles. Their only operational long-range bomber was what NATO designated the Bear, a turbo-prop with a maximum range of 4,000 miles and a maximum speed of 450 miles per hour. No Bears were stationed at forward bases, and it is unlikely that any could have penetrated the U.S. air defense. The myth of the fleet of operational Bisons was a joint creation of Soviet and U.S. intelligence, each functioning with contrary purposes.

At the Soviet Air Day Show in Moscow of July, 1955, flight after flight of Bisons swept by. Based on this, the U.S. Air Force submitted to the Symington Subcommittee on the Air Force of the Senate Committee on Armed Services in 1956 a report entitled *Study of Airpower* describing the famous "bomber gap" (precursor of the even more famous and just as bogus "missile gap"). The entire United States, we were told, now lay almost naked before this vast Soviet bomber armada. But Air Force intelligence knew perfectly well that the Bison was not operational. The swarms of Bisons flying over Moscow actually consisted of ten planes, all prototypes, flying in a large circle and reappearing again and again. Allen Dulles, former Director of the CIA, admitted this in 1963 in *The Craft of Intelligence* (New York: Harper & Row, 1963, p. 149). Furthermore, the maximum range of the Bison was only three thousand miles at most, and the Soviet Union had no bomber base within three thousand miles of the continental United States. (Kissinger's "advanced base" on the Chukchi Peninsula across the Bering Straits from Alaska was a U.S. Air Force concoction.) And, even as late as 1958, the Soviet Air Force had no operational midair refueling units.

In mid-1958, I received a top-secret report about a Soviet attempt at midair refueling. They were trying to use the flexible-hose system, similar to that used by the U.S. Navy, unlike our rigid-boom method. And clearly they were trying to convince us that they could really carry out such missions, for this one took place right over Moscow. Unfortunately, the entire refueling system broke loose from the tanker and crashed into an apartment complex in Moscow, killing a family and starting a major fire. The story was carried in the European press, and these press reports were dutifully included in this top-secret document. Why the top-secret classification? Clearly the Russians knew that it had happened. And, since it happened in Moscow and was reported in the European press, surely they knew that we knew. And we knew that they knew that we knew, the third-level intelligence criterion. Obviously there was only one group that Air Force intelligence wanted to keep from knowing: the American people.

The Soviet motive for trying to convince us that they had a strategic nuclear capability was simple: they wanted to prevent us from launching a strategic nuclear attack against them. But what was the motive of the U.S. Air Force, particularly SAC?

First there was the obvious desire to keep getting huge appropriations to augment the SAC force of 1,400 B-47s, 350 B-36s, and 400 B-52s set up with nuclear bombs in a ring of bases surrounding the Soviet Union and manned by a force of almost 200,000 military personnel. This kept SAC officers in a well-paid, honored position. Tied to this was the fact that most retiring Air Force officers were getting even fatter jobs in the mushrooming aerospace industry. But the cynical and greedy desires of individual Air Force officers were not as dangerous as the cynical and greedy ideology defining the purpose of SAC.

Many of the ideologues in the military, like their counterparts in industry, finance, and government, were primarily concerned about what they called "future national security." This meant the ability of the United States to mold a world-wide system known as the "Free World," that is, a world where U.S. "free enterprise" could have free play. "National security" was clearly threatened by world revolution, which was supported by the Soviet Union. If the Communists could offset the U.S. nuclear monopoly, world revolutionary movements could run amuck and the balance of strategic power would shift toward the Communists. The logic pointed for many of these ideologues toward a clear immediate goal: a preemptive nuclear strike on our part *before* the Soviet Union had the ability to retaliate.

On April 7, 1958, President Eisenhower wrote that the SAC strategic strike force had actually launched toward the Soviet Union many times, "by alerts created by meteoric flights registered on the DEW Line radar scopes, or by interference of high-frequency transmitters creating artificial 'blips' or by the appearance of foreign objects on the scope flying in seeming formation, which have never been explained" (*New York Times*, April 20, 1958, quoted in D. F. Fleming, *The Cold War*, II, p. 917). Usually when the strike force launched, no explanation was given, not even to squadron intelligence officers. But on two occasions I did find out specific causes.

Once a flight of four multi-engine jets heading south was picked up on the Distant Early Warning (DEW) Line in the Canadian Arctic and then again on the second radar fence, the Mid-Canada Line. The planes failed to identify themselves, despite repeated warnings. It turned out that it was a flight of B-52s. Why they failed to identify themselves I do not know.

Another time a prowler was detected by a guard in a "Special Weapons" (i.e., nuclear bombs) storage area at a SAC base. The guard raised his weapon. The intruder fired a weapon, killing the guard, and escaped. Since SAC intelligence actually believed in a Communist conspiracy inside the United States, many people in intelligence thought that this might be the beginning of a full-scale assault. I never learned who the intruder was, though it was commonplace for SAC headquarters in Omaha to send teams of armed intruders to test out the defenses of a base.

It is difficult to determine how much of SAC's paranoia about internal security was actual fear of a Communist attack, how much was self-serving scare tactics, and how much was just fun and games.

One night, I think it was in late 1957, a six-man SAC infiltration team drove up in a single car to the main base at Dow at 2 A.M. They flashed phony I.D.s at the Air Police officers (one of the cards actually bore a picture of Mickey Mouse), who saluted and waved them on through. They drove directly to Air Police headquarters, kicked open the door, and walked in with leveled submachine guns. "Bang, bang," they said. "You're all dead."

Then one of them picked up the phone and called the wing commander: "Sir, this is Sergeant Smith, desk sergeant at Air Police headquarters," he said. "Something very serious has happened, sir. I don't think I should discuss it on the phone. Could you come on down here, sir?"

"Right, sergeant, I'll be right down."

The same routine was pulled on the base commander. So the two top-ranking officers on base were quickly taken prisoner. Next, the team called all the numbers on the Air Police alert list, informing everybody that this was a "Siegfried Seven Level Alert." "Report immediately to your Siegfried Seven Alert post," they concluded, and hung up. Within fifteen minutes the base switchboard was jammed and every key person on the base was trying to call some other key person to ask what a "Siegfried Seven Alert" was.

Then three men from the infiltration team piled into an Air Police armored half-track, parked out front, with a recoilless rifle on top. They nonchalantly drove up and down the flight line, alternately aiming the recoilless rifle at each plane and pasting big stickers marked "BOMB" on the fuselage of each plane.

In January, 1958, the wing instituted a new competitive program designed to boost our SAC "war readiness" scores. Each month the outstanding flight crew was named "Crew of the Month" and given their choice of a vacation flight to any part of the country. Our crew was the first winner, and we decided to go to California, where most of us had never been.

In March, we flew to Castle AFB, and then had a couple of days off in San Francisco. To cover our vacation with an official purpose, we were to take a group of NCO mechanics who had received special training at Castle back to their home base, Westover AFB, Massachusetts, then headquarters for SAC's Eighth Air Force.

We landed at Westover and received taxi instructions. We were asked to hold at an intersection. As I was finishing out my log, I happened to glance out the little window at my position. There were two machine guns manned by four men, plus a recoilless rifle mounted on an Air Police armored half-track pointing right at me. I gave a little yell, just as everybody else in the control cabin had the same reaction. We were surrounded by machine guns, recoilless rifles, and dozens of Air Police. Major Schoppe, our squadron operations officer, who had bootlegged himself along on the ride for fun, grabbed the mike and started yelling at the tower. We were told to "stand by for boarding by the A.O." (Airdome Officer). A jeep sped up to the plane, and out stepped a first lieutenant wearing a white silk scarf and carrying a leveled .45. We opened the main door and he climbed in, .45 still leveled.

"What the hell is going on?" bellowed Major Schoppe.

"That's just what we'd like to know," answered the lieutenant. "But this is one time we're not falling for any of your tricks. You will have exactly five minutes after I disembark to get this craft off our base."

We began to realize that they had taken us for a SAC infiltration team. It turned out that our SAC clearance, a form we all had to file in addition to other clearance papers, had not reached the base.

"Listen, Lieutenant," said Major Schoppe, "we have your own men on board here. Besides, we just flew all the way from California, and we don't even have fuel for another takeoff."

"That's your problem, Major," said the lieutenant, his .45 now pointed at Major Schoppe's stomach.

At this point, the tower called to inform us that our SAC clearance had been located.

With the announcement of the Soviet launch of their experimental ICBM in 1957, things had gotten even loonier than normal. Although all those military experts, including the ones in SAC intelligence, knew perfectly well that it would be several years before the Soviet Union would have an operational ICBM, SAC intelligence went on an intensive campaign to convince every flight crew that a Russian nuclear holocaust could be just fifteen minutes away. Fifteen minutes was the key. Of course, we pointed out, the first target of the Russians would be the SAC bases. At the most, those bases would have fifteen minutes' warning. So each base is now just fifteen minutes away from devastation, and that's how it has to run.

A quarter of the crews were on fifteen-minute alert at all times, meaning they had to be able to be airborne within fifteen minutes. Each crew had to stay together twenty-four hours a day. Alert disrupted daily life and was physically exhausting. Often we would fly a mission, which might last as long as fourteen hours, preceded by four hours of preflight and followed by two hours of debriefing, go home, only to be waked up a few hours later on an alert call, from which we might not return for a week. Minor accidents were happening frequently, and there were constant rumors about major disasters.

On April 10, 1958, our crew was on a one-plane refueling sortie. We were holding in orbit at fifteen thousand feet near Erie, Pennsylvania, on the southern shore of Lake Erie. The B-47 we were waiting for was now half an hour late, so we had to request a new flight clearance.

"Tomcat 89, you are cleared for refueling on airways to Buffalo and then on over Rochester and Syracuse."

Chuck, our A/C, asked the co-pilot, whom we called Charlie

Brown, and me what we thought of that. The idea of refueling on airways over cities, we told him, didn't exactly thrill us with joy. So Chuck asked for, and got, clearance to refuel on a track parallel to the airways and twelve miles south. Since the weather was clear, we got clearance to fly the mission VFR (Visual Flight Rules), which meant that we would take responsibility for our own separation from traffic.

Just then, the first signal from the B-47 showed up on my transponder scope. I established radio contact and began talking him into rendezvous. We broke out of orbit and down the refueling track at the right point, and everything was going routinely.

At one-quarter-mile range, the B-47 was just slightly off dead center on my scope. I gave him a final correction, "Queen 76, five degree right turn . . . now." Their A/C came back: "Roger, Tomcat 89, I am now in visual con—"

His transmission broke off sharply in the middle of the last word. At exactly the same instant, the green squiggle that represented the '47 on my scope disappeared.

"Queen 76," I called, "this is Tomcat 89. Do you read me?"

No answer.

Chuck called back on our interphone to the boom operator, "Rector, do you see him back there?"

No answer from Rector.

"Rector, what the hell is going on? Are you all right back there?"

After a moment that seemed very long, Rector came over in a stammer: "Y-yes s-s-sir. He just blew up. Right behind us. I'm O.K."

Chuck quickly put us into a steep bank to the left. A big fireball and a smaller fireball, each about two hundred yards away, were arcing forward following the path we had just left and slowly dropping toward the ground. We started circling above the two fireballs, which seemed just slowly drifting down. We hopelessly scanned for chutes or free-falling bodies. Before the two fireballs hit the ground, two small planes were circling below us. We watched as the two fireballs hit and exploded about half a mile from a highway, where traffic was stopping. The two explosions bracketed a farmhouse and started fires in some fields.

I got a quick fix on our position. We were exactly twelve miles south of Buffalo, a city of over a half-million population, where most people were living in old wood-frame houses. Even out there in the fields, we learned later, the fires had burned for forty-eight hours. I figured that if we had taken that original clearance a lot of people in Buffalo would have died in the flames.

Within fifteen minutes, twelve private planes, a small commercial airliner, and two rescue helicopters Chuck had called from the nearest airbase were circling the area. We watched as the firetrucks tried to get past the long line of stalled traffic. I checked my watch again: it was 5:30 P.M. Rush hour.

"A/C, this is the navigator," I said into the intercom. "Let's get back on that track so I can get an accurate reading on the wind for the accident report."

We followed all our checklists all the way back to the base. Everything was turned back into our normal flight routines. When we got back and reported to the wing commander, Chuck had to get on the phone with the commanding officer of the B-47's wing back at Lockbourne AFB, Ohio. We learned that there had been four men on board.

None of us seemed to have much of a recognizable emotional response for a while. It was all too unreal, something like watching a movie, but with dull checklists instead of exciting background music and dramatic line. It hit a couple of people that night. But I didn't wake up screaming until the middle of the next night.

The investigation was extremely scientific, and they pinpointed the cause of the accident, despite the fact that many small pieces of the B-47 were gathered by souvenir hunters and despite the contradictory reports of hundreds of eyewitnesses. A number of people had observed a midair collision between two planes. Some saw one plane, trailing flames and dense clouds of black smoke for miles, heading toward another. Two or three saw a plane flying upside down before it exploded. Some saw a plane flying straight down into the ground.

But the real cause was easy to diagnose from spectrographic tests of the parts and the pattern of their distribution on the ground: it was metal fatigue in the center wing section. The wings of big jets are not rigid but flexible. This B-47 had metal fatigue from too much movement in the very center where the wings join. It's like bending a thin beer can back and forth until it rips. When the center wing section had snapped, the fuel lines running through it had ruptured. The plane had exploded almost instantaneously.

One of the rumors we had been hearing was that B-47s were falling out of the sky like clay pigeons. Then on April 15, five days after the B-47 blew up behind our plane, two more B-47s blew up, one out of Pease AFB, New Hampshire, and one over Tampa Bay, Florida. Ten days later a B-47 crashed at Goose Bay, Labrador.

Meanwhile, on April 19, the Soviet Union denounced, in the UN Security Council, the constant overflights of Soviet territory by armed B-47s and B-52s. On May 1, both Khrushchev and Malinovsky spoke of these flights as "provocative." Malinovsky charged that SAC bombers carrying hydrogen bombs were constantly hurtling to, and often over, the Soviet border. On May 2, Secretary of State John Foster Dulles claimed these flights never crossed the Soviet border, were merely for reconnaissance, and had to take place because of legitimate U.S. fears of surprise Soviet nuclear attack from secret air and missile bases in the northern part of the Soviet Union.

On May 3, the U.S. Air Force put out a public story admitting losing fourteen B-47s through accidents since January 1, blaming this on "structural inadequacies." It declared that the remaining fourteen hundred B-47s would be "beefed up." All SAC combat units were informed that all B-47s would be grounded until the center wing sections could be reinforced.

I decided to use my position in intelligence to do some private investigating. It turned out that at the end of 1957 SAC had decided that the B-47 was obsolescent. Flying at its ceiling of about forty thousand feet and its maximum speed of approximately six hundred miles per hour, it could not penetrate the sophisticated Soviet radar and antiaircraft defense. So they began practicing with the B-47 for "toss-bombing." The bomber would fly at extremely low altitude, using the landscape and curvature of the earth to block defensive radar. Then it would pull up slightly, and simulate the release of a nuclear bomb, which then presumably would continue in a long forward arc. The B-47, with its six jet engines slung under wings almost 120 feet from tip to tip, would then pull up and back in a loop, as though it were a fighter plane. Enormous stress was placed on the center wing section, which, needless to say, had not been designed for acrobatics. Within a few months, B-47s were routinely disintegrating just like the one we had been about to refuel.

I also discovered that SAC had been trying out their new technique—without actually releasing any bombs, of course—on the Soviet air defense. Some of those B-47s we had been refueling in the far North would descend to under one thousand feet, streak toward the Soviet Union, fly through their radar line, and then simulate "toss-bombing." These were some of the flights that the Soviet Union had denounced as "provocative" flights, explained away by Dulles as purely defensive in nature.

On the night of July 15, 1958, we refueled a B-52 on a single-plane, radio-silence mission not far from the Arctic Circle. As we approached the Gaspé Peninsula on our way home, our number-three engine conked out. We received permission to make an emergency landing at Loring, the big B-52 base in northern Maine. We landed and started taxiing in. Suddenly klaxon horns started squawking all over the base, and we received a call to pull immediately off the runway. Jeeps with flashing red lights came careering out of the darkness and sped to the row of B-52s on standby alert. These were all loaded with thermonuclear weapons. Flight crews raced from the jeeps to the planes. One after another, the B-52s started their eight engines, taxied out, and launched into the night.

When we finally got to the operations building, we asked what was going on.

"We've just moved into Lebanon," was the answer.

The Arab world in the early and mid 1950s was being swept by rebellion against European and American imperialism and their own feudal monarchies. King Farouk of Egypt had been deposed in 1952 by a group of nationalist army officers led by Gamal Nasser, who had assumed the presidency in June, 1956. In July of that year, the United States and Great Britain, trying to undermine the new government, withdrew their promised support for the construction of the Aswan Dam. Nasser promptly nationalized the Suez Canal. In October and November, Israel invaded Egypt's Sinai Peninsula. France and Britain then began air raids on Egypt and actually landed troops. In February, 1958, Egypt and Syria formed the United Arab Republic.

Eisenhower and Dulles now had only one staunch ally in the area, King Faisal of Iraq, who had led his nation into Washington's Baghdad Pact. So the United States now got the most pro-Washington forces in Lebanon to rig the election of June, 1958, to bring that nation into the alliance. The rigging was so blatant that civil war broke out throughout Lebanon. The United States and its puppets in Iraq moved rapidly for a joint military intervention.

By sea came a vast armada of U.S. planes and ships, carrying combat-ready marines. By land, the government of Iraq moved crack units from its frontier with Iran westward, planning to attack across Syria to Lebanon. There were only two small problems with the plan: some of the troops were commanded by the nationalist General Kassem, and these were to pass through Baghdad itself on the way to Syria and Lebanon. When these troops arrived in the capital on July 14, Kassem and his fellow officers led them directly to the palace, where they shot King Faisal and proclaimed a republic. So the next day, when the United States sent an invasion force of thousands of marines into Lebanon (no doubt marching to the tune of ". . . to the shores of Tripoli"), Washington found itself almost totally isolated in the world.

We managed to return with our plane to Dow the following day, July 16, where we found all crews on full-scale alert. Late in the day the combat crews of both squadrons had a briefing on the situation from the wing intelligence officer. It turned out to be the scene of my one and only act of political rebellion during my career in the Air Force.

Captain Westerly strode to the map in front of the briefing room and explained things quite simply.

"Over here is Egypt," he indicated. "It is now run by a man named Nasser. Nasser is a Communist dictator. The first thing he did when he took over was to seize the Suez Canal from its legal owners and start to run it in the interest of his bosses in Moscow. A few months ago he grabbed Syria, which is over here.

"This country over here is Iraq. A few days ago Nasser's fifth column inside Iraq overthrew the democratic government and set up another Communist state.

"Now, notice the position of Lebanon. Lebanon is right in the middle. It is the next target for Nasser's Communist aggression. Last month the Communists in Lebanon began open warfare against the democratically elected government. We have landed in Lebanon to protect the legitimate government, to safeguard world peace, and to show the Communists they can't keep making incursions into the Free World. If we don't hold the line here, the entire Mideast will fall to Moscow.

"Any questions?" he concluded. "Lieutenant Franklin, you have a question?"

"Well, sir," I said, "it's more of a statement. Nasser is not a Communist, and there are no Communist governments in the Mideast. I think that we're driving these people into the arms of the Communists by invading their country. And I also think we here in the wing should be told the truth about these events."

I sat down abruptly. Nothing like this had ever happened, and the fact that I was the intelligence officer of one of the two squadrons probably made matters worse for Captain Westerly. He reddened, and then walked over to whisper with Colonel Oxenham, the wing commander.

"Lieutenant Franklin," he said finally, "we just want the men here to understand the basic facts of the situation. I'll be glad to discuss these more intricate details with you privately. Please report to me at wing tomorrow."

When I went up to wing headquarters, I expected at least a reprimand and possibly a threat of a court-martial. But all I found was a crestfallen Captain Westerly, who asked me as a favor "not to confuse the men." "After all," he said, "we're not being asked to make policy, just implement it. Our responsibility in intelligence is to explain it in such a way that the men are willing to carry it out."

Morale was generally disintegrating in the squadron. We had pulled double alert from January 1 through June 30, doing both our own and that assigned to another refueling squadron at a different base. We had been promised no alert duty from July 1 through December 31. Now, instead, we were on constant alert, and our flying missions were often sandwiched in when we were already physically and emotionally exhausted. A study completed sometime in 1958 found that SAC flight crews had the highest rate of suicide, divorce, alcoholism, and nervous breakdown of any occupational group in the country.

Chuck, our A/C, seemed to have been particularly affected by the B-47 blowing up behind us. By midsummer, he was on the edge of panic during every mission. And, with a kind of self-fulfilling prophecy, he was turning every flight into a potential disaster. One example among many:

One night we were hooked up to a B-47 at 12,500 feet. On board was Major Bryneldson, a blubbery old bureaucrat who got flight pay for sitting at a desk about thirty-five hours a week and then spending four hours a month as a passenger on a flight. The major was in the back watching the refueling. Suddenly he burst into the control cabin screaming, "A fuel leak! A fuel leak! We've got a fuel leak! There's fuel spurting out all over back there!"

Chuck instantly reached up and hit the emergency decompression button. Then he immediately hit the master switch, knocking out in one instant all the electrical power on board. The plane was plunged into blackness. All our electrical equipment, including practically every instrument on the boards in the control cabin, stopped functioning. And, since we had lost our electromagnetic disconnect, we were now mechanically locked to the bomber.

Chuck then pushed the nose of the plane down into a virtual power dive. We ripped loose by brute force from the B-47 and plunged down like a fighter plane. I caught a glimpse of the bomber circling overhead, apparently trying to figure out what had happened to us. Of course, we could have no radio communication without electricity.

Chuck leveled off at about two thousand or three thousand feet. I crawled around on the floor and found my flashlight. Then I persuaded the reluctant Major Bryneldson to go back to show me the fuel leak. It turned out to be a dripping valve. I fixed it by tightening a connection, and mopped up the spillage with one rag. Then I went back to the control cabin, and yelled at Chuck to turn on the goddamned power. It took me a few minutes to find my maps, get the radar functioning, and figure out where we were. (I later received a ridiculous commendation on my officer efficiency report for "exceptional courage and coolness faced with extreme danger" for this.)

When things got back to more or less normal, Charlie Brown, Master Sergeant Emard, the flight engineer, and I all started demanding that Chuck explain why the hell he had done all this. "I hit the decompression button to clear the fumes," he said. "Then I hit the master switch so there wouldn't be any sparks to ignite the fumes." We all pointed out that when you hit the master switch before shutting down most of the equipment you get the absolute maximum possibility of serious electrical arcing, either in the electronic equipment, where the capacitors and condensers hold a charge, or as the circuit breakers all snap at once.

"But, anyhow, why the power dive?" asked Charlie Brown.

"That was because I had hit the decompression button. We had to immediately dive down to an altitude where there was enough oxygen to breathe."

I looked at Charlie Brown and Sergeant Emard, as we all sat there in silent disbelief. Finally Sergeant Emard said quietly, "But, sir, lots of people actually *live* at 12,500-foot altitude."

About this time, a SAC directive went out allowing anybody who had been accepted by a college or graduate school to get out up to thirty days before his scheduled date of release, if this was necessary to begin a new term. I was due out on February 3, 1959. I ransacked the college catalogs at the base library looking for a graduate school where a term started on January 3. I found one: Stanford University.

The thought of going back to school was grim, but what was there better to do? A career in teaching looked like a way to be of real service to other people, an opportunity not offered by too many jobs in this society. Jane and I had long agonized discussions about what I saw as the other choices: go back to the tugboats or do something to make a lot of money. Neither of us looked at these three choices explicitly in terms of social class. But now, to my Marxist eye, it sure looks like we were rejecting both a life in the working class and an attempt to penetrate the capitalist class, opting for the professional career as a petty-bourgeois intellectual that I had been tracked for. What options might be open to Jane was a world of possibilities that never entered our conversation.

Just before I got out, the incompetence of the squadron seemed to be heading for a new low. The best personification of it all was someone known as Captain Overlook. Being a captain and a pilot, Captain Overlook had to qualify as an aircraft commander, not a co-pilot. But he was simply incapable of doing the job. He had been in the squadron almost an entire year, and had flunked checkout flight after checkout flight. Finally, through a fluke or someone's misguided charity, he passed. He was now officially a combat-ready aircraft commander, with his own crew.

One week later our wing was due to fly a big EWP (Emergency War Plan) mission, refueling two wings of B-52s over the north Atlantic with almost no rest in between missions. Our performance would be closely graded by Eighth Air Force and SAC. What in the world could be done with Captain Overlook? Obviously he would be a major menace if he was sent up on a refueling sortie, where he would have to fly and refuel in close formation with three other tankers and four B-52s. But all crews had to participate, because our score was based on the performances of each and every combat-ready crew and aircraft.

Major Schoppe came up with the solution. Captain Overlook would pilot the command ship. All he had to do was orbit fifty miles from the refueling area, with the squadron commander on board. Everything went routinely on the mission. The command ship, with Captain Overlook at the controls, and with the squadron commander on board, came in for Captain Overlook's very first landing as a checked-out combat-ready A/C. Touchdown was a little rough, but the plane did end up on the runway. Captain Overlook reached out to reverse the inboard engines, numbers 2 and 3, to slow the plane down. But instead his fingers pulled engines 1 and 2, the two engines on the left wing, into full reverse. The command ship spun around and around until it finally ended up stuck in a snowbank. As I was leaving the 341st Air Refueling Squadron, nobody had yet figured out what to do next with Captain Overlook.

Months later we were living in Stanford Village, World War II hospital barracks converted into housing for Stanford's graduate students (and now converted into laboratories for war research conducted by Stanford Research Institute). Two doors down from us lived George Sheldon, a co-pilot from the 341st who had also gotten out thirty days early, to go to Stanford Business School.

On August 25, 1959, George burst through our back door laughing and whooping and waving a newspaper. On the front cover was a picture of Captain Overlook, taken at Vandenberg AFB, California. Captain Overlook now belonged to the 1st Missile Division of SAC. He had just been placed in command of our first operational intercontinental ballistic missile.

A New Life

I REMEMBER DECEMBER 7, 1941, the day the United States officially entered World War II. I was seven years old. My parents and I were visiting relatives in a big apartment building in Manhattan. A bulletin came over the radio: the Japanese, without warning, had attacked Hawaii from the air and sea. I kept peering out the window, fearing and hoping that Japanese planes would suddenly appear.

I remember when we learned that the United States was fighting in Korea, though it wasn't called a war and the date is not made memorable. I was sixteen years old. Four other guys and I were working in New Hampshire, clearing land and constructing buildings for a summer camp my high-school coach was setting up. It was June, 1950. Somebody brought us a newspaper, whose huge headline and front-page story told us that the Communists, without warning, had launched an invasion of South Korea, and that U.S. Marines, who happened to be there, were fighting back. We were all glad to read that the United States was finally going to stand up to the Communists. We didn't discuss why combat units of U.S. Marines were in Korea five years after World War II. Two of the other guys were eighteen. They were worried about getting drafted. I wished I were old enough to fight.

But when was it that the United States entered the Indochina War? The bulletins and the headlines all came years later. And at what point did Vietnam become an important part of my life? Tens of millions of people in this country must have asked themselves that question. The harder I try to answer it, the more the Vietnam War seems at first to have been for me like a mosquito buzzing around while I was asleep. Whenever that whining buzz got right down next to my ear, I would abruptly half wake up and impulsively swat at it. Of course I didn't hit it; the war went right on. But, since most of my swats landed on my own head, at least it helped wake me from slumber and illusory dreams about the society and world I lived in. And, at the same time, there seems to have been another disturbance: the major cities of the United States had become battlefields where troops, tanks, and helicopters moved against a Black nation in revolt.

Much of my dream life had to do with teaching in the university. Most of us who have gone into university and college teaching were moved, at least sometime in our lives, by a vision of a community of scholars working in the service of our society. We wallowed through graduate school, trying to ignore what we were seeing of the actual world of the academy—petty, smug, committed to the safest ideas, ruled by big money, and motivated by careerism. We tried to preserve our naïve, archaic, utopian, and elitist ideal until we could implement it as teachers.

Most professional academics end up affluent, blandly cynical, and fanatically committed to a particularly conservative and genteel brand of liberalism. The main escapes within the profession are alcohol, gossip, sexual fantasies, and a careerist quest for its highest goals: an endowed chair or a post within the administration, each worth upward of $40,000 a year these days.

The purges of the late 1940s and early 1950s swept from the academy all those who would rock the boat or even point out that it was sailing on a dangerous sea. So the storms that burst over the academy in the mid-1960s seemed to come out of the blue. When the rebellion of Black people and reaction against the Indochina War combined to hurl the society as a whole into a turmoil of energy and change undreamed of in the 1950s, a movement of political activism swept the campus. Even some professors participated. That movement taught some of us that our early ideal was too narrow and too precious, that the community we sought could not be realized in the cloisters around an ivory tower, but only by the society as a whole.

Since my first intellectual awakening back in Brooklyn Friends School, there had flitted before me a beckoning image combining the best of Plato's Academy, the university of the early Renaissance humanists, the Mermaid Tavern, and some of my own friendships. I was looking for a place where people could live, think, and create together in friendship. So eager was I for this arcadia that I convinced myself that elements of it could be found in the elegant sophistry of the Amherst College English Department. Stanford Graduate School turned out to be another mirage. Three years as an assistant professor in the Stanford English Department convinced me that this was no oasis either.

Then in early 1964 I deceived myself about still another English Department, this one at Johns Hopkins University in Baltimore. Of course it was foolish to measure any university department against such a preposterous ideal, though the university's own rhetoric still paints itself as just such a selfless community of scholars. But early 1964 was a different era. It is only since then that most of us have learned that the self-portraits of the institutions of our society are just make-up painted over their internal rottenness.

The department at Johns Hopkins did share much of my own disgust for the polite inanity and philistinism of most of academia. These scholars were unquestionably brilliant at what they did, turning out works of literary criticism more complex, and filled with even more types of irony, than the works they criticized. They seemed to make criticism an art form in its own right. They also stressed the importance of a department working together intellectually. So, when they asked me to join them, I enthusiastically accepted.

As soon as the year at Stanford was over, Jane and I began our pilgrimage to the mecca—or rather my mecca—in the East, camping across country with our three children. We came down from the Sierras in late June, bought our first newspaper in a week, and learned that three civil-rights workers in Mississippi named Schwerner, Goodman, and Chaney were missing. We felt a few twinges of guilt for not being part of Mississippi Freedom Summer. We vaguely considered driving to Mississippi then, but gave it up as impractical. Instead, we drove on to Jane's family's farm in North Carolina. We arrived in time to watch on TV the opening of the Republican convention that was to nominate Barry Goldwater, which delighted Jane's parents and frightened us (we were rooting for the liberal hope, Nelson Rockefeller).

On July 17 we got to Baltimore. We were looking forward to living in a real city, rather than the rarefied suburbia of Palo Alto. We planned to live in an integrated neighborhood. Everyone we talked to in Baltimore said no such thing existed. We had previously written of our plan to several of my new colleagues at Johns Hopkins and their wives (all the colleagues of course being male), who patiently explained that this would be impossible, since, as one put it, "Baltimore is not California." We got in touch with about a dozen real-estate agents, who either lectured us on the dangers of living among "the colored," gave us the run-around, or refused point-blank to show us any listings.

From July 18 through 21 the front pages of our newspapers told of the "Negro riots" that were sweeping Harlem, Rochester, and the Bedford-Stuyvesant section of Brooklyn. There was no hint that this was to be the first of the "long, hot summers" that were to culminate in April, 1968, with simultaneous rebellions in 110 U.S. cities. We felt even more determined to find a home that was in neither a lily-white suburb nor a Black ghetto, but in a neighborhood where Black and white people lived together. So we turned from the front pages to the classified section and pored over the houses-for-sale columns.

We almost skipped over the one-line ad from the Windsor Hills Improvement Association, a name that sounded like a parody of a segregationist home-owners outfit. But the Windsor Hills Improvement Association, it turned out, was an organization of Black and white people many of whom shared our liberal ideas.

Windsor Hills, a gently rolling area of west Baltimore, had once been an exclusive, prestige neighborhood. Jews had moved in after World War II, and many of the wealthy WASPs flew out. Then Blacks began moving in from the ghettoes just to the east. Surprisingly, a significant, though hardly overwhelming, percentage of the white residents had stayed. By the time a couple of officers of the Windsor Hills Improvement Association took us around to look at the homes for sale there, the neighborhood had stabilized at about 80 percent Black, and there was a high level of Black-white cooperation and community spirit. Although there was nothing bohemian about the area—in fact it was almost entirely working and professional people living typical family lives—there was a small number of men who lived in openly gay, stable relationships and who participated, sometimes as leaders, in the social and political life of the community. The neighborhood was united in its determination to resist the downtown Baltimore political machine, which periodically made assaults on the community, taking forms as varied as cutting back garbage pickups to conducting police sweeps, with roadblocks and door-to-door house raids.

By the end of July we had signed a contract to buy a beautiful nineteenth-century frame house in Windsor Hills. I was now able to go daily to Johns Hopkins, where my colleagues told me that I was expected to eat regularly at the Faculty Club, which I dutifully joined.

At this point in our lives, Jane was much more concerned about Vietnam than I was. Or at least she had been trying since 1962 to do something about it, such as writing letters to senators and systematically clipping news stories about the U.S. involvement.

There were then, according to official sources, sixteen thousand U.S. "advisers" in South Vietnam, teaching the Vietnamese how to resist "Communist terrorists" and the "invasion from the North."

On August 3 and August 4, the American people were told about alleged unprovoked attacks on U.S. warships by North Vietnamese PT boats in the Gulf of Tonkin, off the coast of North Vietnam. A close reading of the news stories, however, indicated that it was the U.S. warships that had initiated the attacks. On August 5, we were told of a massive air assault on North Vietnam, in "retaliation" for their "unprovoked aggression." Hearings were held by the Senate. Jane sent telegrams, and tried to get the major Baltimore radio stations to cover the developing story. On August 7 the Senate passed the Gulf of Tonkin resolution, which was to serve as the supposed legal basis for later U.S. intervention.

A year later, I put together the first accurate, systematic account of the Gulf of Tonkin incidents and tried unsuccessfully to get it published. It was ultimately printed in the spring, 1966, issue of *Sequoia*, the Stanford student literary magazine. For several more years, I vainly tried to get these materials printed in the establishment press, which to this day still persists in referring to the "attack by North Vietnamese PT boats on the U.S. destroyer *Maddox*." Here, excerpted from that article, is what Jane and I knew was actually happening in August, 1964:

In late July of 1964 . . . relatively little attention was given to a bizarre but ominous news conference in Saigon. . . . When the commander of what was nominally called the South Vietnamese Air Force —consisting of American planes, carrying American bombs and rockets, serviced by Americans, but flown by South Vietnamese—revealed what had really been going on, his American "advisers" were visibly disturbed.

That indiscreet young commander was Air Commodore Nguyen Cao Ky, a native of North Vietnam who had flown bombing missions for the French against his countrymen in all parts of Vietnam.

> The commander of South Vietnam's Air Force confirmed today that "combat teams" had been sent on sabotage missions inside

Communist North Vietnam and that Vietnamese pilots were being trained for possible larger-scale attacks.

Teams have entered North Vietnam by "air, sea, and land," Air Commodore Nguyen Cao Ky said at a news conference.

He said that clandestine missions had been dispatched at intervals for at least three years.

—*N.Y. Times*, July 23, 1964

Commodore Ky in effect was openly boasting that combat teams, transported by American planes and ships, had been infiltrating North Vietnam before the alleged infiltration of North Vietnamese combat teams into South Vietnam. No wonder Ky's own American adviser, Air Force General Joseph H. Moore, who stood at his elbow, nervously and hastily "tried to suggest that Commodore Ky did not have a complete command of English and might be misinterpreting questions" and must be talking about "ancient history." (*Ibid.*) But unabashed and not to be so easily shut up, "Commodore Ky disclosed that he had personally piloted a plane over North Vietnam and that the raids were continuing." (*Ibid.*)

General Taylor, however, asserted the next day that an extension of the war to North Vietnam "would be contrary to the United States' policy." (*N.Y. Times*, July 24.) On the other hand, the South Vietnamese Defense Ministry "did not deny Air Commodore Ky's acknowledgment that South Vietnamese 'combat teams' had been dropped inside North Vietnam," and "one of General Taylor's main points at this morning's meeting . . . was that no such acknowledgment should have been given." (*Ibid.*) What was being affirmed was the principle of keeping American military attacks on North Vietnam secret not from the North Vietnamese, not from the South Vietnamese, but from the American public. . . .

The next week, on July 31 and August 1, South Vietnamese commandos, under cover of naval barrage, attacked the North Vietnamese islands of Hon Me and Hon Ngu. (*N.Y. Times*, August 4; *Le Monde*, August 7.) While this was going on, the destroyer *USS Maddox* was someplace in the vicinity. Whether it was (as Senator Morse and many others have contended) three miles away, well within firing range; or thirty miles away (as the State Department at first argued); or ten miles away (as Admiral Robert B. Moore admitted on August 11); it was at any rate close enough so that it recognized "in the vicinity of Hon Me Island" several PT boats it was to meet again within "several hours." (*N.Y. Times*, August 5.)

In the early morning hours of August 2, the *Maddox* was steaming away from Hon Me Island, heading toward the middle of the Gulf of Tonkin. About 10:00 A.M. the destroyer became aware that it was being followed by three PT boats. We can now pick up the official U.S. Navy version of what happened, as colorfully reported in *Time* and *Life* of August 14 and *U.S. News and World Report* of August 17. From the smokescreen of this official version several important points emerge:

1. The North Vietnamese PT boats trailed the *Maddox* for four hours before any hostile action was taken by either side.

2. At 2:40 P.M. Captain Osier of the *Maddox* opened fire in the direction of the PT boats. According to his account he fired "three warning shots across their bows." (*Time*, August 14.) Since they were due astern, the PT boats were clearly not in a position to attack a destroyer and shots could hardly be fired across their bows. There is no such thing as a warning shot between two vessels of war; shots of any kind are the opening of hostilities.

3. The range at which the *Maddox* commenced hostilities was well over 8,000 yards, which is over four and a half statute miles. That is, our ship fired at North Vietnamese patrol boats off the coast of North Vietnam because they approached to almost one and a half times the distance which we recognize as territorial limits. Apparently we claim that our warships have the right to come within three miles of another country but also have the right to fire on that country's warships if they then come within four and a half miles. The ultimate absurdity of this position is that our warships could rightfully move into a position three or four miles from another country and then shell the ships in a harbor because they were too close.

4. The PT boats did not return this fire. "Still they came on. Two of them moved into a range of 8,000 yards (over four and a half statute miles) off the *Maddox* starboard quarter and headed toward her stern." (*Time*, August 14.)

5. Although the PT boats were still not even in position to attack a destroyer (a PT boat can hardly attack a destroyer from astern or from several miles off its quarter), the *Maddox* opened fire with the guns that could be brought to bear. "The battle began at 3:08. The *Maddox* opened up with her aft five-inchers and her 3-inch and 40-mm guns. The two *trailing* [italics added] craft closed to 5,000 yards [almost three statute miles] and launched one 18-inch torpedo apiece." (*Ibid.*)

So a U.S. warship participating in what at best can be called dubious activities off the North Vietnamese coast opened fire on patrol boats which were trailing it. At first the Administration thought it best to play down the incident, saying it "was not regarded as a major crisis" and "the U.S. did not plan to make an immediate diplomatic protest." (*N.Y. Times*, August 3.) But by the next day, the Administration had apparently seen the possibilities in the incident, and had officially proclaimed it "an unprovoked offensive military action against United States forces"; "The United States Government takes an extremely serious view of the unprovoked attack made by Communist North Vietnamese torpedo boats on an American naval vessel, the *USS Maddox*, operating on the high seas in the Gulf of Tonkin on August 2nd." (Official Note of Protest, August 4.)

So the Administration was finally able to acknowledge an engagement between U.S. and North Vietnamese military forces. And they were not only able to acknowledge it, but actually to turn it into one of two pretexts for a greatly escalated air assault on North Vietnam.

In the hours between these two events—the note of protest and the aerial assault—came the second pretext, another incident off the North Vietnamese coast in the Gulf of Tonkin.

As William Buckley aptly put it, "about the only thing sure concerning this Tonkin affair is that it enabled the president to stiffen the domestic image of his backbone, to make a dramatic TV appearance at prime time, and to get an overwhelming blank check vote from Congress." (*National Review*, September 22, 1964.) The first official Pentagon statement mentions an unprovoked attack by North Vietnamese PT boats, but fails to give any details about the nature of the attack:

> The attack came at 10:30 P.M. local time (10:30 A.M., August 4, Washington time).
>
> PT boats were taken under fire by the destroyers, and thereafter by attack aircraft from the Ticonderoga and the Constellation.
>
> The attackers were driven off with no United States casualties, no hits and no damage to either destroyer.
>
> (Official Pentagon Statement, August 5.)

We learn that this alleged attack came "65 miles from the nearest land" and "lasted about three hours in rough sea, with bad weather and low visibility." (*N.Y. Times*, August 5.) Of course since our government is the soul of honesty and Communists never tell the truth, we should certainly not listen to the North Vietnamese contention that the whole battle was a fabrication. Although, admittedly, the circumstances are so suspicious that William Buckley approvingly quotes this argument from the *Peking Review* of August 14:

According to the "chronology," at 7:40 P.M., local time, U.S. warships encountered these "surface vessels" and at 9:52 an "engagement" took place. Fierce fighting continued for more than three hours and lasted till 1:30 on August 5. The whole process lasted for nearly six hours. This was truly a sea battle of considerable scale. But anybody with a little knowledge of military science knows that torpedo boats have high speed and short range and are fit for short distance surprise attack and hit-and-run tactics. How could they be engaged in fierce fighting with powerful U.S. destroyers for three hours on high seas more than 60 nautical miles off the coast? Secondly, if these vessels were, as alleged by Johnson, "hostile vessels of the Government of North Vietnam," which made "deliberate, wilful, and systematic attack on U.S. vessels," why didn't they start the attack immediately after spotting the U.S. vessels, instead of paralleling the tracks of U.S. vessels until 9:52, that is, more than two hours after the U.S. spotted them, got everything ready, and even had time to call in an escort of aircraft?

(*National Review*, September 22.)

At any rate, within hours American planes (for the first time admittedly piloted by Americans) were devastating both industrial and military targets all along the North Vietnamese coast—in retaliation for this attack which had inflicted so much damage upon our innocent forces. These targets were presented to the American public as PT bases, and therefore appropriate for our rightful vengeance. But, as Bernard Fall pointed out, "none of the targets attacked was previously known as a regular port or base area. Hon-Gay, for example, was one of the largest open-pit coal mining operations in Asia, if not the world." (*Washington Post*, August 9.)

At the same time, President Johnson, apparently not satisfied that we were sufficiently displaying our unflinching bravery, asked Congress for a resolution expressing our determination to defend ourselves. The President's relation to the Congress at this time is well described by *Time*, August 14: After making the decision to bomb North Vietnam,

He made it clear he was informing his old Capitol Hill colleagues, not asking their advice. "These are our plans," he snapped. Johnson also asked the legislators to move swiftly for a resolution expressing congressional approval and support of the determination of the President, as Commander-in-Chief, to take all necessary measures to repel any armed attack against the forces of the U.S.

> and to prevent any further aggression. Solemnly, Johnson looked to each man around the table for his agreement. No one dissented. Republican Senator Everett Dirksen, the key figure, waved his O.K.

By August 7, President Johnson had his resolution. The House, after a forty-minute debate, had passed it 416–0. The Senate, however, had not been stampeded; they sagaciously had taken nine whole hours to debate before voting, 88–2, to surrender their powers to the President.

We were all supposed to sleep soundly now. On August 12, President Johnson, speaking before the American Bar Association, solemnly vowed that he would never "supply American boys to do the job that Asian boys should do."

While U.S. planes were conducting their August 4 raids on North Vietnam, the bodies of Schwerner, Goodman, and Chaney were being dug up from a levee in Mississippi. Chaney, the one Black, had been severely tortured before being shot three times. From August 2 through August 17, Black rebellions broke out in a Chicago suburb and in the New Jersey cities of Paterson, Elizabeth, and Jersey City. On August 26, LBJ was nominated for President by the Democratic convention in Atlantic City, New Jersey. In Philadelphia, sixty miles away, a massive Black uprising began two days later.

Johnson renewed his promise not to send American troops to Vietnam. Jane and I were not so naïve as to trust him. But the alternative, Barry Goldwater, was stumping the country threatening to do exactly what Johnson was vowing he would never do. We rushed to Democratic party headquarters in downtown Baltimore to volunteer to help stop the madman from Arizona. I found myself delegated the precinct captain for our neighborhood in Windsor Hills, while Jane was assigned to register voters in an inner-city Black ghetto.

The Windsor Hills Improvement Association, almost unanimously opposed to Goldwater, immediately got active in the precinct. Help appeared in the person of a middle-aged Black man accompanied by two young Black men in army field jackets who showed up at my house one day explicitly to check me out. The two young men were different from any Black people I had ever met. They made a point of showing that they didn't care what I thought of them. They were neither friendly nor hostile, but extremely businesslike, and very correctly polite. My immediate impression was of career diplomats or military attachés from some foreign nation, a view I now think fairly accurate. The older man—let's call him Raymond—seemed satisfied with the inspection. He agreed to take charge of organizing half the blocks in the precinct.

Despite my repeated requests to downtown Democratic party headquarters, we got no help in the precinct, where we could not find the regular local Democratic organization. This surprised me, for the Baltimore machine, with its Chicago-style ward bosses, was notoriously efficient. So we organized the precinct ourselves. We soon had an active block captain on each block. We took a voter registration campaign to every home in the precinct. In the poorer Black houses and all-Black apartment buildings, where I went usually with one of Raymond's young friends, I found an intense interest in the presidential campaign. There was no illusion that Johnson was any less of a racist than Goldwater or that he would do any more about civil rights or the economic conditions of Black people. What they were interested in was Vietnam, and there they shared my own wishful thinking. Old men and women who had never registered filled out the forms with great effort, getting help in spelling almost every word. They told us with quiet certainty that if the United States got any more involved in that Vietnam thing, it would be Black people who would be doing the fighting and dying. Goldwater was saying right out that he was going to widen the war. So you had to take your chances on Johnson, because he was promising not to.

In the last week of the campaign, the Democratic party machine suddenly made its appearance. On street corners throughout the entire 7th Congressional District, which was about 90 percent Black and included our precinct, groups of three were passing out official-looking sample ballots with the heading "OFFICIAL GOOD GOVERN-

MENT BALLOT" filled in with the straight Democratic slate except for U.S. Senate, where Republican J. Glenn Beall was substituted for Democrat Joseph Tydings. Raymond immediately telephoned and asked me to come over. He explained to me that Tydings' reform activities had infuriated the Baltimore machine, and that this was the crucial test of whether the bosses would run this district or whether "the people's own organization" would have control.

He told me that we had to deal with this "directly" and outlined a plan. While he was talking, his phone was constantly busy and small groups of his young friends were steadily arriving. By the time we were ready to go, there were about thirty or forty of us. I was the only white. We went in groups of four, with a car containing another four as cover, up to each group of three handing out the bogus sample ballots. We politely and firmly informed them that we were the regular Democratic organization, that their activities were not authorized, and that they had to give us those ballots and leave the area. The typical threesome we accosted consisted of two Blacks and an older white man. We discovered that the white men were all part of the ward machine, and that the Blacks had been hired at two dollars an hour to hand out what they had been told was the official Democratic party ballot. All the Black people immediately complied with our "request." Most of them were visibly surprised that they had been hoodwinked, some were angry, and a few joined with us in going around to the other groups.

Only one of the groups we encountered offered any problem. Late in our roundup, we ran into four burly leafleters, two white and two Black, clustered close together on a street corner. As we pulled up, one of the white men muttered something, and all four turned to face us. It was obviously a goon squad sent out to stop our activities. Raymond went through our little speech. One of them suggested that if we were "so interested in the leaflets," we "might try taking them." We started to, and there was a little scuffling, which ended abruptly when the four men in the car covering us jumped out and got into the scene.

The machine reappeared on election day in the form of armed, uniformed guards from a private police agency, sitting as "official Democratic party poll watchers" at every polling place in the 7th Congressional District. In actuality, we were the official Democratic party poll watchers and there were laws against private police, their weapons, and their uniforms being in the polling places. This time Raymond not only mobilized his own forces but called his "contacts," who were having similar problems in the districts of the Black ghettoes to the east of us. We went around in sizable numbers in our own and these adjacent districts, successfully ejected the private police, and never saw another sign of the machine.

The election returns in our precinct confirmed all the appearances of the campaign. A record turnout gave Johnson 1,024 and Goldwater 42 votes, or 4 percent of the total. The machine's efforts to show its own strength by mobilizing a sizable vote for Beall resulted in a switchover of only a few dozen votes: Tydings got 940, Beall 100. I was elated by the national returns that night, and just as happy about the broad-based local community organization we had built.

There did seem to me something mysterious about Raymond and his organization, which obviously had existed prior to the campaign. It had a level of efficiency and purposefulness somehow disproportionate either to our electoral activities or to the limited concerns of our community. I felt something there clearly beyond my comprehension. Now I wonder whether they were part of a revolutionary organization. But such a question never crossed my mind at the time, because "revolutionary organization" was simply not a category of my thought.

Meanwhile, what I was doing with most of my time was being a professor of English and American literature at Johns Hopkins University. My colleagues at Hopkins, unlike most of those at Stanford, did lead an active intellectual life, and literature, or rather the "professional" study of literature, was at the heart of it. Lunchtime was the focus of faculty life for the Hopkins English Department. There were only eight of us in the department, and we were all expected to eat at the same table in the faculty club. This fraternal luncheon had sounded appealing back at Stanford, where members of the department seldom ate together. But my picture of intellectual comradeship at Hopkins had not included table service by Black waitresses to white gentlemen dining at an elegantly set table on thick, regal carpet under the austere but approving stares from oil portraits of the illustrious white gentlemen who had created the university and its traditions.

The table conversation was extraordinary, though also not as I had imagined. With one exception, each member of the department was supposed to be the most brilliant and learned scholar-critic in his particular period. As for the exception, each colleague privately apologized to me for his embarrassing presence. Since we were all superstars, the lunchtime atmosphere was charged—not with any crass competition or attempts to cut down anyone at the table—but with great mutual expectations. Each of us was expected by the others to display, without ostentation, our exceptional learning and wit. Sometimes it seemed to me like being in a gang made up of the top gunfighters of the West: we were happy to be with each other in the same outfit, but you didn't want to make any sudden move or thoughtless remark. At other times the image came from *All Star Comics:* each member of the alliance had unique talents, and all combined in one unbeatable unit. I wondered when I would be detected as both a social and intellectual impostor.

The aptly-named Tudor and Stuart Club, which met, as I recall, every other week, provided our other regularly scheduled intellectual gathering. At each meeting, a learned paper was read by a faculty member or graduate student from the English Department. Jane was interested in the first announced topic, but I was informed that no females—not even our own women graduate students—were permitted to attend the Tudor and Stuart Club. I told my colleagues I could not in good conscience attend a segregated meeting, and then quietly abstained from the meetings without further protest.

The department was ruthless in applying its standards. They

prided themselves, for example, on the attrition rate among their own graduate students. Several members of the department individually boasted to me about the fact that, of the eighteen students admitted to graduate study two years before, fifteen had been asked to leave and two had quit voluntarily. Those who survived were treasured as apostles who would spread the "Hopkins method" throughout the university world. This process has, in fact, been going on with increasing success.

The department saw itself as a vanguard creating a new synthesis in literary criticism. New Criticism had provided them the formal discipline, traditional literary scholarship and intellectual history (such as that developed by the great Hopkins scholar Arthur Lovejoy) had given them the learning, and European structuralism had pointed the way toward a new methodology. (The intellectual event of the year was a lecture by the great European master, Paul De Man. He made a brilliant and vastly complex comparison of European and American literary criticism in a lecture marred only by his ignorance of the most basic facts about American literary criticism.) For them, the Hopkins method was the fine art that made available to a highly selected elite an orchestrated rendering of the interrelationships among the subjective world of the writer, the objective world around him, and the created world of his art considered as a single corpus. That is, one was not to be concerned with the structure of a writer's individual work (a poem, a novel, a play), like the obsession of the New Critics, but rather, in the process of interacting with the mind-world-art structure of the writer, one was to create an even richer critical structure. Lunchtime brought these critical works in progress from the different periods into subtle but enriching contact with one another.

The real world around them, either in the persons of the Black waitresses, whose rat-infested inner-city Baltimore ghettoes were about to blow up, or a political campaign waged around a war in Southeast Asia, had to be pushed back into a place where it could not interfere with these creations, which were, like all great art, relatively timeless, eternal, and transcendent. Their role was not to fight mindless political battles but to show that pure mind could rise above and outlast them.

I kept hoping that my colleagues might come to share some of my extracurricular interests and see their relationship to the study and teaching of literature. For instance, Jane and I went one night to hear Martin Luther King speak at a "freedom rally" held in the Cornerstone Baptist Church of Christ in the heart of a Baltimore ghetto. The audience of over a thousand included about five other whites. King's talk overwhelmed the entire church, including us. The world of brotherhood he projected seemed to exist right there as we all sang "We Shall Overcome," our arms and hands intertwined with those of our neighbors in the pews. The next day I described King's speech, which was not mentioned in the regular media, to some of the other Hopkins professors of English. My presentation may have been a little overenthusiastic. Most seemed embarrassed. The only comment came from the senior man in American literature, who explained, a bit impatiently, that Martin Luther King was effective simply because he had mastered all the rhetorical tricks of Negro preachers. In vain I argued that sermons are taught as literary works in American literature courses, where attention is paid primarily to their content, and that those seventeenth-century Puritan, eighteenth-century revivalist, and nineteenth-century Unitarian sermons were probably less significant than what Martin Luther King was preaching.

Meanwhile, the Stanford English Department and I had been discussing the possibility of my returning. They offered an associate professorship. I remember a phone conversation with the chairman, Tom Moser:

"Does this carry tenure?" I asked. "I know my ideas are controversial and some people in the university get upset by them. I don't want to wake up one day to find I'm being fired for expressing my views."

"No sweat," said Tom.

On February 2, 1965, Hanoi and the National Liberation Front proposed negotiations. The February 5th *New York Times* discussed "the apparent readiness" of "the Reds" to seek a "face-saving" settlement. On Sunday morning, February 7, the *New York Times* came to our home with the news that Soviet Premier Kosygin, arriving in Hanoi on a peace mission, had been received enthusiastically. It also told of two "Viet Cong" guerrilla attacks that had killed eight American "advisers."

While Jane was washing the breakfast dishes, the radio brought an interview with Secretary of Defense McNamara, who announced that American planes had been launched in a massive air assault on North Vietnam in retaliation for the previous day's guerrilla attacks, a "brazen example" of "North Vietnamese aggression." As she listened to McNamara's lies, she realized how badly we had been fooled, despite all our suspicions, by LBJ, the peace candidate. She called the Friends Meeting House and asked if they were going to do anything. She was referred to a woman from the Baltimore chapter of Women Strike for Peace, which, it turned out, had disbanded. Jane got the numbers of former members, and managed to pull the chapter back together again in time to join the Women Strike for Peace mobilization in Washington on February 10. Jane had become an antiwar activist.

Meanwhile, I agonized. On Monday, February 8, I bought a newspaper at school and read President Johnson's reassurance that the air strikes were "a limited response," that "we seek no wider war," and that this was certainly not the beginning of regular air raids against North Vietnam. As everybody now knows, that single retaliatory raid turned into a continual aerial bombardment that went on, with a few pauses, for almost seven years.

I decided to eat lunch that day with Professor Maurice Mandelbaum of the Philosophy Department. Compared to most Hopkins professors, Maury seemed down-to-earth and less uncomfortable dealing with the world outside the pages of books. Besides, his field was ethics, one hard to separate from that surrounding world, and he had written what many considered a leading American work in that field. I assumed that Maury would share my anguish and outrage about the bombings, and that he would have given some thought to the predicament that conscionable intellectuals now found themselves in. As soon as I mentioned the raids, he cut me off by saying, "Oh, that's just preliminary to negotiations," and hurriedly changed the subject. A moment later, I made the conscious decision to become a class traitor to the professors of the U.S. empire.

From that day on, I ate lunch in the student cafeteria, which was indeed interpreted by the other members of the English Department as an act of open treachery. In the cafeteria, I met three other deserters from faculty social ranks. We started the first faculty antiwar group, which put antiwar ads in newspapers and eventually brought a Vietnam teach-in to Hopkins.

One day President Milton Eisenhower called in two representatives of the group. He ordered them to cease using the name Johns Hopkins University in identifying the organization or any of its members. "No member of the faculty," he told them, "may indicate his affiliation with Hopkins while making statements about the war or engaging in any other political activity." They reminded him that he had been introduced as president of Johns Hopkins University when he had made a nominating speech at the Republican convention the preceding summer. Ignoring this point, Eisenhower insisted "the name of Johns Hopkins University cannot be used in any way in connection with views about the war in Vietnam." "The university is not to be used to strengthen any position on Vietnam," he repeated. "That is all, gentlemen."

On April 3, McGeorge Bundy was invited to Hopkins to give a presentation defending administration policy in Vietnam. On April 7, President Milton Eisenhower himself introduced President Lyndon Baines Johnson, who gave the address known as the Hopkins statement, in which he told of our determination to punish "aggression" and to defend "freedom" and "the independence of South Vietnam":

> We will not be defeated.
> We will not grow tired.

We will not withdraw, either openly or under the cloak of a meaningless agreement.

We know that air attacks alone will not accomplish all these purposes. But it is our best and prayerful judgment that they are a necessary part of the surest road to peace.

(*The Johns Hopkins Magazine*, April, 1965, p. 4.)

On April 9, Henry Cabot Lodge came to speak at Johns Hopkins, where he said, ". . . the North Vietnamese seem only to understand force, and of course when they use force they must be met by force, as they were in the Gulf of Tonkin." (*The Johns Hopkins Magazine*, April, 1965, p. 14.)

Producing Napalm and Revolutionaries

It was early 1966. A woman in the suburban community of Redwood City, California, answered her door. She was asked to sign a petition about the local production of napalm. "Napalm? No thank you," she said. "I'm not interested. I always use Tide."

She was in the majority, for in early 1966 most Americans had never heard of napalm. By the end of that year, there was a national and global campaign against its use. That campaign had been started by a handful of individuals in and around Stanford in January, 1966. It was the single most important event in turning Jane and me, and many other people, into revolutionaries.

I happened to know a fair amount about napalm and its history, mainly through my Air Force experience. So I was assigned to do much of the research for our materials and to make a number of public presentations.

Napalm is a highly flammable sticky jelly originally made by adding to aviation gas a chemical compound of aluminum *naph*thenates and *palm*itates. The Chemical Warfare Service developed napalm in 1944–45 for two purposes. First, it is an antipersonnel weapon, effective because it sticks to clothing and flesh and continues to burn into the bone. This is its tactical purpose. Its second usage in World War II was strategic. Under contract to the Chemical Warfare Service, university professors and other scientists supervised the construction of replicas of the working-class districts of Japanese industrial cities, including the homes made of paper and wood. Their goal was to develop an incendiary weapon that would leave flaming materials in contact with structures long enough to generate a fire storm so intense that the winds it caused would make it self-sustaining and unextinguishable in any city having at least 25 percent of its space covered by roofs.

"Conventional" incendiary weapons were used on a total of three or four bombing missions in Europe, the worst being the firebomb raid on Dresden. Napalm as a strategic weapon was to be reserved for non-white people. It was designed to be used against the Japanese, and the thousand-plane napalm raids on Japanese cities were far more devastating than the Dresden inferno. In fact, one raid on Tokyo killed more people and destroyed more property than either the Hiroshima or Nagasaki atomic bombs. The overall effect was described by Major General Aden H. Waitt, chief of Chemical Warfare Service during World War II: "Sixty-six of Nippon's war centers with . . . 20 million population received more than 100,000 tons of incendiaries in 15,000 sorties. More than 100 square miles were burned out in five major cities, while incendiary destruction amounted to about 40% in the urban areas involved." Napalm was used again in the Korean War, so effectively that in vast areas almost all life was destroyed. To this date, Koreans in the northern half of the country will show visitors a lone tree that survived the holocausts, referring to it as a "prewar tree."

But U.S. weapons technology never stands still. In early January, 1966, a worker from a local corporation, United Technology Center, secretly communicated to a few of us antiwar activists the news that his company had just received a subcontract from Dow Chemical to develop a new, improved kind of napalm. The contract, we discovered, was for the development of Napalm-B, a thicker jelly, that would ignite more reliably, burn more intensely, and stick more tenaciously.

Napalm-B consisted of 25 percent gasoline, 25 percent benzene, and 50 percent polystyrene, the marvelous new thickener, which was to be manufactured in quantity especially for napalm by Dow Chemical at Torrance, California. If UTC (United Technology Center) could successfully complete the research and development, production was scheduled to reach mammoth proportions. Our original research was later verified in *Chemical and Engineering News* (March, 1966), which reported that the forthcoming use of polystyrene in Napalm-B would be 25 million pounds a month, so much that the normal industrial supplies would be severely overstrained. According to this figure, which I think conservative, the production of Napalm-B was to reach 600 million pounds a year, three times the total dropped on Japan in World War II.

The antiwar movement at Stanford was then almost entirely embodied by the Stanford Committee for Peace in Vietnam, accurately described by its vague, innocuous name. SCPV consisted of about two dozen individuals more or less fitfully active against the war. It included a few people who called themselves pacifists, fewer who called themselves Marxists, and most who no longer knew what to call themselves.

Jane and I fitted into that last category. We still didn't allow Robert, our two-and-a-half-year-old son, to play with toy guns, and we were in favor of "militant, nonviolent protest." But we no longer considered ourselves pacifists, and our opposition to "violent" protest was not philosophical but tactical (it might "alienate" people). We were staunchly opposed to aggressive anti-Communism, but deeply suspicious of communists. We avoided political ideology, particularly Marxism, about which we knew virtually nothing except that it was a musty old nineteenth-century dogma of little relevance to the modern world, especially to an advanced industrial society like the United States. We were in favor of anything that would work to stop the war.

SCPV as a whole expressed a similar outlook. Each weekly meeting was mainly spent debating proposals for actions to take the following week. We were looking for the one spectacular action that would quickly educate the American people, bring the government to its senses, and end "the senseless killing" in Vietnam. We felt this was urgent because we believed that the Vietnamese would soon be destroyed as a people. SCPV had no interest in any long-term programs to change U.S. society.

When SCPV got the word about the local contract to develop Napalm-B, we thought we could at last do something concrete—stop this local production. And practically everybody saw a great potential for some kind of mass campaign that would swiftly educate people about the "immoral" nature of the war and the dishonesty of our government. There were only two who disagreed.

One of the people, who called himself a Marxist, argued: "A campaign against napalm would only build false consciousness. It would suggest that the Vietnam War would be acceptable if it were fought with conventional weapons. This kind of campaign would only appeal to middle-class liberals. In fact, it will alienate working-class people, because they want to use whatever weapons are necessary to support our troops. We must focus all our efforts on demanding immediate withdrawal of all our troops. This is the only demand that working-class people can support."

Another person—whose name and appearance I could not possibly recall—took a position that seemed almost the exact opposite: "There is only one way to deal with a napalm plant, and that's to deal with it. Anybody who is interested, see me after this bullshit meeting is over."

In fact, these two seemingly opposite positions had a good deal in common, for they were both based on the assumption that we could not build an effective mass opposition to napalm. I do not believe that either of the courses of action these two proposed was wrong. We did have an obligation to build a mass movement calling for withdrawal of the troops. At some point the napalm plant should have been sabotaged. And there were also many other things that should have been done. But a mass movement against napalm, as it turned out, was certainly not a diversion for any of these goals.

One person, and I think only one, understood all that back then.

That was Keith Lowe. Looking back, I see that Keith understood both the potential and the limitations of the situation. He also had the patience to lead some of the rest of us step by step through a process of political and personal development that produced not only a mass anti-napalm campaign spreading from the San Francisco Peninsula across the country and around the world, but also a number of Marxist-Leninist revolutionaries, including Jane and me.

Keith was very slight, unintimidating, modest, affectionate. He was Jamaican, and his features seemed a mixture of all the European, Asian, and African peoples who had mingled on that multinational island. He responded to other human beings as though he were a stranger to none of them. He not only loved "the" people, but deeply loved people. Keith kept undermining my stereotyped image of the communist activist as cold, unfeeling, ruthless, and calmly calculating. He was warm, passionate, kind—and calmly calculating. Keith was later rewarded appropriately for all he had done by the administration of the United States and the administration of Stanford University, who worked together closely on his case. In 1969, Keith Lowe, then assistant professor of English at the University of California, San Diego, was denied a visa to re-enter the United States from Jamaica. The main evidence against him in his immigration file consisted of statements from the administration of Stanford identifying him as a "subversive."

Keith's response to the news of the napalm contract was something unheard of—at least to most of us—at that time. He proposed that we carry the issue right to the people in the napalm company. Most of the members of SCPV were excited by this proposal, but there were two quite different views of how to apply it. Some thought this meant we should go directly to the workers, and try to persuade them not to help develop and produce the new form of napalm. Others thought that only the management had the power to pull the company out of the napalm business, so we should go to them. Most groups of activists I have seen would then have plunged into endless debate. One side would have argued it was hopelessly impractical to go to the workers. The other side would have attacked this argument, and those who put it forth, as anti–working class. They in turn would have been attacked as dogmatists. Soon the argument would have been on the level not only of theory but of basic philosophy, and if any action had come out of the discussion it would have been crippled by the divisive struggle that had brought it forth. What Keith apparently understood was that all the people in the debate were lacking the experience necessary to resolve it rationally, and that most of us would use the debate, if we could, as an excuse to avoid the arena of practical struggle. Neither Keith then nor I now would argue that the intellectual struggle is unimportant. But it would have been purely metaphysical if actual practice had not been made primary. So, under Keith's gentle but firm leadership, we soon found ourselves testing both lines. Because we ourselves were so naïve, we followed each in a somewhat ridiculous manner. We leafleted the workers as if a leaflet could convince them to quit their "immoral" jobs, and we sat down with the top management to convince them that they should cease being war profiteers.

The main office of United Technology was in Sunnyvale, about ten miles south of Stanford. In 1950, Sunnyvale had been a sleepy little town with a population of 9,800. The Stanford "community of technical scholars" had changed all that. The aerospace and electronics complex developed by Stanford turned Sunnyvale into a boom town. By 1960, its population was almost 53,000. In 1966 it reached 100,000. Five delegates were selected to visit the ultramodern office complex of UTC, strung out amidst the similarly well-landscaped offices of the other corporate, manufacturing, and banking centers of Sunnyvale. Our mission: to meet with the president of UTC and convince him, through rational dialogue, that the development and manufacture of napalm were immoral and so his company should refuse the contract. Off we went on January 25, 1966, all neatly attired in our most conservative suits and dresses.

After some last-minute dickering, we were admitted into the office of Barnet Adelman, the president. He was flanked by three other officers of UTC; two of them were retired generals, one a retired admiral. We then had our rational dialogue about the Vietnam War and Napalm-B.

Mr. Adelman was just a nice, ordinary, mild-mannered Jewish scientist, who had gotten his master's degree in chemical engineering from Columbia in 1948, and then worked in rocketry for the Jet Propulsion Lab, Cal Tech; the rocket-fuels division of Phillips Petroleum; and Ramo-Wooldridge. He belonged to the American Ordnance Association and the American Rocket Society. He assured us that he was just as interested in having the Vietnam War end quickly as we were.

"After all," he said, "our business has suffered a great deal from the war. Our main work is in long-range liquid-fueled space rockets. These have no immediate military application. The Defense Department has taken away all our funds for these rockets because of Vietnam. So we have no choice. Even if we didn't want to work on napalm, we would have to just to stay in business."

"So you would do anything just for money?" asked an Asian-American Stanford student who was part of our delegation.

"Napalm will help shorten the war," responded President Adelman. "Isn't that what we all want? Besides, whatever our government asks us to do is right."

Elena Greene, who had visited China and Vietnam with her husband Felix Greene, brought up Nuremberg, and pointed out that one of the main defenses of the war criminals there was that their government had ordered them to do it.

"But that was not a legally elected government," said Mr. Adelman.

Someone appealed to Mr. Adelman directly as a person whose own people had been the victim of war crimes. He responded, "That was Germany. This is America." I then went into some of the history of Dow Chemical itself and its connections with Nazi war crimes, reading from my research notes:

"In the 1930s, Dow Chemical and the giant German chemical corporation I. G. Farben formed an international cartel. They agreed to restrain U.S. production of magnesium and allow Germany to take world leadership in this element. So, when World War II began, Germany was producing five times as much magnesium as we were.

"During the war, it was the Farben subsidiary, Badische Anilin and Soda-Fabrik, that developed and manufactured Zyklon-B, the poison gas used at Auschwitz and Dachau. Actually Dow maintained secret ties with Badische throughout the war. As soon as the war was over, they formally renewed their prewar connection with Farben by going directly through Badische. Right now, Dow Chemical and Badische are in partnership in a giant chemical plant in Freeport, Texas, called the Dow-Badische Company."

My little speech had no visible effect on Mr. Adelman, not to mention his three colleagues. Finally one of the other delegates asked if we could have an opportunity to discuss the issue with the employees.

"I *am* the employees of UTC," said Mr. Adelman. He then informed us he had to "take care of other business," and our discussion was "terminated."

So, no matter how little we wanted to deal with ideology, we were forced to face the central ideological concern of our historical epoch: the relation between the workers and the means of production. We now went to the workers, taking with us a leaflet asking, "*Is* Barnet Adelman the employees of UTC?"

UTC's napalm test site was located on a rambling old ranch off a dirt road several miles from the rural crossroads community of Coyote, south of San Jose. A few hundred yards back from the little dirt road were several mysterious-looking low buildings, a small tower, and some large chemical storage tanks. Along the road, there was a barbed-wire fence, and the property stretched as far back as the eye could see into the hills.

We were all nervous the first day, particularly since all the workers in America, according to the media, staunchly supported the war. We stood at the gate in the barbed-wire fence, and tried to hand leaflets to the workers as they drove through. That first day, most of the workers stopped to take the leaflet. Some went out of their way to be friendly. A few tried to run us down. On the second day, the company posted plainclothes security guards and a photographer at the gate. Almost every worker driving through now pretended we didn't exist, except for a few who again tried to run us down. It looked as though the workers were as reactionary as the media said. Then two people took leaflets back down the road to where it met the main highway, three miles away from the company guards and photographer. Here the response was even more friendly than the first day. Some workers got out of their cars to talk. They told us that the management was very nervous, and had posted plainclothes security guards inside the plant to keep an eye on the workers. Most people, they explained, were very fearful of losing their jobs if they showed any sympathy for our position.

One of our leaflets asked the workers, of all things, to quit their jobs in protest. Two or three actually did, and were quickly blacklisted from all employment in the area.

In the first week of February, we had an open meeting at Stanford to get people together for a caravan to Coyote, where we would hold a rally as the workers were leaving the day shift. At the Stanford meeting, one of the speakers was a young Black man from the Student Nonviolent Coordinating Committee (SNCC). He was tall, thin, unsmiling, and so tense he looked as if he might explode. Speaking in a soft voice, filled with barely restrained anger, he told us about a new political party he had helped organize in Alabama. It had split off from the regular Democratic party of Alabama in order to conduct voter registration and run candidates in predominantly Black Lowndes County. Since the symbol of the Alabama Democratic party was a snowy white rooster, they had chosen the Black Panther as their symbol. The speaker, Stokely Carmichael, then said he had just received his draft induction notice. He spoke of draft resistance. "I intend to walk right into that draft office and tell them," he said so quietly you had to cock your head to hear, " 'I don't belong to you, so you have no power over me.' " I heard this then as an existentialist affirmation, an act in the individualist tradition of Thoreau. I realize now that I missed altogether the significance of what Carmichael was saying, because I knew nothing then about revolutionary Black nationalism. I heard Carmichael projecting himself as a representative of every individual human being. In reality he was defying the draft as a representative of the Black nation. He was disputing the power of the draft board to claim ownership not so much of his own human essence, but of the lives of a people kidnaped from Africa.

At the Coyote rally, Carmichael spoke again. Standing at a microphone directly facing the gate in the barbed-wire fence across the dirt road, covered with the dust churned up by the workers' cars, he spoke about the Vietnam War itself, his voice now loud, his words ringing out toward the napalm test site and the rolling hills beyond. Afterward, I walked up in my sports jacket, white shirt, and tie, and was introduced. I enthusiastically put out my hand and said, "That was a wonderful speech." Carmichael limply put his hand in mine for a second, glanced at me, stared past my head toward the chemical storage tanks, and mumbled something like, "Yeah?"

Several weeks later, SNCC held a national conference, at which Stokely Carmichael was elected chairman. It was this conference that issued the historic paper entitled "The Basis of Black Power," a modest statement demanding self-determination for Blacks and asking "progressive whites" to organize in the white communities. The mass media suddenly barraged the country with the name of Stokely Carmichael, depicting him as a "Black racist," a "disciple of hatred and race war," "a fiery inciter of passions." This obviously didn't describe the man who had come to help in our campaign against napalm. It never occurred to me then that Carmichael had stuck his neck out to try to ally the Black movement with the anti-war movement, and that we ought to be thinking about what we could do to further that alliance. I was too busy working to stop napalm.

About this time, both Jane and I began to notice cars following us and mysterious things happening on our phone. Jane then spent a lot of time on the phone, turning the San Francisco call-in shows into discussions of the war. Once, after dialing and before the phone was picked up at the other end, she heard a man's voice say, "Oh, she's just calling one of those damned shows again." One afternoon one of the workers who had quit UTC telephoned and asked me to come to his home in Santa Clara. After supper, I drove to his moderately prosperous suburban community, and, wary enough already to try to conceal our meeting, parked a few blocks away. He was still in contact with some of the other UTC workers, who said that many workers privately were opposed to making napalm, but the plant had been turned into a virtual police state. Their casual conversations were being spied on, and even their personal reading matter was being inspected surreptitiously. On my way home, I thought I was being followed on the freeway. When I got to Palo Alto, I drove to a gas station and went to a telephone to call Jane to find out where SCPV was meeting that night. Suddenly a car pulled in and rolled right up to the phone booth, blocking the door and fixing me in its headlights. I could barely make out the silhouettes of two men, wearing what seemed to be felt hats and business suits, in the front seat. I quickly told Jane what was happening. I could see the front license plate, so I made it obvious to the men in the car that I was reading its numbers into the phone. I continued facing the car and kept talking to Jane. I felt as though I was no longer in Palo Alto, but back home in Brooklyn. After what seemed like a very long time, probably a few minutes, the car backed up and sped off, burning rubber.

By the middle of March, UTC had completed its contract for the development of Napalm-B. They received their reward: a large contract for the production of actual napalm bombs. They selected as the site for this production an unused Standard Oil storage facility in the port of Redwood City, at the end of a causeway sticking two miles out into the San Francisco Bay. This site was on publicly owned tidal land. Therefore, all leases and uses of it were under the jurisdiction of the Redwood City Port Commission, and its rulings were legally subject to override by the citizens of Redwood City.

On March 21, the Port Commission convened in an old frame building amidst the unused petroleum storage tanks Standard Oil was asking to sublease to UTC. About fifty protesters showed up. Some were members of Concerned Citizens, a Palo Alto peace organization. Others came from a Unitarian congregation in Redwood City. Most of us wore suits and dresses. The most casually dressed were a few Stanford students. The room where the commissioners met could hold only about a dozen of us, so we presented them with our formal written protest and asked them to move to a larger facility. After much arguing, they agreed to adjourn to an auditorium in the county office building in downtown Redwood City.

By the time the meeting reconvened, almost two hundred people had gathered. The middle-aged white gentlemen on the commission set up ground rules for public participation, specifically ruling out of order "the moral question" and "the federal policy of war in Vietnam." Speaker after speaker rose to reason with the commissioners: a local minister, several Redwood City housewives, workers, students. Olive Mayer, an engineer from Redwood City who had inspected the gas ovens of Belsen, calmly stated: "As a professional engineer I knew that other members of my profession planned and engineered these ovens as execution chambers. The manufacturer's name was proudly displayed over the door of the ovens. Engineers had to calculate the number of victims to be accommodated, means of ingress and egress, how many to be executed at one time, etc. Local government and professional people had to be involved in providing for locations for the manufacture of these ovens, just as you commissioners are now called upon to make a decision concerning a napalm factory."

I rose, intending to speak about the specific qualities of napalm, based on my Air Force experience and recent research. I got as far as my name. The chairman turned bright red and burst out angrily, "We know who you are and what you have to say, and we don't want to hear it. Sit down!" I couldn't believe my ears. I tried to ask why I shouldn't be allowed my opportunity to speak. The chairman yelled to the police at the back of the room, "Get that man out of here! Right now!" Two cops rushed up, twisted one arm behind my back, and started dragging me backward down the aisle. My seven-year-old daughter Gretchen burst into tears. The people in the audience were all staring in shock and disbelief at the scene in the aisle. By the time the police got me to the rear door, I noticed that the commissioners were packing their briefcases and starting to leave. I broke loose, ran back down the aisle, and demanded, "What are you doing?" People began calling out: "What's going on?" "Why are you leaving?" "Aren't you going to discuss it?" "Aren't you even going to bother to vote?" The chairman looked over his shoulder, laughed, bent down to a microphone, and said: "We just did vote to grant the sublease. We also voted to adjourn. You probably couldn't hear because of all the commotion you were making."

During the next few days, I investigated the legal options open to us. I discovered that the vote of the commission could be overturned in a referendum called by an initiative petition signed by 10 percent of the registered voters of Redwood City. When our lawyer went for help in preparing the papers, the City Attorney gave him false information that cheated us out of thirteen days of the thirty we were supposed to have. So we had only seventeen days to find volunteers, build an organization, and get signatures of 10 percent of the voters. And this was the period when, according to the media and their polls, everybody but a handful of "dissidents" supported the war.

Signatures could be solicited only by registered voters of Redwood City. Redwood City was a suburban bedroom community of about fifty thousand, almost 100 percent white, mostly middle-income working class, small business, and professional people. The city boundaries had been drawn to exclude the sizable population of Chicano, Black, and poorer white working-class people, mostly concentrated in the unincorporated area known informally as East

Redwood City. Redwood City had no history of radical politics. There wasn't even a liberal political organization to be found in town. On top of all these obstacles, the local press launched a campaign to block the petition. The Redwood City *Tribune* called us "treasonous." The influential Palo Alto *Times* tried to urge and incite violence against us, and then later, in two most revealing editorials, explained that if the people were allowed to vote on such matters, the country would be unable to wage war and the national government would collapse:

> There is no question that considerable pressure is being brought by a small but vocal minority that objects to our use of napalm in the Viet Nam war. It is the same minority that objects to our involvement in the war at all. . . . The voters of Redwood City do not have the right to preempt these decisions for themselves, to make the decisions for the rest of the country.
>
> . . . to place on a municipal ballot decisions on military and foreign policy is to invite chaos. If all cities in the United States were to decide for themselves whether to permit the manufacture of military aircraft, bombs, rifles, grenades, rockets, torpedoes and other war material, they would wreck our armed forces. If all of them were to arrogate to themselves decisions on foreign policy, they would wreck the national government. (April 16, 1966.)

> While there may be some question about the use of napalm in warfare, it is not a question to be decided by the voters of Redwood City or any other municipality. These are matters of foreign policy and military policy. The proper place to debate them and to make the decision is at the national level, in the halls of Congress.
>
> It is easy to see what would happen if every city were to be allowed to make its own decision as to what war material is acceptable to its citizens.
>
> The people of Sunnyvale could vote on whether Polaris missiles should be manufactured by Lockheed. The people of Palo Alto could vote on whether electronics equipment for guided missiles should be built in the city. The citizens of San Francisco or Oakland could vote on whether their municipal port facilities should be permitted to load materials of war, such as napalm and atomic weapons, onto ships headed for the war.
>
> The result would be chaos. (April 20, 1966.)

But in a few days we had our volunteers and an organization. One hundred and ten citizens of Redwood City, most of them working people, were out actively soliciting signatures. The regional warehousemen's local of the ILWU sent a telegram of support, a small donation, and three volunteers. The press thundered on about treason. One canvasser was roughed up. The Huntley-Brinkley show covered the campaign, to report that the people of Redwood City ranged from indifferent to hostile. On the seventeenth day we stayed up all night verifying and counting the signatures on the petitions. Fifteen percent of the registered voters of Redwood City had signed.

Anyone who has done petition work knows this figure represents overwhelming support. In a petition campaign, it's good work just to *see* 15 percent of the registered voters in *thirty* days. On April 20, as we officially filed the petitions, we were confident we were going to win the election, and we knew this would have national and international significance.

Meanwhile, UTC had started production of napalm bombs. As you drove out along the causeway to the napalm facility, you now passed acres of stacked crates of 500- to 750-pound bombs. You could even stand at the high chain-link fence to watch as the empty bomb casings were swung over to a raised platform and pumped full of napalm. On May 1, a barge partly loaded with napalm bombs mysteriously developed two holes in its hull and began to sink. A vigil began across from the plant. On May 16 and 17, a Palo Alto psychiatrist, two students from Stanford, and a Chicano jazz musician named Aaron Manganiello were arrested for lying down in front of some trucks bringing empty bomb shells to be filled.

The signatures on the petitions still lay, uncounted, in the city clerk's office. The City Attorney had been using one legal maneuver after another to block the election. On May 20, Superior Court Judge Melvin Cohn ruled that the petition was invalid because it had attacked the original sublease from Standard Oil to UTC. He disclosed that on April 26, six days after we had filed the petition, Standard Oil, UTC, and the Port Commission had secretly scrapped the old sublease and arranged a new one. Judge Cohn informed us that, in order to be valid, a petition would have to attack this new lease. Since this new lease had gone into effect on April 26, we would have until May 26, only six days, to draw up a new petition, get signatures, and have it filed. It was now obvious that, even if we could have performed that miracle, Standard Oil, UTC, and the Port Commission would merely draw up still another lease. A few weeks later we discovered that Judge Cohn was a personal friend of Barnet Adelman, president of UTC, and their children attended the same Sunday-school class. But we now knew that had little to do with his clearly illegal decision. We had been forced to recognize that judges—like port authority commissions, city attorneys, policemen, FBI agents, newspapers, and armies—were there to do whatever the corporations required of them.

The following day, Aaron Manganiello began a one-man fast and vigil across the road from the napalm plant. Aaron had just been suspended from the College of San Mateo, the local public community college where he had been studying music, for distributing literature against the Vietnam War. Each night of his vigil and fast, men from UTC would hose him down every hour. After six days, Aaron had pneumonia and had to give up the vigil.

On May 28 we officially launched the national campaign against napalm with a rally and a four-mile march through downtown Redwood City and out along the causeway to the gates of the napalm plant. Despite a virtually complete news blackout, thirty-five hundred people showed up. Most wore suits and dresses. There were many families with small children. Robert, who was then three years old, pedaled the entire way on his tricycle.

The march ended with more speeches, delivered from a flatbed truck outside the front gates of the napalm plant. The principal speaker was Senator Wayne Morse, who rambled on for half an hour, telling a couple of anecdotes to show he was still good friends with Lyndon Johnson and never once mentioning napalm. The rally concluded, and people began strolling to the buses we had chartered to take them back to their cars. Suddenly dozens of squad cars appeared, as if from no place. They had been carefully concealed behind buildings surrounding the rally. We counted hundreds of police from five different agencies. Most of the squad cars displayed shotguns and contained six police in full riot gear, something most people there had seen only on TV. The Redwood City police and the San Mateo County sheriffs had prepared an elaborate ambush, and they were obviously disappointed they had not found a chance to "teach you some patriotism," as one yelled out his window.

Only the local newspapers reported that the march and rally had taken place, and they vastly underestimated the size of the crowd, reporting that the citizens of Redwood City were all hostile to such activities. Even a mere twenty miles away, the press and radio in San Francisco imposed a total news blackout. On one hand, this did keep many people in ignorance. But, on the other, it deepened the education of many tens of thousands about the role of the media. Almost everyone in the area knew an important event had taken place and could not help but wonder why it was not reported and how many events from other areas were not reported to us.

In fact, we had succeeded in breaking through the media isolation. The national boycott of Dow Chemical Corporation products, announced at the rally, had already begun. That very day, fifty pickets demonstrated outside the New York offices of Dow Chemical, and over two hundred picketed Dow's big plant for production of polystyrene in Torrance, outside Los Angeles. But none of us would have predicted the hundreds of mass demonstrations against Dow Chemical that were to take place in the next several years.

The napalm campaign changed my view of U.S. society and of my own relationship to it. Not that I had had any overwhelming illusions about corporations, politicians, generals, judges, security agents, police, and the media. But I had never before grasped either their interconnectedness or how their behavior was determined by their functions. I had never understood that the entire state apparatus and the mass media exist primarily to carry out tasks defined by the needs of the corporations. More potentially far-reaching was what I learned about the people. I began to understand why the media in general blacked out this mass movement, and why the liberal media continued to present an image of the people as mindless Yahoos, indifferent to the war or jingoistically supporting it.

Up to this point, I had still been refusing to open my mind to Marxist-Leninist theory. I was fond of saying to the two or three Marxists who chided me about my ignorance, "Later for theory. Right now there's too much to do." But that spring I found myself beginning to shift in my graduate seminar in Utopian and Anti-Utopian Literature. Up until then, I had been presenting a little Marx and Engels as examples of "utopians," while I extolled the brilliance of the great anti-utopians—Dostoyevsky, Zamiatin, Huxley, Orwell, Burgess, etc.—with their cynicism about "human nature," particularly as manifested in the common people. Now I took a new look at Engels' *Socialism: Utopian and Scientific*, and realized that its analysis helped me to understand my present experience. Somebody finally persuaded me to read a few works by Mao Tse-tung. The first one was "On Practice." Underlined in red in my copy are these words:

> If you want to know a certain thing or a certain class of things directly, you must personally participate in the practical struggle to change reality, to change that thing or class of things, for only thus can you come into contact with them as phenomena; only through personal participation in the practical struggle to change reality can you uncover the essence of that thing or class of things and comprehend them. . . . If you want knowledge, you must take part in the practice of changing reality. If you want to know the taste of a pear, you must change the pear by eating it yourself. . . . If you want to know the theory and methods of revolution, you must take part in revolution.

Why did this passage have such a revolutionizing effect on my thinking? After all, many readers will think, isn't all this just common sense? Well, there is some truth in that. This is common sense, though raised to the level of practical revolutionary theory.

Or, as Mao puts it, ". . . take the ideas of the masses (scattered and unsystematic ideas) and concentrate them (through study turn them into concentrated and systematic ideas), then go to the masses and propagate and explain these ideas until the masses embrace them as their own, hold fast to them and translate them into action, and test the correctness of these ideas in such action." But I had been systematically deprived of my common sense. I had been educated to be a philosophical solipsist, and a cynic. Mao's oft-quoted remark about eating a pear gets to the heart of the matter.

I had been trained in a system of thought that I now feel comfortable in calling bourgeois. It had developed with the rise of the bourgeois social class and the dominance of capitalism. True, experimental science has been fundamental to bourgeois thought, and did not begin with Marx or Mao. But equally fundamental is that radical cleavage between mind and body, subject and object. This is a reflection of social relations within bourgeois society, and also within feudal society. On one side of capitalist society are those who use their minds, including the intellectuals in the university. They have, as far as their ideas are concerned, no bodily existence. On the other side are the workers, those who build everything used in the society, including the buildings, libraries, laboratories, computers, typewriters, pencils, mouse cages, and paper of the university. The goal of bourgeois science has been to arrive at an "objective" understanding of the material world. Correctly enough, bourgeois science began by attempting to remove from that material world the subjective qualities put in it by feudal metaphysics. Bourgeois physics has striven toward a purely objective model of the universe. We do not live, however, in a dualistic universe, but a dialectical one. One's only means of perceiving reality is one's mind, and one's mind itself is matter that thinks. One's mind is both material and part of the reality it is trying to comprehend. So inevitably bourgeois physics reached an impasse, expressed variously by Heisenberg, Einstein, and Arthur Eddington. The impasse is that all the experiments of bourgeois science are "null" experiments, because the perceiving mind is actually part of the experiment. Dialectical materialism, the science of Marxism-Leninism, transcends this impasse precisely because its foundation is consciously purposeful, not supposedly "neutral" and "objective," and its purpose is in part to smash the alienation of mind and body. Mao's simple example of the pear is so easy to understand that bourgeois savants, trained to equate truth with obscurity and complexity, cannot grasp its significance. Mao is saying that true knowledge comes from apprehending the interpenetration of subject and object, not by trying to separate them.

Where did that leave me? For I was still part of an institution whose fundamental reason for existence was supposedly to step outside the rest of society, into an "ivory tower," in order to perceive and communicate the truth.

A Declaration of Independence

I. Stanford-in-France

> Bruce Franklin, an articulate prophet of the coming American revolution, was an assistant professor at Stanford University. During a sabbatical interlude, Franklin and his wife were sent to France. While in France, Franklin began reading Marxist texts and during that period declared his conversion to Marxist/Leninist Communism.
>
> From report by Evelle Younger, Attorney General of the State of California, entitled "Terrorism in California," July 9, 1974.

In June, 1940, the Nazi army sweeping southward from Paris was halted on the north side of the Loire River in the outskirts of the city of Tours. Its artillery fired almost point-blank across the river into the city, where the French forces held out, only to be taken over in a few days by the collaborationist Vichy government. After World War II, an apartment building was put up on the south bank of the Loire in place of buildings destroyed by the Nazi shelling. This apartment house has since been converted into the dormitory, dining room, offices, and classrooms constituting "Stanford-in-France." Seminannually, eighty Stanford students, along with two professors and their families, go there to absorb the culture of France and the rest of Europe. Very few of the students ever learn the history of their building.

The students' main activities are much the same as in California: bridge, dope, drinking, sex, skiing on weekends, and whatever study is required of them, which isn't much, because the professors are busy trying to make the most of this paid European vacation. The whole group takes field trips to the châteaux of the Loire Valley and other cultural centers of France, Italy, and Spain. Each student is assigned to a French family for an occasional meal. The families are carefully selected to make sure they are of the proper social class (petit bourgeois) and political sentiments (anti-Communist and pro-American).

Across the street from the main building and overlooking Saint Julien, a twelfth-century church scarred by the Nazi barrage, is a small but elegant apartment reserved for the Stanford professor with the larger family. Here Jane and I and our three children began living in September, 1966. We ate with the Stanford students. Jane got Karen and Gretchen started in the local public school. I started teaching my classes in literature. Everything was beginning as it was supposed to.

We were surprised to find on the newsstands, displayed just like any other newspaper, stacks of *L'Humanité*, the daily tabloid of the French Communist Party, and we bought an occasional copy. The second week we were there, Jane found in *L'Humanité* a notice of a meeting to be held in Tours. A delegation from Vietnam—representatives of both the Democratic Republic of Vietnam and the National Liberation Front—were to appear at a "soirée" celebrating the forty-sixth anniversary of the founding of the French Communist Party. Tours, the article explained, had been the scene in 1920 of the decisive conference at which the French Socialist Party had joined Lenin's Third International, thus becoming the Communist Party of France. One of the most influential speakers in favor of this move had been a young man named Ho Chi Minh.

(The article did not explain what we learned later: that Ho Chi Minh had caused an uproar when he rose to demand that the Party take a position on Vietnam and the other French colonies.)

When Jane and I got to the big movie theater where the meeting was to be held, we found it closed. Jane, whose French was much better than mine, inquired of some people chatting under the marquee. They looked at us with obvious curiosity.

"You are Americans?" We nodded. They whispered.

"Talk to that man over there."

The man over there was craggy-faced, thin-lipped, unsmiling, about forty-five years old, in a trench coat and a black wool watch cap pulled down at an angle across his forehead, with a cigarette dangling from the corner of his mouth. Jane and I timidly walked over and meekly introduced ourselves as Americans who had come to attend the soirée with the Vietnamese.

"You are tourists?"

"No," I said. "I am a professor at Stanford-in-France."

"You must see Labeyrie," he said flatly.

"What is 'Labeyrie'?" I asked.

"Labeyrie," he said, with a hint of a smile, "is the *man* you must see." He took our telephone number and told us that the soirée was postponed one week.

"Before then," he added dramatically, "you will hear from Labeyrie."

Two days later, Labeyrie called and arranged to come over. He was a stocky, forceful-looking man in his early or mid-fifties, a professor of biology at the University of Orléans. Labeyrie was friendly, charming, disarming, and obviously there to figure out who and what we might be. Most of what we learned about him we found out later. He had been in the Communist Party since 1941. During the German occupation, he had been in a Resistance cell which had machine-gunned several Gestapo officers. Madeleine Riffaud, another member of the cell, had been captured by the Nazis, who had cut off her breasts. Labeyrie was now a fairly high official in the Communist Party in the region. Before he left, we asked him if it would be appropriate for Stanford students to come to the soirée. He was enthusiastic about the possibility.

I announced the meeting at supper, giving some background on the local history and making sure the students understood they would be welcome. None of the students showed any interest. The local director of Stanford-in-France, M. Paul LeMoal, rushed up to say he didn't think it "proper" for American students to be associating with "the enemy." But Alice and Steve Mick, a married couple who had both recently graduated from Stanford and who served as counselors, said they would like very much to go along with us.

Labeyrie was waiting for us when we got there, and the four of us sat with him and some companions. The theater quickly filled. A young Frenchwoman went to the microphone on stage and welcomed everybody to this celebration of the unity between the peoples of France and Vietnam. She talked of Ho Chi Minh's role in the foundation of the Communist Party of France in this very city, and of the duty of the people of France to support the Vietnamese now in the hour of their need. She omitted, I noticed, any mention of the role of the Communist Party of France during the 1946–54 French war against Vietnam. Then she introduced the four Vietnamese guests. Each, she explained, had had at least one close relative killed by U.S. forces.

The first speaker was a young peasant woman from the North who had shot down more U.S. planes than anybody else that year. She described the daily life in the countryside under continuous attack by American planes, and how the people of her village had devised means for protecting the children and developing crossfire against the strafing attacks. A somewhat older factory worker from Hanoi then spoke. He described how his plant had overfulfilled its production quota, despite frequent raids on the city by U.S. planes, including direct hits on the factory. The last two speakers were a student from Saigon now studying in Paris and a diplomat representing the Democratic Republic of Vietnam in France. They spoke mainly about the antiwar movement in France and around the world, and how it inspired their struggle.

At the end of the program, Labeyrie took me by the arm and walked up to the Vietnamese, saying, "I would like you to meet an American who has been very active in the movement against the war, Professor Bruce Franklin."

I was sorry he had done this. Besides the guilt and shame I felt for being an American, I now felt like a fraud. What had I done to stop the war, except inconvenience myself a bit from time to time? And how could these Vietnamese possibly respond politely to a U.S. citizen? They didn't. They threw their arms around me, hugged me, kissed me. Tears streamed down their faces. Tears started to trickle out of my own eyes. A cynical thought flashed through my mind. Weren't they just putting on an act carefully calculated to move me toward greater support? But the pressure of their bodies, the human passion burning in their eyes and cutting through my conditioned responses to "Oriental eyes," their embarrassed attempts to express what they felt in French, a language foreign to all five of us—all this made me more ashamed of my cynicism than I had been for our national guilt and part-time activism. Then came another explanation, less vicious but more degrading: this was merely a cultural expression of "the beautiful, simple Vietnamese people." Months later I saw a Vietnamese friend show a rare burst of anger when an American liberal openly attributed the heroism of the Vietnamese national liberation struggle to the "culture" of "the beautiful Vietnamese people."

"Diem is also part of the Vietnamese people" was his response, "and so are the landlords and businessmen who work with every foreign invader. And so are the pimps in Saigon, and the secret police who put your electric instruments to the testicles and breasts of our comrades. What gives us our internationalism and our sure knowledge that we will win is our understanding of history. And that comes from the Marxist-Leninist science that Ho Chi Minh has taught us."

That night in Tours, I managed to tell the Vietnamese a few words about the struggle against the napalm plant in Redwood City. I also informed them there were certain things about the latest napalm production they should know. They asked if I could meet privately in two days, and I agreed.

With new misgivings, I went to the address I had been given. It was on a narrow cobblestoned street in a workers' district of Tours. I rang. Footsteps on a stair, and a challenging voice: "Who's there?"

"The American friend of Labeyrie," I said as instructed.

The door was unbolted. I was led up a rickety staircase and asked to have a seat on a chair in the bare upstairs hallway. After a few minutes, I was ushered into a bare room almost filled with an old conference table around which were seated Labeyrie, the craggy-faced man we had met at the theater the first night, another Frenchman, and eight Vietnamese men all dressed in inexpensive, plain dark suits and ties.

After some awkward attempts at small talk, one of the Vietnamese said, "You told our comrades you had some information you wished to give us."

Was I a traitor for what I was about to do? Or would I be a traitor for not doing it? I hesitated, then, in my primitive French, helped by sketches to illustrate some technical points, I made the long statement I had been mentally rehearsing.

I briefly told of the napalm struggle. I next described the napalm bombs being made in Redwood City. Up until then, napalm had been used in Vietnam almost entirely by fighter-bombers carrying one bomb under each wing. I explained that many of the bombs in Redwood City were built to be racked in B-52s. I gave them the figures on the vastly expanded total production of napalm. I noted that the bombs were all marked "MUST BE USED WITHIN ONE YEAR."

"What this all means," I said, "is that the U.S. is going to use napalm now as a strategic weapon. Waves of B-52s will saturate entire areas with napalm. The fire will become so hot it will generate big winds, fire storms burning all vegetation and consuming the oxygen. Nothing will live in these areas."

After a brief conference, a somewhat elderly Vietnamese said:

"Comrade, we are grateful for this information. We promise to send it on immediately to the comrades in Vietnam. We see that you are worried about what this weapon will do to us.

"No weapon can frighten us into submission. What you have told us is very grave. It means we will suffer and pay a high price for our freedom. But we have known all along that your government has many terrible weapons, including nuclear bombs. But not even nuclear weapons can turn back history. The people are more powerful than any weapon. Eventually we will free our entire homeland. And every weapon used against us will bring more of the people of the world to our side."

At the end of our meeting, one of the Vietnamese presented me with a small box. Inside was an aluminum comb, shaped like a jet fighter, inscribed in Vietnamese.

"This comb," he said, "is a little symbol of our friendship. It was made from the metal of another terrible weapon, a plane that could fly much faster than sound. The plane was brought down by a peasant woman armed with a rifle from World War I."

The next morning, when I started combing my hair with this symbol, I recoiled in shock. Wasn't the pilot of that downed plane someone like me when I was in the Air Force? Shouldn't my loyalties be with him, rather than with these people whose life was foreign to my own? How could I make light of his death, or captivity, by combing my hair with a piece of his plane's wreckage? But a great sense of liberation swept away these doubts. Yes, I was switching sides, but it was from the side of LBJ, UTC, ROTC, Dow-Badische, Napalm-B and Zyklon-B, the Palo Alto *Times*, the cops and bankers, the New York Port Authority and the Redwood City Port Commission, Judge Cohn and President Adelman, Milton Eisenhower and Richard Nixon, Amherst fraternities and the Strategic Air Command, General MacArthur and Captain Vere, New Criticism and Madison Avenue, my father's exploiters on Wall Street, Mr. Carb and the Syndicate, Leland Stanford and the faceless management of the Pennsylvania Railroad, the administration in Washington and its counterpart at Stanford—switching from that side to the side of those trying to create a decent future for humanity. I cheerfully returned to combing my hair.

A few nights later, Labeyrie took Jane and me on a wild ride, careering through the fog along the banks of the Loire, to attend a workers' antiwar meeting in Blois, a small industrial city thirty-five miles up the river from Tours. The meeting, of about eighty factory workers, was held in a large classroom. Labeyrie chaired from the teacher's desk. The speakers were workers, who discussed Vietnam and gave detailed reports on the antiwar organizing in each factory in Blois and the surrounding region. My French was not only poor but very bookish, so I could barely get the gist of this living, working-class French.

Toward the end of the meeting, Labeyrie announced, "We are most fortunate to have with us tonight a comrade from the United States. He is going to tell us all about the movement against the war in the United States." Applause. When I realized who he meant, my blood felt like ice. How could I speak to French workers? When I thought of France I thought of avant-garde movies, bourgeois novels, Impressionist paintings, medieval churches and castles, gourmet restaurants and elegant wines, and tales of how the French loathe most a foreigner, especially an American, who mutilates their language.

I couldn't speak in English, because there was nobody there to translate. There was no way out. I took my time getting to the front of the room, trying to organize a few sentences, embarrassed by the continuing applause. When I got there and looked directly into the faces of these French workers, a very surprising thing happened. I saw that the faces were friendly, and found myself being sustained by a warm feedback, a sense of recognition dissolving national boundaries. Something told me that I had more in common with these workers of another nation than with my "colleagues" of the English departments of Johns Hopkins and Stanford. I can't remember anything of what I said, except for criticism of the backward role of the U.S. Communist Party. But we all knew that my words were not our main communication. For days after, my ribs were sore from their embraces.

Labeyrie was continuing to single out me, a fellow male and a fellow professor, as the local representative of the U.S. antiwar movement. It was probably good I was sick the day of the next antiwar event, as Jane for once got to go as a separate individual rather than the professor's wife. The occasion was a massive demonstration in Paris organized by the two giant labor confederations, the Communist-led CGT and the big Catholic union.

Jane left around 5 A.M. to board a chartered train, already almost filled with workers. Into Paris, the hub at the center of the rail network of France, came similar trains from all regions of the country. Delegations were selected to meet with the embassies of each country still supporting the United States in Vietnam. Jane was chosen to visit the South Korean embassy. The main spokesman for her group of four was a tough twenty-five-year-old factory worker from Paris, who wore a black leather jacket and spoke with enough authority to make the South Korean diplomat who met them begin to shake. He introduced Jane as a representative of the U.S. people opposed to the war. When she began to condemn the activities of the South Korean brigades in Vietnam, the diplomat snuffed out his cigarette on the desk, missing the ashtray by two inches, and hurriedly fled from the room. The demonstration ended with huge marches converging, under a steady downpour, from all quarters of Paris into the Place de la Bastille.

One of the Vietnamese we had met the night of the soirée was Nguyen Ngoc Giao, secretary of the Union of Vietnamese Students in France. Giao had enthusiastically accepted my invitation to come talk to the Stanford students. After a couple of months, during which, we later learned, Giao and a comrade gave themselves a crash course in English, they came. By this time, Alice, Steve, Jane, and I had convinced most of the Stanford students to attend.

The Vietnamese brought two films, one made in each half of Vietnam. The one from the North showed numerous bombing raids on cities, villages, farms, schools, and hospitals. It also showed the air defense we had heard described by the Vietnamese woman at the soirée. One sequence showed a group of Vietnamese peasant women, armed with bolt-action World War I Springfield rifles, blazing away at a flight of four F4 Phantom jets strafing the fields. One of the jets suddenly started trailing dense black smoke, spun wildly out of control, then crashed and exploded in a wooded area. Several of us clapped. A few angry hisses came back at us from the darkened room.

The other film, made by the National Liberation Front, showed the development of hospitals, schools, child-care centers, and small-weapons manufacture in the liberated areas of the South. People told in interviews of activities they had seen performed by U.S. forces: torture, rape, looting, the burning of villages, and massacres. One film segment, shot astonishingly from hand-held hidden cameras, showed U.S. troops entering a village. We saw torture, houses put to the torch, bags of rice being slit open and scattered around, medical supplies stomped into the ground under GI boots. Most of the villagers conformed to the media image of the "South" Vietnamese peasantry: timelessly indifferent to both sides, they wanted only to be left alone. There they were, in their age-old peasant garb and their age-old peasant stoop, looking blank, numb, merely enduring. The GIs marched out of the village. Suddenly, everything was transformed. An impromptu guerrilla theater broke out, with the villagers doing exaggerated imitations of both the U.S. soldiers and themselves, now stooped over even more, looking even blanker and more obsequious. The camera followed a party of the villagers to a carefully concealed trap door. They took out a variety of weapons, Springfield and Mauser rifles, M1 carbines, two AK 47s, assorted pistols, one mortar, and one tripod-mounted machine gun. The weapons were carried to the village center and distributed to a group of men and women sitting in a circle sketching plans in the dirt. The last scene showed this group setting off, singing, on the same trail the U.S. troops had taken to leave.

After the films, the two Vietnamese gave a brief outline of Vietnamese history and the present military and political situation. Then they announced they would answer all the questions they could. The discussion lasted three hours.

Most of the questions asked by the Stanford students showed a total ignorance of history, the grossest insensitivity to the feelings of the Vietnamese, and a lack of common sense. "Why should we allow the democratic nation of South Vietnam to be destroyed by a Communist dictatorship?" "Do you think we Americans enjoy having to go around the world policing people who can't take care of their own affairs?" "Isn't it true that all Catholics in North Vietnam were tortured to death or put in slave-labor camps?" "Why won't North Vietnam allow free elections to be held?" "If we don't stop the Communists here, where will we be able to stop them?" "Why don't you people appreciate all our economic aid?"

With what seemed superhuman patience, the Vietnamese answered each one, never, with one exception, showing even irritation. Were Asians, as we have all been taught, less emotional and more cunning than other people? Only months later did we learn Giao had such a severe ulcer there were very few foods he could eat. The one question to provoke anger came late.

"Don't you realize," said a six-foot-two blond, healthy, boyish, amiable Stanford sophomore, the son of an executive of a big bank, "that we are only in Vietnam to protect you from the Chinese?"

"Are you actually saying to us," shouted Giao's comrade, "that you have invaded our land and butchered our people to protect us from foreign invasion? First of all, you better understand the Chinese people are our brothers and sisters. They give us now a firm rear area, and they are prepared to support us any way we ask. But suppose that were not true, and the Chinese people wanted to invade Vietnam, as you think. Don't you Americans understand by now that we are quite capable of defending ourselves, and nobody can invade Vietnam? Even your forces, with all your great weapons, will not conquer us. We do not need America to protect us from anybody."

Then he added, in a subdued voice, with his face once more composed, "I am sorry to have spoken in anger. But you do not comprehend what it is to have your homeland invaded and destroyed."

One day Labeyrie invited me to attend a *déjeuner-débat,* a luncheon discussion meeting for Communist Party cadres. The subject was to be "Marxism and Art." Somehow—I can't even remember how—it was decided that Steve, but not Jane or Alice, would also go. Though I was now beginning to think of myself as a Marxist, I was apprehensive about participating in a Communist ideological meeting. Back came the old images of sinister, manipulative, dogmatic Communist fanatics. And would they find out I was just a liberal American academic?

Steve and I followed the directions. To our surprise they led us to one of the most elegant restaurants in the region, actually built into a cave out in the country. We introduced ourselves at the door and were admitted into the main dining room, where several dozen leading Communist Party cadres from the surrounding region soon arrived. We were introduced to the guest of honor and main speaker, none other than Roger Garaudy, then chief theoretician of the Party. We all assembled at the splendidly set banquet tables, where we were served a magnificent luncheon.

The time came for the main speech. Garaudy gave a witty presentation. Then followed a general discussion of his central theme, posed just like this: "Do we want to raise the level of the workers up to the level of the culture, or lower the level of the culture down to the level of the workers?"

The answer, needless to say, was that we should try to raise the level of the workers up to the level of the culture. I was terribly confused. All during Garaudy's talk, I kept thinking I must be misunderstanding because of my poor French. After all, this was a meeting of the Communist Party of France, not some wealthy cultural do-gooders from Westchester or Beverly Hills. Steve, whose French was excellent, assured me the problem didn't lie in my French.

Steve and I consulted and framed a question, which Steve asked:

"Couldn't there be a culture that came from the workers themselves, that spoke to their needs, that they could understand and appreciate without lessons?"

"No," said Garaudy, smiling patiently, "there is only one culture. That is the culture of Tchaikovsky and Beethoven, of Goethe and Shakespeare, of Michelangelo and Rodin."

I tried to think of an example of an artist, known both to us and to them, who at least drew his art from the culture and needs of the people, who spoke directly to them, and was therefore widely popular. The most obvious person at the time was Bob Dylan. I offered him as just such an example, not necessarily of a "great" artist, but of an important artist, popular among millions of working- and middle-class youth. The response was polite scattered laughter. I thought at first I must have made a mistake in French. But they would not be so impolite as to laugh out loud, and the laughter was too friendly to be aimed at me. The truth sank in. They thought I was making a sophisticated joke. To them, the popularity of Dylan was just more evidence that the masses were hopelessly backward.

The discussion got back to business. A young woman described her experience in Saint-Pierre-des-Corps, a nearby town, mostly inhabited by railroad workers, that had been a Communist stronghold, with a Communist mayor, since the end of World War II: "Well, out in Saint-Pierre-des-Corps we have no difficulty getting the workers to go to the cinema. Our trouble comes in getting them to discuss it afterward." The subject now became: How do you get workers to *discuss* culture?

While all this was going on, we were being served cheeses, wines, sherbet, coffee, mints, and cordials by a precision corps of waiters, waitresses, and busboys, all clad in starched, ironed, spotlessly white uniforms. It would have been unthinkable to turn around to ask any of these workers what they thought of this discussion. For the assembled cadres of the "Communist" Party, the people serving them food and taking away their dirty plates were as beautifully trained, and as tactfully unobtrusive, as the most perfect robots of science fiction. And certainly there was never the flicker of a sign on any of the faces of the people doing the work that they had heard any of the words being spoken at the tables.

I have thought a lot about this scene since. More than any other single event, it changed my attitudes toward art, its study and teaching, and its relationships with the rest of human activities. Of course it is easy to caricature the luncheon and the elegant "Communist" diners. But the problems of what I would now freely call proletarian culture are not so simple. After all, bourgeois culture has been developing for centuries, most of that time as the culture of a ruling class. At its disposal has been an entire educational system and a virtual monopoly on the means of communicating culture: publishing houses, theaters, concert halls, museums, motion-picture companies, and so on. It has developed close to its complete potential, and, now, even in the period of decay, it is rich in formal perfection. The culture of the modern industrial working class, on the other hand, has been developing under the most difficult conditions. It is primitive, in the sense of being young and relatively undeveloped. Bourgeois culture is bound to be, for the most part, "better" in aesthetic terms—at least bourgeois aesthetic terms—than the proletarian culture that has developed up to the present moment. So there is the very real necessity of raising the level of proletarian culture. But does this mean that it aspires to rival bourgeois culture in its own arena, and with its own rules?

After the luncheon meeting on "Marxism and Art," I went back to our apartment and read Mao Tse-tung's "Talks at the Yenan Forum on Literature and Art." Mao, I discovered, dealt directly with the question of raising standards, but from a far different point of view from the French CP's:

> There must be a basis from which to raise. Take a bucket of water, for instance; where is it to be raised from if not from the ground? From mid-air? From what basis, then, are literature and art to be raised? From the basis of the feudal classes? From the basis of the bourgeoisie? From the basis of the petty-bourgeois intellectuals? No, not from any of these; only from the basis of the masses of workers, peasants and soldiers. Nor

does this mean raising the workers, peasants and soldiers to the "heights" of the feudal classes, the bourgeoisie or the petty-bourgeois intellectuals; it means raising the level of literature and art in the direction in which the workers, peasants and soldiers are themselves advancing, in the direction in which the proletariat is advancing. (*Selected Readings*, p. 215.)

Though I saw that Mao had cut through the pretensions of the *déjeuner-débat*, and though I accepted his fundamental solution to the problem of raising the level of proletarian culture, there was much about his formulation that struck me as simplistic, jargonistic, and far removed from my own cultural experience, in Brooklyn as well as at Amherst and Stanford. "Workers, peasants, and soldiers" seemed to fit China, but how did it apply to the United States? Insofar as Black people in the United States were mostly workers and peasants, I could translate Mao's formulation into our own experience. Certainly in the United States it was obvious that Afro-American culture was *different* from the culture that ruled the academies, and in many ways it was *better*, by almost any standard. I was beginning to grasp the difference between the culture of white workers and that of white professors of literature. But soldiers? Surely that had little relevance for the United States.

A few months later I was arranging for the clandestine printing of a leaflet, written by a GI who had just deserted, and intended for publication on U.S. Army bases throughout Europe. The man who wrote it, the son of a beer-truck driver from Detroit, had always been told in school he was stupid and illiterate. He entitled the leaflet "To Those Guys Still in the Army." He put the heart of his message in a pun based on a misspelling, apparently in his own mind connecting what he had been taught about himself in school with what was being done to him, and the other members of his class, in the army:

I used to be in there too. Now you guys listen good cause I am going to tell you some good things.

First—There have been more than 10 guys that I know of that have gotten papers and I am one of them.

Listen. Second—I have a job—I go dancing and my pay is more than a P.F.C. gets and I'm getting a raise shortly.

Third—life is a great deal better than being in Vietnam. Fighting for a cause that isn't what it's built up to be.

What this thing means is this: DESSERT.

Notice the spelling in DESSERT—It's not a bitter thing to Desert, it's the sweetest thing in the world.

II. Paris: 1967

It was April in Paris. The sun was rising on a beautiful day and the city was astir, waiting to greet its distinguished visitor from the United States, Vice President Hubert H. Humphrey. *L'Humanité* had printed a map of the Vice President's itinerary, along with the hope that "the citizens of Paris would give M. Humphrey an appropriate welcome." *L'Humanité Nouvelle,* organ of the pro-Chinese party, urged the workers and students not to be outdone by their comrades in Italy, hundreds of thousands of whom were shown in photographs fighting through police lines surrounding Humphrey.

Humphrey's first official duty in Paris was to lay a wreath before the equestrian statue of George Washington in the Place d'Iéna. The "Paris American Committee to Stopwar" (PACS), a group of mainly older American exiles we had begun to work with shortly after we had moved in March to Paris for six months, had picked this as the appropriate spot for us Americans to greet our Vice President. Jane and several other women carried along a big American flag, carefully furled to conceal an NLF banner. With her was Robert, then almost four.

As we arrived at Place d'Iéna, a large crowd was already drifting in. There were local dignitaries and American officials, French and American military officers, middle-aged affluent American tourists and middle-aged affluent Parisians, a brightly uniformed band, a color guard with the U.S. and French flags, swarms of police with their dramatic dark-blue capes (weighted with lead to be swung at demonstrators), and mostly large numbers of young French men and women.

I carried a stack of PACS leaflets, which consisted of what seemed to me a rather innocuous brief declaration in French and English:

Vice-President Humphrey!

This statue of George Washington is: "Given by the women of the United States of America in memory of the Friendship and Fraternal Aid given by France to their fathers during their fight for Independence."

Is napalm burning "Friendship and Fraternal Aid"?

Today Americans are fighting the Vietnamese who want:

their FREEDOM

their INDEPENDENCE

their OWN COUNTRY!

What are we doing in Vietnam?

Washington and Lafayette would be ashamed of us.

VIETNAM FOR THE VIETNAMESE!

(signed) Americans in Paris

For about ten minutes, I politely handed out my leaflets to some of the thousands of people streaming into the plaza. Suddenly two men dashed up behind me. Each grabbed an arm and twisted it behind my back. At the same instant, another man snatched my stack of leaflets, and then stood glowering at me, waving them in my face.

"What are these, eh?" he snarled in French.

I tried desperately to think of the French word for leaflets, but my mind went blank.

"Des papiers," I said lamely.

"Des papiers? Des papiers? Des papiers, eh?" he roared, now furious. "What kind of fool do you think I am?" Then to the two holding my arms, "Away with him!"

They dragged me over to a truck, heaved me in, and locked me up. A few minutes later, the back was opened again and a young man was thrown in, blood streaming from his nose and mouth. Within another few minutes, two more were prodded in with clubs.

Then we heard motorcycles and the band playing "The Star-Spangled Banner." We figured Humphrey must be arriving. The band started "La Marseillaise." Then came sounds of pandemonium: shouting, police whistles and sirens, screeches of tires, thuds, running, screams. In the background we could still hear a singer:

. . . Contre nous de la tyrannie,
L'étendard sanglant est levé . . .

Our truck was soon packed with prisoners, some very badly beaten. As we worked on the injuries, they told us the latest news from the street. The police had trapped hundreds, who were being beaten and arrested. I had awful visions of Jane and Robert. People in the back were able to see trucks and busses behind us loaded with prisoners. Soon we went in a caravan to a massive old church whose sprawling basement had been turned into a temporary prison.

We were unloaded in small groups, booked, and shoved into our dungeon. As the hours went by, truckload after truckload of prisoners were brought in. We cheered each group as they came. Steve was brought in. He said Alice had also been arrested, but he thought Jane and Robert might have gotten away. Each truckload brought the latest news. At Place d'Iéna, several groups had broken through the police lines. For a while Humphrey had been cut off from his motorcycle escort. The police had managed to extricate him and take him straight back to his hotel, around which they had thrown ring upon ring of riot police. In the earliest hours, the heaviest fighting had been between police and students in the Latin Quarter, with the police getting the better of it. But then work had ended at a number of factories. Soon two hundred thousand workers joined the battle. During the first hour after the workers got into it, sixty police were hospitalized, according to a police admission on the radio. The American Cultural Centers in Paris, notorious fronts for the CIA, had all been sacked. The main American Express office was under siege. Two major train depots were now controlled by the people. Several hundred thousand people were in the streets, most of which had been conceded to them by the police.

I have never met anyone living in the United States at that time who was aware through the media of any protest against Humphrey. (Most people I've described it to thought at first I must be thinking of May, 1968, not April, 1967.) Weeks later, I worked on *Loin du Vietnam*, the film made jointly by Roger Pic, Jean-Luc Godard, William Klein, Alain Resnais, Chris Marker, and other *cinéastes*. I saw the footage of Place d'Iéna, which even shows Jane with Robert in her arms barely escaping as the police sweep in, their lead-weighted capes and clubs flying. There were reels and reels of the fighting from all over Paris. In the final version, Chris Marker spliced together scenes of Humphrey's actual Paris reception with the U.S. news coverage of the event: "Vice-President Humphrey arrived today in Paris and received a warm welcome. The expected antiwar protest failed to materialize."

This was the first time I had ever been arrested for political activities (the last time I had been arrested it was as a "juvenile delinquent" in Brooklyn). Each hour I spent in our makeshift prison, one of the many filling up around Paris that day, deepened new loyalties and erased old ones.

Our dungeon eventually held about seven hundred men. Two or three hundred women were on the other side of a massive wall. The women started a chant and we joined in. Dozens of guards came running and we all stopped. As soon as they left, we started again. After we tired of this cat-and-mouse game, someone began singing the "Communist Internationale." I had never heard that song before, but the thousand voices joined in those words made my heart pound. I picked up the refrain after the first stanza:

> C'est la lutte finale,
> Groupons-nous, et demain
> L'Internationale
> Sera le genre humain.

After the "Internationale" was sung in French, some people started it in Italian, with most of the prisoners joining in the chorus.

People then started shouting "En anglais! En anglais!," looking to us Americans to begin. There were about a dozen of us, and we gathered in a little ring while two older men wrote out the words for the rest of us. A short, fat, balding man with beady eyes and a square black mustache, who had been following me around from a distance, now slithered up and stood on tiptoe, trying to peer at the conspiratorial plan we were drafting. As soon as we realized what he was, he scurried to the door and whistled for the guards, who let him out.

After we had sung the "Internationale" in English, someone called out, "Let's have a meeting." The meeting was a prolonged discussion of what should be done to organize the antiwar movement in Paris during the next few months. As it went on, I became aware of some of the political differences dividing the French movement, although, partly because of my poor French and mainly because of the primitiveness of my own political education, I could not comprehend the importance of the differences or see why the debate was getting so hot. That I was to discover soon. Late that night, we were all released.

In the next couple of weeks, I was ordered in twice by French police agencies for questioning. Each interrogation lasted almost a full day. Two-man teams of interrogators took each other's place and went over the same ground again and again. I pretended my French was even worse than it was. Each team consisted of the Mutt and Jeff act common to all police interrogation. One of my questioners was always harsh, mean, threatening. The other would say little, except for an occasional word on my behalf. Then the first would invariably drift off, searching for a pack of cigarettes or answering a phone or getting more "evidence." While he was gone, the other would then whisper confidentially, in the friendliest tone, that he thought I was a decent fellow, that this other guy was known as a mean bastard, that I would be out of there in ten minutes if I just told them the things they needed to know, that his pal wanted to torture me, and that he couldn't restrain him much longer.

Operatives of the CIA and countless other U.S. agencies were swarming all over Europe, particularly in Paris, which was a nest of intrigue. The contacts some of us had with the Vietnamese brought special attention. When the Union of Vietnamese Students in France began working with some of us to put on joint American-Vietnamese film and lecture shows, the intelligence operatives frantically tried to infiltrate the Vietnamese and disrupt our programs.

There were then several hundred Vietnamese students who had been hand-picked by the Saigon government to study in France. These were the most loyal students Saigon could find. As soon as they got to France, practically every one openly supported the National Liberation Front. Saigon stopped sending students to France because, as they put it, "the Viet Cong were too strong in Paris."

The CIA went to the handful of remaining students and proposed the formation of another American-Vietnamese friendship organization, which would also put on programs, these intended to show how the United States was supporting democracy in Vietnam and protecting the Vietnamese people from the "invasion from the North." Two of the Vietnamese said they would like to do this. The first meeting of this new organization was publicly announced for a room in the Cité Universitaire at 8 P.M. But the CIA operatives had no intention of holding a public meeting, because they knew that most of the people who would come would be against the war. So they connived with their two "loyal" Vietnamese to have a notice put up at Cité Universitaire at 8 P.M. explaining that the meeting had been changed to 7 P.M. in a building at the opposite side of Paris. Unfortunately for this brilliant plan, both of the "loyal" Vietnamese were secretly reporting every CIA move. When the three CIA operatives showed up at the new meeting room at 6:30 P.M., they were met by a group of twelve members of the Union of Vietnamese Students and two of us from PACS. Their faces collapsed. One of them blurted out, "But how did you . . ." He was deftly interrupted by the man obviously in charge, who asked us all to wait a few minutes while they "conferred." We surreptitiously observed that their conference included a five-minute telephone call. When they emerged, their senior man announced, "We think a meeting among us all might be useful." The Vietnamese agreed to meet.

At the meeting, the CIA men dropped all their inept covers, including the dull-witted drawl affected by the one who had infiltrated PACS. What they openly proposed was the creation of a "third force" in Vietnam, "neither Communist nor under orders from Washington, but an honest patriotic group." This was put forth as a novel approach to "solve" the Vietnam "problem." My training as a professor of English literature now proved not entirely useless, for I recalled this was exactly the same formula used by the CIA in Graham Greene's novel *The Quiet American*, first published in 1955–56. The Vietnamese response was simple and direct: they gave a brief outline of Vietnamese history, explained patiently that the United States had no legitimate business meddling with their internal affairs, and calmly affirmed their determination to win independence and reunite their homeland.

Working directly with the Vietnamese shattered some of our fundamental beliefs. In the United States we have been taught that collective life prevents the development and fulfillment of the individual. We are trained from birth to advance our own selves at the expense of others, and, even more fundamentally, to perceive all our successes and failures as personal. Many people now recognize that collectivization has produced great material progress, as in China, but they think this has been paid for by the crushing of the individual. The Vietnamese taught us the opposite: a true collective depends on the development of the individuals within it. These Vietnamese Communists were, in fact, the most highly developed human individuals we had ever met.

When I found myself functioning in collective situations with them, I discovered a new form of human relationship. For they acted upon the knowledge that the individual human self is not fulfilled by egoism but destroyed by it. People respected each other fully because nobody was being put down or stepped on. I could express my opinions, as primitive as they were, with a freedom I had never known in the United States, for these opinions would never be held against me. My opinion was not *my* property, but something of value to us all, part of a collective effort to discover the most accurate and productive ideas. If people disagreed with me, they saw this not as my fault but our problem. Since my opinion was not a vehicle for my ego, I had no more reason than anybody else to defend it. I began to get a glimmer of why the Vietnamese projected liberation.

It was the Vietnamese, strangely enough, who also made Jane and me overcome our sense of guilt and shame for being Americans. This was partly an intellectual process, a deepening Marxist-Leninist understanding of the contradiction between the U.S. government and those of us ruled by it. But beyond this, and growing out of it, was that feeling of international love we had encountered first the night of the soirée, based on an appreciation, not a denial, of the differences in our cultures. They did not want us to behave like Vietnamese, any more than we expected them to behave like Americans. Our comradeship united, on a small scale, two vastly different cultures.

It was about this time that deserters from units of the U.S. Army ordered to Vietnam from their bases in Germany began to arrive in Paris. They came mostly as individuals, though a few were smuggled in by a small organization in the Netherlands. No government in Europe was yet willing to give deserters political asylum because none was ready to face the wrath of the U.S. government. So, wherever they went, these men had to be hidden, fed, clothed, and kept out of trouble. Meanwhile, public and private pressure was being applied to induce at least one government to grant asylum, following established usage.

The importance of these desertions was obvious. Word was already leaking out in the French press of the large-scale mutinies starting to break out among GIs in Vietnam. If GIs in Europe now began deserting because of the Vietnam War, and were free to make public statements, the U.S. government would be even more isolated, both internally and internationally. More important, it would help lead to what eventually did happen: the internal collapse of the U.S. military in Vietnam. (See, for example, Colonel Robert D. Heinl, Jr., "The Collapse of the Armed Forces," *Armed Forces Journal,* June 7, 1971, pp. 30–38.)

The risks in aiding the deserters were of course high. Many people were asked to help. Few refused, except for every member of the French Communist Party, which had issued strict orders not to get involved. The word "revisionism" began to take on new meaning.

De Gaulle was then actively trying to cut France loose from its virtually neo-colonial ties to the United States, and the Foreign Ministry was the strongest center of Gaullist power. So the people active in the underground deserter network concentrated their pressure there. It looked as though this work was about to pay off when the Foreign Minister himself signed a pledge to grant U.S. political deserters both asylum and work permits. But meanwhile the other side was hard at work on the Ministry of the Interior, where U.S. influence was strongest, mainly because of the interpenetration of police apparatus. The issue came to a head unexpectedly when Paris police finally nabbed their first deserter. It ended the next day with agents of the Interior and Foreign ministries having a physical tug of war over the deserter, who had one arm and one leg in the grasp of each. The Foreign Ministry outpulled the Interior Ministry. From then on deserters began to pour into Paris.

Meanwhile, the deserter network was spreading throughout Europe and reaching directly into every U.S. Army base. A Marxist-Leninist organization in Sweden launched a public campaign to have their government go even further than the French government, openly denouncing the Vietnam War while opening its borders to the GIs.

The U.S. intelligence agencies throughout Europe were frantic. Only a little less panicked were the various "Communist" parties, who were trying to keep the struggle against the war on the lowest possible political level. They were particularly anxious to prevent revolutionary ideas and forces from developing inside the antiwar movement.

Jane and I meanwhile had helped organize a Marxist-Leninist study group. It included Black and white Americans, as well as people from France, Greece, Vietnam, Brazil, and Ethiopia. It spanned a wide political spectrum, including apologists for the Soviet Union, Trotskyites, Debrayists, and those of us who looked to Mao and China for leadership (and also at least three agents of the CIA). "Revisionism" was a word debated in every meeting, and external events forced us to realize this was no idle debate.

One day, after a big antiwar march, several members of the study group came to the meeting with bruises and bandages.

"What happened?" someone asked. "The police?"

"No, the revisionists."

They had been with a contingent that had chanted "*FNL vaincra*" (NLF will win), a slogan strictly banned by the Communist Party. The Party usually tried to drown out all potentially revolutionary slogans by chanting "*Johnson assassin,*" which made it sound as if the war were the work of a lone killer, or, even worse, "*Paix aux Vietnam*" (Peace in Vietnam), which even LBJ himself would have been happy to yell. The group had been ordered to cease chanting about an NLF victory, and, when they refused, were beaten by the CP "*service d'ordre.*"

Later, the pro-Chinese Mouvement Communiste Française, which had been doing community organizing against the war, rented the grand hall of the Mutualité for an "evening of solidarity with Vietnam." The CP *service d'ordre* was there, armed with clubs and iron bars. They attacked the MCF people as they entered the hall, and tore up the huge portrait of Ho Chi Minh as well as stacks of literature printed in Vietnam and China.

The Cultural Revolution had just broken out in China. Jane and I were beginning to understand that the Chinese people were trying to resolve the basic ideological and practical question of our time: Can the working people actually run a society, particularly a large industrial society, or must they always be ruled by a state controlled by some form of ruling elite? It was not until years later that we realized the ongoing Chinese Cultural Revolution may be the most important single event in human history. The international edition of the *Herald Tribune* was presenting quite a different version, with sensational stories of mobs running amok, looting, fighting, and even hanging people from lampposts along a street in downtown Canton. *Le Monde*, certainly the most responsible capitalist newspaper in the world, was at the same time printing stories from French, German, Swiss, and Italian businessmen who walked down the very street where the bodies were supposedly hanging, seeing nothing but the usual throngs of passers-by, except for a few young people hanging up big-character wall posters.

Ironically it was in Paris that I began to grasp the significance of the Black liberation movement in the United States. There for the first time I met Afro-American Marxist-Leninists, who had been driven into exile. And there I saw the internationalism of the Afro-American movement. In the United States we are conditioned to think of Blacks as a "minority group." Even within the revolutionary movement today, there are still many self-proclaimed Marxist-Leninists who think of Black people as just a particularly oppressed and militant section of the United States working class. But, within the international revolutionary movement, the 25–30 million Afro-Americans are seen, accurately, as a large and powerful nation of people with a distinct history, culture, and global role. When I was invited to speak as a white American revolutionary on the subject of Black Power before Présence Africaine (La Société Africaine de Culture), where two of the other speakers were the African revolutionaries Aimé Cesaire and Alioune Diop, I learned that in the Third World, especially Africa, the freedom of the Afro-American people was seen as a key to their own destiny.

I consider July 4, 1967, a special date in my life. On that day, the Union of Vietnamese Students and a number of us Americans put on a joint Vietnamese-American Independence Day program. We rented an auditorium seating over a thousand. Our leafleting was concentrated on Americans visiting or living in Paris. An overflow crowd showed up. There were songs, speeches, displays of U.S. weapons and atrocities. Ten-year-old Karen read the famous poem from an American girl to the Vietnamese, and a Vietnamese student read the response from one of Vietnam's great poets. Giao spoke, brilliantly analyzing the military and political situation in Vietnam. He closed by expressing his confidence that "the American people will also triumph" on what he called " 'the second front' in the United States": "This common victory, dear friends, will be the promise of a true friendship between our two peoples." I also spoke, summing up my entire political education to that point in my life. That speech represented to me a personal declaration of independence—and of commitment.

A Declaration of Independence

(Speech delivered at the joint Vietnamese-American Independence Day Program: Independence—1776 United States-Vietnam 1967; Paris, July 4, 1967.)

TODAY, the 4th of July, in America is traditionally a day to demonstate one's loyalty. Yet it commemorates a day when disloyalty was proclaimed, when revolution was declared. The tradition of this day is to celebrate a new loyalty, a loyalty that displaces an old one. Suddenly on July 4th, 1776, the old loyalty became treason, conservatives were traitors. What I propose tonight is that we all perform a similar act, that we declare an old loyalty treason and go forth dedicated to a new loyalty.

The eighteenth-century American revolutionaries declared the king of England an enemy of the American colonies, and for the sake of their revolution solemnly pledged to each other their lives. What I propose is that we here declare the government of the United States of America in 1967 to be the enemy of mankind, the number-one public criminal of the world, wanted dead or alive. I propose that we declare a new loyalty, a loyalty to the overwhelming masses of mankind, to the peoples of the whole world.

For those of us who are Americans, why should our loyalty be to the Kennedys, the Rockefellers, the Johnsons, the H. L. Hunts rather than to the Vietnamese who are here with us tonight? Some of you are sitting here at this moment with draft induction papers in your pocket. What was your reaction when the men of the Vietnamese Men's Choral Group sang from this platform a few minutes ago? Soon you may be asked to kill them, and then they will have to kill you to defend their homeland. Who is doing this to us? These Vietnamese people are not our enemies. They are our comrades, our brothers. Our mutual enemy is not in Hanoi; he is in Washington.

Have you thought that of all the dozens of Vietnamese men and women here tonight almost every one has had relatives, many of them close relatives, killed in this war? Some Americans here have had relatives and friends killed in this war. Yet we come together here tonight. We come together as comrades, and we know who is the murderer of our friends and relatives.

Our enemy has told us to march to "support our boys in Vietnam." We know what this really means. We have read the letters from our "boys" in Vietnam; they say, "Get us the hell out of here." In this room tonight are young men who have risked prison and public scorn by refusing to serve in the army or by deserting from the army in order not to kill and be killed for our enemy. Here tonight are also some who have supported these "boys" by working in the American Underground, themselves risking prison and public scorn. We should all support our men in Vietnam—by bringing them back home to help deal with our real enemy.

At this moment, loyalty to the government of the United States is the most profound treason to all of humanity. To be loyal to this government is to join forces with death, with starvation, disease, fire, flood. It is no coincidence that these four great natural enemies of humanity are the artificially produced allies of this monster in Vietnam. Flood. Now begins the annual season for the attacks on Vietnam's dike system, because now the water levels are high and a serious breach in the dikes means a flood that will overwhelm millions. Fire. The favorite weapon of this monster is napalm, a weapon intentionally designed to create the most horrible imaginable fires among a civilian population; the most horrible, that is, with the exception of their blackmail weapon. Disease. You have heard tonight eyewitness accounts of what was inflicted on the great Vietnamese leprosarium at Quynh Lap. Thirty-nine raids; the demolition bombing of every building marked with a red cross; the fragmentation bombing, fire bombing, and, finally, strafing of lepers, doctors, and nurses; all done as part of a conscious policy, defined by the Air Force as "psycho-social targets," to create terror among the people. What kind of deformed monster joins forces with leprosy? And now this government has developed an entirely new strain of bubonic plague, one that is resistant to all treatment. Starvation. Last year the government of the United States, by its own admission—or, rather, bragging—destroyed over one million acres of rice crops in Vietnam. Then there is rice blast, a crop disease which has been for centuries the greatest natural enemy in Southeast Asia. The government of the Democratic Republic of Vietnam and the Vietnamese people have struggled to overcome this enemy, developing resistant strains of rice and chemical treatment. The government of the United States of America provides a perfect contrast: recently the United States Army awarded the highest honor it can bestow upon a civilian, granting it to the researcher who has just developed a brand-new strain of rice blast that is resistant to all treatment.

Let me be clear on one point. When I say the government of the United States I do not mean this particular administration. The Johnson administration has the same basic aims as its predecessors, and the only political disputes among the two major parties are about tactics and the division of the spoils. They all agree on one policy that joins forces with starvation not only in Vietnam but all over the world, even in the United States, where children now starve amidst the computers and space ships. That policy is to wage counterrevolution against the peoples of the world, most of whom are hungry, who not only want their planet back but are engaged in global revolution to take it back.

Our problem is not how to stop *the* war. It is how to stop War. Since the people should not and cannot be stopped from waging war for their world, their lives, and the lives of their children, the solution must lie in stopping the War Machine, the enemy of the people.

The war is not simply a war in Vietnam anyhow. It is a global struggle, a world war between revolution and counterrevolution, between the exploited and the exploiters, between the billions of people deprived of their world and a privileged few who have expropriated the land and riches and labor of the planet for their own selfish ends, and who now try to use the lives of some of us to defend their ill-gotten gains from the rest of us.

The war is a world war. At this moment, American forces are engaged in combat not only in Vietnam, but in Laos, Thailand, Bolivia, Venezuela, Guatemala, Colombia, the Dominican Republic. American combat planes are flying over China. American special forces and military advisers are working with the forces of international fascism in Spain, Portugal, South Africa, Greece, South Korea, Taiwan. The same American electric-shock equipment used to torture prisoners in Vietnam is used to torture political prisoners in Brazil, where political activists have been turned into human vegetables in one week of torture. Operation Prometheus, used to set up the fascist dictatorship in Greece, has a counterpart not only in every NATO country (as reported in the international *Herald Tribune*) but in the United States as well, where it is called Operation Dragnet. There eight concentration camps are ready and waiting for the moment when the President signs one piece of paper which will authorize the FBI to arrest anyone they think fit without any legal formality or right to examine witnesses or evidence. American napalm has burned the flesh of people of at least fifteen countries. In the United States itself, the monster is mortgaging our future for its filthy ends, while it poisons our water, our air, our minds.

Vietnam is the front where the heaviest fighting is going on, and where the Vietnamese people have proved to be the most heroic people of recorded history. But Vietnam is not the only fighting front, and soon it may prove to be not the most important. Because now the home front is opening, and there is now no sanctuary for the enemy, no sanctuary in the entire world, not even in his own great cities.

There is now also no neutrality in the world. And because of this the "peace movement" is rapidly becoming a misnomer. Like all peace movements since the first began in 1835, the present one has been a somewhat uneasy alliance between pacifists and revolutionaries. Now the dove is no longer an appropriate emblem. More and more Americans, many millions of Americans, have now realized the essential problem in pacifism: to preach pacifism to slaves is to side with the slaveowner and with slavery.

Until fairly recently the main purpose of the peace movement has been to "stop the war" by having our elected representatives stop it. Three basic avenues seemed possible: (1) Directly convince our present elected representatives to stop it, using reason, facts, argument, testaments of conscience, symbolic acts of disaffection, demonstrations, protests. (2) Convince a majority of the people to agree that the war should be stopped, and then persuade them to use method number one on our existing representatives. (3) Convince the majority and elect representatives pledged to stop the war. Even stating the assumptions like this should show how pathetically unrealistic they are. Behind the last one looms this procedure: (a) Persuade a majority. (b) Get this majority to agree to vote on a particular policy. (c) Get a candidate nominated and (d) elected on this policy. (e) Have the candidate work successfully to implement this policy. In 1964 we got a, b, c, d—and then our candidate began openly implementing the policies of his opponent (Mr. Not-a-choice-but-an-echo, or was it the other way round?), and of course he had been preparing for this all during the election. While he was promising never to send "American boys to Asia to do the job Asian boys should do," he was getting them ready to go. Now he implies that we are traitors when we say he should bring them back.

Many of you no doubt still believe that you are represented more or less by this government, or at least could be by a different administration operating under the same system. This is something neither I nor anybody else is going to convince you about in a speech. You can only learn the truth from your own experience. Millions have learned from the 1964 experience that what we are offered is a choice between which member of the ruling class we want to misrepresent us for the next few years. Many millions of Black Americans had previously learned the same thing from their experience.

In 1966 in Redwood City people had a fine educating experience. Redwood City is, or rather was, a very conservative community, whose congressman for many years has had the second-lowest ADA rating, where there wasn't even a liberal much less a radical political organization to be found. Hundreds of radical orators could have talked on thousands of platforms without convincing anyone that there was such a thing as "the power structure"—comprising the news media, the local government, business interests, and the courts—which was intent on keeping the good citizens from threatening it in any way. But when these people overwhelmingly asserted that they wanted to exercise a basic democratic right, one guaranteed by all California legal precedent and by their own city charter, to vote on whether a napalm factory should be permitted to operate on their *public* land, suddenly the mask was torn away. The newspaper said that the people should not be allowed to vote, because if people in general were allowed to vote on issues of war and peace the government wouldn't be able to conduct its war-making! (An interesting point, for would the American people ever have voted to send troops to Vietnam? Or would they now be voting to send troops to fight in two other countries in Southeast Asia and six countries in Latin America?) The local government, by violating every pertinent provision in the city charter, finally managed to throw the case into a court where the judge was none other than a close personal friend of the president of the napalm company. Now in Redwood City there are many thousands of people with an understanding of the real nature of American democracy.

What is the alternative for the movement against the war in Vietnam? The first step is to make an analysis of the two basic positions from which opposition has been made, positions well defined in advertisements run by the Revolutionary Contingent in the April 15th march, the liberal argument and the radical argument. Liberals argue that "both" sides are to blame for the war. Like Bernard Malamud, they conceive of the "gentle Vietnamese people caught between two warring armies," thus displaying as little common sense as political understanding. Radicals recognize the basic distinction between the aggressor, the government of the United States, fighting for neo-colonial domination of Southeast Asia, and the Vietnamese people, who are fighting for national liberation. Liberals are willing to accept almost any peace (except the peace offered by the Pentagon, the peace of cemeteries); radicals demand a peace based on Vietnamese self-determination. Liberals accept Johnson's most beguiling defense, his implication that the war in Vietnam is really an unfortunate accident that he's doing his best to get "us" out of. Radicals recognize that the war against Vietnam is a deliberate policy consistent with historic American expansionism and absolutely necessary to American capitalism; they know that American troops are fighting in Vietnam today for the same reasons that they fought against the Filipino war of national independence in 1899, against the Chinese rebellion of 1900, against the Russian Revolution, in every time and place where American business interests have been threatened by social revolution. The liberals think that the war is the work of a clique in the ruling circles known as hawks; radicals know that the only disputes among the ruling class are about tactics. Liberals think that communists are active in National Liberation Movements to further their own nefarious and selfish ends. Radicals know that true communists will make any sacrifice, face any torture, brave any death, and they recognize as true comrades all communists who lead revolutions against oppression and exploitation.

Then—and this is the most important, and for many of us the most difficult thing to do, for we have been brought up in an environment of images designed to make us feel all alone—we must stop thinking of ourselves as an alienated minority, a handful of kooks, an impotent band of idealists. We must start thinking of ourselves as what we in fact are—part of the overwhelming majority of people in the world. Forget all those who want to wait for the Gallup poll to tell them when a revolutionary struggle can begin. We are billions strong already. And even as billions we are only representatives of all the unborn generations of humanity. Besides, the revolution has already begun, even in America.

We who are Americans have potentially a glorious historical role to play, for we live in the strongest, really the last, stronghold of the monster, and that monster must have our loyalty if it is to win. If instead we are loyal to humanity, humanity will win.

The heroic Vietnamese people have shown us the way. The mightiest military machine in history has been exposed as a political Frankenstein's monster. And on the home front, students, Blacks, young workers, housewives, intellectuals have moved from protest to active resistance. The antidraft movement is creating deep concern in the supposedly omnipotent government, although the movement is just being born. Armed struggle is breaking out in every major city and many smaller ones. The reserves and National Guard cannot fight overseas because they are tied down on the home front. The Black vanguard of the American revolution is showing all of us what needs to be done.

In the world today one has to choose one side of the barricades.

There is no neutrality. And what is pitiful is not the suffering and torture and death of the Vietnamese people, nor that of the revolutionary people of Bolivia, Angola, Spain, and Watts. Heroes are not to be pitied. What is pitiful is all those who are oppressed and don't know how to join the world liberation movement, and all those who wallow in meaningless desperation as they try in one form or another to repress this movement. Some try to repress it with napalm, others use despair. The first say, Stop it or we'll kill you. The others say, It's hopeless, they'll kill you if you don't stop. Both are traitors to humanity; truly the first are more hateful, the second more pitiful—but also more effective.

So let us declare our independence, and our new loyalty. Let us defy the forces of death, and break our pledge of allegiance to those who place more belief in the machine than in humanity. Tonight is a fitting night to join with the peoples of the world and their revolution. For us in America that will mean resistance now, our own new American revolution before long, and liberation in the process.

And Now...

SOMETIMES IT'S HARD TO TELL where you're going unless you look back to see where you've been. That's also one way to walk a straight path if you are lost in the woods and want to get out.

When I was born, in 1934, the world was reeling from three unprecedented historical events: a world war, a triumphant Communist revolution, and a global economic crisis of the capitalist system. Most of the peoples of the world were still colonial and neo-colonial subjects of five European nations (Great Britain, France, Belgium, the Netherlands, and Portugal). But the colonial empires, vast and powerful as they appeared, were dinosaurs. The major capitalist powers, trying to redivide the world, had succeeded only in losing all of Russia and the Czar's immense Asian empire, so there was already one area of the world free from imperialism. Within the existing empires, revolutionary and national liberation movements were rapidly developing. Fascism was emerging as the most plausible way to save capitalism, and Germany, Japan, Italy, and their allies of Eastern Europe were moving to reconquer the Soviet Union and to attempt a new redivision of the world. The economic crisis continued to deepen.

In the midst of this global upheaval, the United States of America, undamaged by the First World War, and having digested its own conquests from Mexico, Spain, and the native peoples of the continent, was preparing to dominate the world. So my first thirty years were lived in the most rapidly expanding of empires, the only one in human history to come close to ruling the entire planet.

By the end of the Second World War, the United States faced no serious rival empire. It stationed its military forces with impunity on the soil of fifty-one nations, from which it threatened the nuclear devastation of any people resisting its hegemony. It reduced the economies of the former capitalist world powers—France, Great Britain, Germany, Japan, the Netherlands, Belgium, Portugal, Italy—to virtually a neo-colonial relationship. It placed its own military chieftains at the head of armies ostensibly representing the "United Nations" of the world. Only one thing stood in the way: those movements for national liberation and socialist revolution.

In 1949, China was "lost." Then half the tiny nation of Korea held the armies of the United States and its allies to a stalemate. In 1959 a socialist revolution triumphed in Cuba, which became a revolutionary outpost just ninety miles from the U.S. coast. Within a few years, the empire met its Waterloo and Stalingrad in Indochina, where it was stopped decisively. Empires must expand, or they die. So since 1963 I have been living in an empire that is decaying and collapsing.

Today it is the peoples of the Third World, the non-white peoples of the former colonies and neo-colonies, who are the motive force of world history. The seemingly passive objects of colonialism have become the movers of the earth. From the Third World, therefore, come the theoretical and practical leaders, the influential philosophers and strategists, for all the peoples of the planet.

Many hundreds of millions study the words of Mao Tse-tung, Amilcar Cabral, Ho Chi Minh, Kwame Nkrumah, Che Guevara, Malcolm X, Vo Nguyen Giap, Kim Il Sung. What political leader of the opposing side expounds an ideology, a philosophy, a strategy commanding even attention, much less respect? Truman's Doctrine, Eisenhower's Crusade, Kennedy's Special Warfare and New Frontier, Johnson's War on Poverty and Great Society—all have been swept into the dustbin. General Motors has a wider view than Gerald Ford. Can you imagine someone studying the writings of Richard Nixon (except a grand jury, a student of psychopathology, or Charles Colson, who claims to have read *Six Crises* fourteen times)? Everything the defenders of capitalism tell us is basically lies or nonsense, because they cannot possibly face one fundamental truth: the uprising of the wretched of the earth is revolutionizing our destiny. No person within the United States can understand his or her historical experience without comprehending that elementary fact.

Of course that's not how things normally appear. The media and the educational institutions, owned and controlled entirely by those who also own and control the means of production, do not tell us that we live in an era of global liberation and that our own freedom is dependent on that of the peasants of Cambodia, the gold and diamond miners of South Africa, the packing-house workers of Uruguay, and the unemployed untouchables of India. For to do so would be to call for the liquidation of their owners—the Hearsts and DuPonts, Hunts and Mellons, Rockefellers and Fords. No, instead our imaginations are filled with two polarized sets of images.

One displays the immutable power of the status quo. Colossal banks and office buildings take over the centers of our cities, sweeping aside slums and modest houses, schools and small businesses, ascending toward heaven on foundations of steel and glass. Rockets speed around the sun to other planets and beyond. The institutions of the republic—especially its presidency, congress, and courts—exist outside historical time, eternally preserved by checking and balancing each other. The business suit and necktie will be, unlike robes and diadems, immortal. Any problems you see come not from this system, which is much less bad than all the others, but from human nature, which is inherently selfish, ambitious, petty, jealous, spiteful, and corrupt. So there is nothing you can do to improve our setup, and if you don't like it here, either amuse yourself at Disneyland, the Superbowl, curled up with *True Romances* or *Inside Linda Lovelace*, with your TV or your RV, or go back where you came from.

The other image is less pleasant. The world is coming to an end. There are too many people, particularly colored people. We are running out of energy, particularly oil. The streets aren't safe any more. All the old values are gone. The sun is dying. A black hole or a Black terrorist may get us. The sky is falling down. You are an impotent little cockroach, who had better not reproduce itself. Maybe you're just a figment of your own diseased imagination. So go abuse yourself with a needle or a fifth, a novel by Vladimir Nabokov or E. Howard Hunt, Krishna or Jesus, a *Last Tango in Paris* or *A Clockwork Orange*, an *Exorcist* or a *Death Wish*.

These seemingly contradictory images of changeless power and catastrophic illusion merge and combine in countless forms. But, despite them all, we slowly awake to a consciousness of where we really are and what our role is to be in replacing the "Free World" with a world of human freedom. This book describes the process of one person's fitful awakening, an experience uniquely individual in form but exceedingly common in content. Only one of us is living this particular life, but that is in a world shared by us all, in a common historical epoch. Each of us is capable of recognizing this world, and collectively we are capable of changing it according to human needs and desires.

I deeply believe this. Yet I must admit that the institutions of our dying system, structured for self-perpetuation, frequently force me into doubts and confusion. "Am I alone in some bizarre fantasy?" I secretly wonder. After all, the majority of the Advisory Board at Stanford, including the chairman of the Department of Psychiatry, drove me out of the garden because my "perception of reality . . . differs drastically from the consensus in the university," and, therefore, unless I had "a dramatic change in perception" they were "highly dubious whether *rehabilitation* is a useful concept in this case."

Malcolm X, whose image was transformed by the media into that of a mad fiend, a real-life boogeyman, understood with precision the purpose of making each individual feel unique in perception of social reality: "Because if you know you're dissatisfied all by yourself and ten others aren't, you play it cool; but if you know that all ten of you are dissatisfied, you get with it. This is what the man knows." (*Malcolm X Speaks*, p. 175.) A few months after saying these words, Malcolm was murdered. But that did not stop millions of dissatisfied people from getting with it together.

It is permissible to recognize that other people in other places are in revolt. Even William Randolph Hearst and CBS now acknowledge that socialism may be a good thing, at least for the time being, for a "backward" nation like China. But to perceive the possibility of similar revolutionary change in our own society is at best silly and naïve. If you deeply believe such ridiculous stuff, you may be suffering from incurable madness:

> We are highly dubious whether *rehabilitation* is a useful concept in this case. Professor Franklin's announced convictions about the guilt of the university appear deeply-held, and his opposition to the institution in its present form seems implacable. We believe him when he expresses his regret that his role in converting the university to "serve the people" is restricted by practical reasons to advocacy rather than action.

The crime for which there can be no pardon or rehabilitation has three components: opposition to the present form of institutions; an unswerving belief that they can be changed into people's institutions; advocating this change to the people when they are in a position to do something about it. That is "urging and inciting."

Thus the main target of the repression of the 1970s has been those people getting together, beginning in the 1960s, on the basis of radical opposition, potentially revolutionary goals, and a commitment to spread both as widely as possible. Our rulers were absolutely correct in perceiving that grouping together as the birth of a revolutionary movement within the United States. The ruling class is always more sensitive to threats to its existence than are those who constitute the threat. As Lenin put it:

Nothing gives our "omnipotent" government away so much as this display of consternation. By this it proves more convincingly than does any "criminal manifesto" to all who have eyes to see and ears to hear that it realizes the complete instability of its position. . . . Decades of experience have taught the government that it is surrounded by inflammable material and that a mere spark, a mere protest . . . may start a conflagration.

That early movement, infantile in an historical sense, was primitive, barely conscious, inchoate, and badly battered by the 1968–71 wave of repression. Now the media try to wash away the historical significance of this new force by shedding crocodile tears over the bygone days of student activism and long hot summers in the ghettoes, as if these same media had not been hysterical about both. The movement is transmuted into a myth, or a daydream that briefly diverted us from the cynicism and careerism of the campus, the boredom and degradation of the factory, the survival games on the block. The movement was just an illusion. Besides it's dead now. And it never did accomplish anything. Some people are seduced by these bland condolences, and give up. They fail to see the deadly wounds already inflicted by that baby human movement on the old dinosaur empire. It is the "United" States which has proven to be an illusion, an empire financed by phony money, menaced by its own army, taping for posterity the empty gaps and blank spaces in its innermost oval rooms, generously pardoning its own professedly nonexistent crimes. The emperor does not even dare walk around inviting admiration of his new clothes, for people might throw rocks and bottles at him.

I believe it is no overstatement to say that the history of the United States since the mid 1960s has been a history of the growth and development of a revolutionary crisis. This book cannot give a history of the revolutionary movement developing as part of that crisis. (In *From the Movement: Toward Revolution* I presented a documentary record with a general analysis.) It would certainly not be appropriate to present the movement through a chronicle of my life in it. My role has been more than sufficiently sensationalized by Senator Eastland's committee; the San Mateo County and San Bernardino County sheriffs; *Time* and *Newsweek;* the House Internal Security Committee; the Stanford Administration, with its bosses in the war industry, its henchmen on the faculty, and its hired pens in public relations; the Palo Alto and San Francisco police departments; the University of Colorado Board of Regents; Joe Pine and Ed Montgomery; the FBI and CIA, Robert Mardian and his Gemstone cops, and various accomplices of these gentlemen masquerading as part of the left. All these share a common view which betrays their own contempt for most people, whom they think of as mindless sheep or buffalo. They have me creating "disruptions," "violence," and even whole revolutionary organizations through the magic power of "rhetoric," "romantic" ideas, or "fanaticism." The latest colorful version runs like this:

> Franklin easily got those . . . "with guts" to train in weapons with him in the hills. At these sessions, Franklin spun hair-raising tales of revolution, a task in which the captain was quite adept—being an instructor in "Science Fiction" at the Stanford English Department. To aid the vividness of his vision, Franklin often administered mescaline, or some other hallucinogen, after the shooting practice. . . . To further isolate his growing crew of bloodthirsty Vietcong, Franklin instituted "secret membership" and many of his faction went "underground" waiting for the war to start. (*New Solidarity*, August 3, 1974.)

The main point of my existence as a revolutionary, as I said at the beginning, is that my life is representative rather than special. This is as true of my life within the movement as of the part of my life leading to it. True, only a minority of Americans have actively participated in the movement, at least consciously, but that minority already consists of tens of millions. How many people have taken some conscious action to end the Indochina War, to help bring about the liberation of the Black nation and other oppressed peoples, to end the oppression of women, or to gain political, economic, social, or cultural power for poor and working people?

Certainly vastly more than the numbers who have served in the Air Force, worked on tugboats, or taught English literature. Far more important, the great majority of the people now share the underlying goals of the movement, though there is precious little agreement on how to achieve them.

Some of the early goals of the movement have actually been reached, but, like conquered foothills, they reveal far higher peaks to be scaled. Black people have the vote and are using it, though many have moved beyond Malcolm's modest formulation of "the ballot or the bullet" to a belief that both are necessary. Black mayors are elected but the city police forces continue their reign of terror in the Black and other Third World communities (Los Angeles, Atlanta, Detroit, Newark, etc.). Equal opportunity programs are developed, and the non-white labor participation rate falls to 56.1 percent in New York City (as of August, 1974), indicating that almost half the adult population is either officially unemployed or unaccounted for. The draft has been ended, but poor and working-class youth are still forced into the army by economic laws. We acknowledge the oppression of women, the legal structure creaks toward an acceptance in principle of the equality of the sexes, and some women are able to move up in the professions, politics, and skilled-labor categories. Yet, at the same time, even more women are forced to work on assembly lines, as waitresses, and at office routines while keeping house, and others are forced into prostitution and the similar jobs now advertised, regardless of sex of course, in the help-wanted columns ("masseuses," "exotic dancers," "intimate talk partners," "bunnies," "bar girls," "hostesses," "photo models," "explicit film stars"). Chicano agricultural workers are allowed to have a union, but only on condition they support laws defining their sisters and brothers in Mexico as "scabs" and "wetbacks." Prison rebellions and prisoner-support groups force a few modest reforms and make the advanced political understanding developed inside the prisons available to those outside. But hundreds of prisoners are murdered, the most articulate, such as George Jackson and Sam Melville, being singled out as targets, while the man in charge of the bloodiest single massacre is appointed Vice President, and university professors work overtime developing new techniques of psychosurgery and behavior modification. Each advance strips away another layer of illusion and reveals the underlying class contradiction concealed by bourgeois "democracy."

Those who still think that "the movement hasn't really accomplished anything" should take a good look at the armed forces, where the antiwar movement first combined with the Black national liberation struggle. By early 1967, small-scale mutinies in Vietnam were common and spreading. In mid-1969, the United States launched what was to prove its last ground offensive, a massive "search-and-destroy" operation in the A Shau Valley. It reached its bloody climax on a height the GIs named "Hamburger Hill," where unit after unit was chopped to pieces as they were senselessly ordered to advance against the entrenched Vietnamese. The entire ground army, including the marines, acting collectively through clandestine papers and a reliable grapevine, vowed, "There will be no more Hamburger Hills." Up to this point, news of the GI resistance had been suppressed fairly well. But then two rifle companies, one from the 196th Light Infantry Brigade and the other from the famed 1st Air Cavalry Division, conducted battlefield sit-ins in front of reporters and TV cameras. By late 1969, fragging (throwing fragmentation hand grenades at officers) was a systematic way of life for the GIs, of death or mutilation for any commander who ordered his men into offensive action. Many combat units were no longer allowed to have grenades or ammunition for their weapons except when on patrols (which now became semi-officially known as "search-and-evade" missions). This separate peace was officially accepted by the National Liberation Front, which announced in Paris that all its units were under orders not to engage American units unless directly attacked by them. By late 1970, the Pentagon was tacitly acknowledging that GI deserters, both white and Black, were fighting on the side of the "Viet Cong." Contingency plans were issued in the event of a full-scale rebellion, and the troop withdrawal was accelerated.

U.S. strategy shifted to a reliance on aircraft carriers massed in the Gulf of Tonkin along the Vietnamese coast. Massive campaigns of sabotage and an unending series of protests and rebellions soon torpedoed this strategy. In 1971, ships were sporadically forced out of action. In 1972, the movement became systematic, and the public began to learn a tiny bit about its existence. In March, the carrier U.S.S. *Midway* received orders to leave San Francisco Bay for Vietnam. A wave of protests and sabotage swept the ship, becoming public knowledge when dissident crewmen deliberately spilled three thousand gallons of oil into the bay. In June, the attack carrier U.S.S. *Ranger* was ordered to sail from San Diego to Vietnam. Naval Investigative Service reported a clandestine movement and at least twenty acts of sabotage, culminating in the destruction of the main reduction gear of one of the engines; repairs forced a four-and-a-half-month delay in the ship's sailing. In July, the carrier U.S.S. *Forrestal* was ordered to sail for the Mediterranean, but was prevented by a massive fire deliberately set by crewmen. In September and October, the crew of the carrier U.S.S. *Coral Sea* organized systematic protests against the war, with over a thousand crewmen signing a petition to "Stop Our Ship"; it was forced to return to San Francisco Bay, where crew members now helped organize support rallies and demonstrations. In October, a massive revolt broke out among the Black sailors on the carrier U.S.S. *Kitty Hawk*, spreading four days later to its oiler, the U.S.S. *Hassayampa*. On November 3, a revolt on the carrier U.S.S. *Constellation* made it return to San Diego, where over 120 men were discharged from the ship, and where it was forced to remain for over two months. The media called this a "racial outbreak," but the picture in the San Francisco *Chronicle* (November 10) captioned, "The dissident sailors raised their fists in the black power salute," shows mainly white sailors with upraised arms and clenched fists. When I went to San Diego on November 10, I found five carriers tied up, all forced out of combat by their crews, each of which was publishing a revolutionary newspaper on board. These crews were now getting together with one another in the San Diego bars and movement centers. In December, the U.S.S. *Ranger*, all repaired now, finally made it to the Gulf of Tonkin, where it was immediately disabled by a deliberately set fire. The Navy admitted this was the sixth major disaster on a Seventh Fleet carrier since October 1. Not since Pearl Harbor had the U.S. Navy been so crippled, and then it was by an enemy that could be defeated in combat.

One measure of the extent of the antiwar movement within the armed forces surfaced in August, 1974, when official talk about "amnesty" evoked some official statistics. In vastly understated numbers, the Justice Department and the Pentagon admitted there were twice as many deserters (28,000) currently liable for criminal prosecution as "draft dodgers" (14,000). In September, 1974, the Departments of Justice and Defense acknowledged there had been 500,000 incidents of desertion and admitted that "206,775 men were referred to United States attorneys as draft delinquents between 1963 and 1973" (*New York Times*, September 17, 1974).

This movement has already damaged U.S. strategy in areas besides Indochina. Take the Middle East, for example. In 1958, when U.S. Marines invaded Lebanon the rest of us in the armed forces dutifully prepared the entire war machine, including the SAC armada, to follow up. After making my little protest speech at the wing briefing, I obediently stood alert with the rest of our crew and no thought of organizing resistance ever flitted across my mind. By late 1971, some units had put themselves on record, in advance of the next crisis, as being unwilling to go to the Middle East. In December of that year, the enlisted men of Headquarters Battery, 1st Battalion, 144th Field Artillery, California National Guard, actually polled themselves and recorded their answer to the question of Middle East service:

If a Middle East crisis occurs and our unit is activated for immediate overseas duty, would you:

willingly go	0%
go, but unwillingly	8%
seek legal means to prevent activation	43%
leave the country	11%
refuse to go under any circumstances	22%
undecided or other	15%

In July, 1972, came that fire preventing the U.S.S. *Forrestal* from sailing for the Mediterranean. Then in November, 1973, there was a Middle East crisis. No attempt was made to activate additional units, nor were any serious preparations made for landing ground troops. But the United States did order its Mediterranean armada to make a show of force. What was shown instead was the farce of U.S. military power: even the flagship of the fleet, the cruiser U.S.S. *Little Rock*(!), had to be removed from action because of a revolt by its Black sailors. Within months, the oligarchs of Wall Street were holding out their homburgs for loans from the sheiks of Araby.

In the good old days, the defeat of a European empire merely meant the U.S. corporations, and often troops, taking over, as from Spain *et al.* in Latin America, France in Indochina, Italy and Great Britain in Libya and Ethiopia, Belgium in the Congo, Holland in Indonesia. But when in 1974 the African colonies of Portugal, under the leadership of Marxist-Leninist revolutionaries, win their independence, U.S. military intervention is unthinkable. This is one of the historical achievements of the U.S. revolutionary movement. What military units of the "Volunteer Army" could be sent? The elite 82nd Airborne, which had to court-martial a dozen of its Black GIs for refusing to go to Chicago to put down the white antiwar protesters at the 1968 Democratic convention? What young Black men would go to fight Africans? Would the unemployed white youth forced into army fatigues go fight? And what ships would transport any willing to go? Direct military intervention in

Latin America is almost as improbable, thanks largely to the Chicano and Puerto Rican liberation movements. So the United States is forced to rely on puppet military forces to maintain its hegemony, a scheme about as well designed as that of Victor Frankenstein. The generals and admirals of Peru, using U.S. planes and ships, prevent the U.S. fishing fleet from looting its ocean resources. The officers of the army of Ethiopia use their U.S. tanks and planes to overthrow the Emperor and begin to redistribute the land. The Greek generals try to use their U.S. equipment to seize Cyprus, but they are overmatched by the Turkish generals with their U.S. equipment. Then they are overthrown by popular forces, who demand that the United States remove its nuclear weapons from Greek soil. And does anyone outside the White House, the Pentagon, the Congress, and the CIA believe the future lies with Generalissimo Chiang Kai-shek, General Pak Jung Hi, General Lon Nol, General Thieu, or General Pinochet?

Even more ominous for our rulers is the domestic significance of the revolutionary movement within the armed forces. During the People's Park demonstrations in Berkeley in 1969, it was necessary to call up the National Guard. Disaffection was so high that the men were not allowed to have ammunition for their weapons, and behind each platoon guarding the fence stood two or three Military Police with loaded 45s and M-16s. The Headquarters Battery, 1st Battalion, 144th Field Artillery, also polled itself on its duties at home. Here is how they answered one question:

You are called up for duty in an Isla Vista student disorder. While making a sweep of a street, you are confronted by a mob of students yelling obscenities and throwing rocks and bottles. You are ordered to fire over the heads of the demonstrators, and you do so, but they continue to harass your unit. You are then ordered to open fire on the crowd itself. What would you do?

obey the order	8%
disobey the order	92%

As all strategies against the world revolutionary movement are thwarted, the internal collapse accelerates. Our rulers kill their own puppets—like Ngo Dinh Diem—and then fall victims themselves to conspiracies and machinations in their own ranks. John F. Kennedy, mastermind of Special Warfare and Commander in Chief of the Bay of Pigs, falls as the first in a string of assassinations, and a government commission then seals all the relevant evidence until the year 2039 "to protect national security." His successor leaves office, discredited, with ugly scars from flames and gun battles marking the cities of America as well as those of Indochina. Then Nixon, Mardian, Mitchell, Kleindienst, Agnew, Connally, Reinecke, and their cronies, coming forward as the restorers of law, order, and a balanced budget, leave the scene exposed as criminals and symbols of political, social, and economic chaos. Next begins the first non-elected government in United States history: a key figure in the cover-up of President Kennedy's assassination is appointed President by the criminal leaving office, and he in turn then appoints as his Vice President the most notorious incarnation of capitalism in the world.

Despite its considerable achievements, the conscious revolutionary movement has been unable to overcome its alienation, to comprehend how broadly representative it truly is, even in its weaknesses. When a movement arose, at first reformist, after the repression of the late 1940s and the 1950s, our entire society had been stripped of the knowledge, and even the vocabulary, necessary to comprehend our situation. What we said and did betrayed our spectacular ignorance. The spontaneous mass movement that burst forth in the mid-1960s surprised everybody. People on both sides of the barricades glimpsed its revolutionary potential. Consciousness began to emerge from spontaneity. Then the conscious movement found itself crippled by the existence within us of the very forces we were attempting to eliminate from U.S. society: elitism, egoism, careerism, the domination of Blacks by whites, women by men, the uneducated by the professional intellectuals. Now, after the ferocious repression has taken a toll, many of the conscious revolutionaries created by the spontaneous mass movement see themselves as isolated. It is as though they had once been part of a crashing wave, only to find themselves stranded, a small pool of water on a desert beach. They begin to doubt the existence of the ocean from which they came. Or they suffer from the preposterous delusion that they created the mass movement, which in fact both created them and offered them an historical role—to synthesize the thoughts of those millions and millions of profoundly dissatisfied people, to provide the theory, organization, and leadership necessary to change social reality rather than merely protest against it.

I have personally had a small taste of the consequences of being perceived (accurately I hope) as a danger to our rulers. But a few arrests and mild police beatings, campaigns of broadcast and whispered vilification, and even blacklisting from employment hardly compare to the murder and torture of Black people in either U.S.A. (Union of South Africa or United States of America), the tiger cages and napalm used on the peoples of Indochina, the U.S.-manufactured electrodes fastened, according to the instruction of U.S. police advisers, to the testicles and breasts of Latin American revolutionaries, or the blockading of food and medicine to whole nations, such as China, Cuba, North Korea, North Vietnam. Whether the men who command these monstrous acts are mad is an academic question. They do it because the system they head has reached the last stage of irrationality. If they refrained from issuing the orders necessary to keep it kicking a few years more, they would be replaced by less squeamish members of their class.

These men know where the real danger to their power lies. So do most of the professors they hire to teach their own children and the millions of youth from other classes they need to have somewhat educated. Their nemesis is so powerful they have trained us to have a strong negative reflex action when anyone calls it by its right name. "Ugh!" we are conditioned to respond. "Someone using that naïve propaganda term out of the 1930s!" The correct name of their nemesis is: the masses.

That explains why their hired professors go berserk when someone from their own ranks betrays them by invoking the millions of people beyond the ivied walls of their cloisters, laboratories, and computers. They even go so far as to say one person uttering such words threatens the very existence of their institution. No matter how many times they and the media proclaim I was fired (and denied employment) for "urging and inciting," the fact remains, documented beyond debate, that the speeches I was fired for giving were analytical statements posing quite a different kind of threat. These speeches all had one central theme: the university as an institution is not separate from imperialism but an important component of it, and the campus movement, though important, is not decisive, for it is the masses beyond the campus who will change U.S. social reality.

The main speech, the only one for which the Advisory Board unanimously held me "guilty," was a response to several speakers who argued that there should be no on-campus antiwar movement, that instead Stanford students should go into "the community" to educate the people. I began with a brief history of the movement at Stanford, and then got to my main thesis:

> We're the last ones in the world to oppose doing anything in the communities. The fact of the matter is that most of our comrades are working full-time in the community, because they come from the community. They are brown and black and white working-class and poor people. See, there's an extreme form of false consciousness that's created on a university campus. We get the illusion, because there are a lot of people gathered here, that this is the most advanced opposition to the war. But that poll that was cited . . . —and remember it was a poll of people over 21, and mostly white—that poll showed something. And that is that 60% of those people with a college education want to get out of Southeast Asia now; 70% of people who only have a high school education want to get out of Southeast Asia now; and 80% of people with only a grade school education want to get out of Southeast Asia now. So when we talk about high consciousness, high consciousness is the consciousness of the people most oppressed by U.S. imperialism, which includes as a main institution of that, Stanford University.

The professors on the Advisory Board held that anyone expressing such thoughts about Stanford was urging and inciting "violent and illegal actions" against the university, that a person so dissatisfied with "the institution in its present form" and so "implacable" in his commitment to "converting the university to serve the people" ought to go back where he came from.

Well, in a sense I have. And I find my beliefs daily reinforced by the people around me. I find myself doing less talking and more listening, especially when I'm not in the groves of academe. I don't by any means intend to disparage the student antiwar movement of 1964–72. Awhile back, I was talking with a man who was checking out my groceries at a discount supermarket. Like most people who work and shop in supermarkets, he was upset about the cost and quality of food. He seemed a particularly angry man, about forty-five, with a crew cut, thin lips, outthrust jaw, and a bony face lined by worry and weather. He told me he used to be a truck driver, and that he knew that a handful of rich people "are getting fat off our work, while we eat their crumbs." Then he started talking about Vietnam, and he became red with rage.

"You know," he said, calming down a little, "when those kids had all those demonstrations, it used to make my blood boil. I told my wife they were just a bunch of spoiled brats, and I'd like to teach them a thing or two about patriotism. Was I wrong. Was I wrong. Was I ever wrong. Those kids were trying to tell us something, and we were too dumb to listen. But we'll never let those bastards get away with another Vietnam."

The last thing he said were the words I hear most around and about these days: "How long do they think we're going to put up with it?" And everybody knows what is meant by *we* and *they*.

The people of the United States are neither fools nor cowards. Every month more of us figure out what kind of society we live in and start thinking about the possibility of replacing it with a decent society for ourselves and our children. Many of those who today call themselves revolutionaries do not understand this, and they remain caught up in their own alienation, careerism, power trips, sectarianism. They are like those members of the Chinese Communist Party castigated by Mao in 1926 because they were blind to the revolutionary stirrings of the Chinese peasants. Thirty million Afro-Americans, and millions of other Third World subjects within the United States have already shown they will not put up with it. Another hundred million poor and working people, students, small farmers, artists, professionals, and even sons and daughters of our own rulers have about reached the end of their toleration of war, hunger, poverty, unemployment, welfare, ignorance, roaches, pollution, secret police raids, Madison Avenue, corrupt politicians and other rats, inflation, meaningless work, drugs, bureaucrats, deceit, and fraud that constitute the empire. We do not intend to continue forever to sell our creative labor to those who daily rob us, and our sisters and brothers around the world, of our human birthright.

We human beings developed as part of the earth, which holds all we need to satisfy all our material requirements, and which gives us the senses to appreciate the beauty of water, air, land, life, and each other. This planet, literally rolling in the heavens, is potentially the paradise imagined in most of our religions. We now confront the last class of men who claim to hold this planet as their own private property, and who force the majority of us to toil to extend these claims. We live in the epoch which will end the private ownership of the earth and of the goods laboring people have brought forth from the earth. We live in the early dawn of human history, when we can see the possibility of communism—a world of peace, abundance, creativity, and freedom.

GLASSBORO STATE COLLEGE